The Lemass Era

The Lemass Era

Politics and Society in the Ireland of Seán Lemass

edited by

BRIAN GIRVIN

GARY MURPHY

UNIVERSITY COLLEGE DUBLIN PRESS

Preas Choláiste Ollscoile Bhaile Átha Cliath

First published 2005
by University College Dublin Press
Newman House
86 St Stephen's Green
Dublin 2
Ireland

www.ucdpress.ie

ISBN 1-904558-29-1

Cataloguing in Publication data available
from the British Library

Typeset in Ireland in Adobe Garamond, Janson and
Trade Gothic by Elaine Shiels, Bantry, Co. Cork
Text design by Lyn Davies
Index by Jane Rogers
Printed on acid-free paper in England
by Athenaeum Press, Gateshead

For Mandy and Rona

Contents

Foreword

JOHN HORGAN

Revisiting the Lemass era little more than three decades after his death, at a time when some of those who witnessed or even participated in the final years of that era are still professionally or politically engaged, may seem at first sight to be hasty, or to raise the possibility that reminiscence and self-justification will take the place of analysis and exploration. Two factors, thankfully, help to prevent this happening. One is the enormous wealth of material that has become available for scholars under the National Archives Act, despite the occasionally haphazard implementation of its provisions. The other is the fact that, while the documents themselves act as a valuable corrective for wayward memories, the lived experience of those participants who are still alive can itself provide invaluable contextual information – about linkages, about personalities, about agendas – without which documentary analysis alone can sometimes lack a vital element. Given the regularity with which archival releases now surface in the news pages of our media, it is to be hoped that the in-built professionalism of our best public servants, and their natural and laudable tendency to insist on the appropriate documentation for all major decisions, will in the end prevail over the dawning realization that the confidentiality to which they have become accustomed may evaporate while many of them, and their former political masters, are still around to face the music.

There is a wider sense, however, in which the Lemass era remains a fruitful area for a wide range of disciplines – political science, economics, sociology and history among them. This is because it can be argued to have been pivotal, not just in the economic, social and political sense, but in relation to the whole area of policy evolution and, in particular, to the complex interplay of factors in policy making between the political, private and administrative spheres.

Each of these areas plays its own part in the formulation of public policy: the notion of the Taoiseach as dictator, or of Cabinet members as the

Olympian masters of all they survey is as misleading as the idea that the civil service is the 'permanent government' of the country, or of the conspiracy theory which depicts politicians and public servants alike as mere puppets of powerful vested interests. And yet it is arguable that the centre of gravity of this complex relationship is never fixed, and is pulled one way or another at various times by powerful forces.

It is tempting to look at the Lemass era, in this context, in comparison with the eras which preceded and succeeded it – to look not only at the lineaments of policy itself, but at the interplay between agency and structure, and at the whole process of policy formulation, with a view to identifying where that elusive centre of gravity is to be found at any given time.

About the de Valera era there can be little doubt. Policies, for the most part, derived from the fertile, if often mistaken, ideals of the man who could discern the deepest wishes of the Irish people by looking into his own heart – policies tempered or enhanced, as the case might be, by the foresight and the subtlety of the Moynihans and the Cremins of the public service. That these policies secured electoral majorities time after time demonstrates, perhaps, less the ineducability of the electorate than the fact that vision and idealism in politics are not to be disregarded, even if they are occasionally wrong-headed or strategically impoverished. The mini-era in which Noel Browne flourished briefly as Minister for Health provides valuable supporting evidence for the same thesis.

Lemass had known for many years that he would never be a leader in the de Valera mode, and that he could not command loyalty to his policies on the same basis. He saw efficiency as an undervalued requirement of Irish public life (it could be argued that it still is). He also – and this is perhaps where he made the most substantial break with de Valera, whose personal magnetism he could not replicate – saw the need, if public policy was to enjoy the political support it required, to engage a wider cast of actors in the whole policy formulation process. In relation to economic policy, this meant primarily business and trade union interests, whom he incorporated in the process of policy formulation to a greater extent than any of his predecessors.

Under Lemass, nonetheless, the centre of gravity of the policy formulation process remained fundamentally political. There were exceptions, of course. It is noteworthy, in particular, that there were a number of areas in which public servants, more generally seen as a brake on change, actively encouraged it: Whitaker in relation to economic policy, and Mac Gearailt and O'Connor in that most unlikely breeding ground for innovation, the Department of Education. It is certainly worth considering, in the light of this, whether this delicate balance between politics and public administration has continued to be the case in the decades which separate us from the 1960s. It could be argued that the main *foci* of policy formulation in the late 1960s and early 1970s were even external to the three main actors I have mentioned, and were effectively environmental: the Northern crisis after 1969, and the economic crises of the mid-1970s. Thereafter, policy formulation seems to have been driven increasingly by short-term considerations. This has meant a larger role for the public service, particularly in relation to the longer-term issues of strategic planning and development, but also in relation to fire-brigade activities. It has also created a larger role for the interest groups in society generally – particularly the more vocal and electorally powerful ones. In all of this, there is the ever-present danger that the centrality and quality of political decision making, and the often harsh choices that have to be made by political actors, can become submerged in a bland managerialism of which Lemass, for all his managerialist efficiencies, would surely have disapproved. In this context, among many others, the studies in this volume provide invaluable matter for reflection, and suggest further avenues for research.

Acknowledgements

The editors would like to take this opportunity to thank our contributors for their efforts during the compilation of this volume. We, and our authors, are grateful to the staff of various archives both in Ireland and abroad without whose efforts no new research would be possible in contemporary history. We are indebted to John Horgan for his contribution of such an eloquent foreword. John has been a mine of information and unfailingly helpful when we have called on him, as we have had to do many times, for advice and information. We would like to thank Michael Moynihan and Declan Ryan of the *Irish Examiner* for providing us with the wonderful cover picture of Seán Lemass and Jack Lynch at the handover of power in November 1966. We are extremely grateful to Barbara Mennell at UCD Press for her marvellous professionalism. She has been a joy to work with. Brian Girvin wishes to thank the British Academy for a research grant to carry out research for his contributions, and to the Department of Politics at the University of Glasgow for providing him with leave to finish the research and editing for the book. Gary Murphy wishes to thank the School of Law and Government at Dublin City University for various research support over the duration of the writing of this book. He would also like to thank Breda Griffith and Dave Hannigan for their friendship and hospitality during various research trips to the United States. Finally we would like to thank Rona and Mandy for their support and encouragement over the years.

BRIAN GIRVIN
GARY MURPHY
Glasgow and Dublin
September 2005

Abbreviations

AIFTA	Anglo-Irish Free Trade Area
BBC	British Broadcasting Corporation
BBFC	British Board of Film Classification
BFI	British Film Institute
CAB	Cabinet Minutes
CCIH	Centre for Contemporary Irish History
CIA	Central Intelligence Agency
CIO	Committee on Industrial Organisation
CIU	Congress of Irish Unions
Dáil Deb	Dáil Éireann, Parliamentary Debates
DC	Department of Communications
DDA	Dublin Diocesan Archives
DETE	Department of Enterprise, Trade and Employment
DF	Department of Finance
DFA	Department of Foreign Affairs, Central Registry Files
DIC	Department of Industry and Commerce
DNC	Democratic National Committee Papers
DT	Department of the Taoiseach
DT S	National Archives of Ireland, Department of the Taoiseach, Files Series
EC	European Communities
ECA	Economic Co-operation Administration
ECSC	European Coal and Steel Community
EEC	European Economic Community
EFTA	European Free Trade Area
EIPP	Education Investment and Planning Programme
EPA	European Productivity Agency
ERP	European Recovery Programme
FDI	Foreign Direct Investment
FII	Federation of Irish Industries

FIM	Federation of Irish Manufacturers
FTA	Free Trade Area
FUE	Federated Union of Employers
GATT	General Agreement on Tariffs and Trade
GPO	General Post Office
HSC	National Joint Committee on the Human Sciences and Their Application to Industry
HST	Harry S. Truman Presidential Library, Independence, Missouri
IAC	Industrial Advisory Council
ICC	Industrial Credit Corporation
ICTU	Irish Congress of Trade Unions
IDA	Industrial Development Authority
IFFC	Irish Film Finance Corporation Ltd
IIRS	Institute for Industrial Research and Standards
IMI	Irish Management Institute
INPC	Irish National Productivity Committee
IPC	Irish Productivity Centre
IRA	Irish Republican Army
ITGWU	Irish Transport and General Workers Union
ITUC	Irish Trade Union Congress
JFK	John F. Kennedy Presidential Library, Boston, Massachusetts
KP	John F. Kennedy Papers
LBJ	Lyndon B. Johnson Presidential Library, Austin, Texas.
LJP	Lyndon Johnson Papers
NAI	National Archives of Ireland
NARA	United States National Archives and Records Administration
NATO	North Atlantic Treaty Organisation
NFA	National Farmers Association
NLI	National Library of Ireland
NUI	National University of Ireland
OECD	Organisation for Economic Co-operation and Development
OEEC	Organisation for European Economic Co-operation
PRO	Public Record Office
PRONI	Public Record Office of Northern Ireland
PUTUO	Provisional United Trade Union Organisation
RTC	Regional Technical Colleges
RTE	Radio Telefís Éireann
RUC	Royal Ulster Constabulary

TCD   Trinity College, Dublin
UCD   University College Dublin
UCDA   University College Dublin, Archives Department
UN   United Nations
VEC   Vocational Education Committees

Contributors to this volume

ENDA DELANEY is a lecturer in modern Irish history at the University of Aberdeen. He is the author of *Demography, State and Society: Irish Migration to Britain, 1921–1971* (2000) and *Irish Emigration Since 1921* (2002). His current project is a monograph on *The Irish in Post-war Britain: Displacement, Memory and Home*, to be published by Oxford University Press in 2007.

MAURICE FITZGERALD is a lecturer in European and International Studies at Loughborough University, and a graduate of University College Cork and the European University Institute, Florence. He has published on Ireland's history of European integration, Irish neutrality, and Irish-American diplomatic relations.

RODDY FLYNN is the director of Film and Television Studies at the School of Communications, Dublin City University, where he lectures on political economy of the media. He is currently working on two cinema-related books: *Cinema and State: Irish Film Policy from 1922 to 2005* and the *Historical Dictionary of Irish Cinema* with Patrick Brereton.

BRIAN GIRVIN is Professor of Comparative Politics at the University Glasgow. Among his principal publications are *Between Two Worlds: Politics and Economy in Independent Ireland* (Dublin 1989), *The Right in the Twentieth Century* (London, 1994), *Ireland and the Second World War: Politics, Society and Remembrance* (edited with Geoffrey Roberts) (Dublin, 2000), *From Union to Union: Nationalism, Democracy and Religion in Ireland* (Dublin, 2002). His book on Ireland during the Second World War, *The Emergency*, will be published by Macmillan in 2006.

MICHAEL KENNEDY is Executive Editor of the Royal Irish Academy's Documents on Irish Foreign Policy Series. He has published widely on Irish diplomatic and political history. His most recent publications include

Ireland, Europe and the Marshall Plan (edited with Till Geiger) (Dublin, 2004), *Division and Consensus: The Politics of Cross Border Relations in Ireland* (Dublin, 2000) and *Ireland and the Council of Europe* (with Eunan O'Halpin, Strasbourg, 2000).

PETER MURRAY is lecturer in sociology at the National University of Ireland, Maynooth, and a research associate of the National Institute for Regional and Spatial Analysis. He has published work on early twentieth-century Irish social and political movements and on industrial work and health issues in contemporary Ireland. His current research on Irish involvement in Europe's productivity drive after the Second World War is being supported by a grant from the Irish Research Council for the Humanities and Social Sciences.

GARY MURPHY is senior lecturer in government in the School of Law and Government at Dublin City University. He is the author of *Economic Realignment and the Politics of EEC Entry, Ireland, 1948–1973* (Bethesda, 2003), and co-editor of *Irish Political Studies*, the leading journal of political science in Ireland. He has published widely on Irish political history and is currently engaged in research on political lobbying.

NIAMH PUIRSÉIL is a research fellow in the Centre for Contemporary Irish History in Trinity College, Dublin. She is the co-editor of *Saothar*, the Irish Journal of Labour History and is currently completing a history of the Irish Labour Party since 1922 to be published by UCD Press.

ROBERT SAVAGE is co-director of the Boston College Irish Studies program. He is an editor of the *Irish Literary Supplement* and serves on the editorial board of *The Historian*. His books include an edited volume, *Ireland in the New Century: Politics, Culture and Identity* (2003), *Seán Lemass: A Biography* (1999), and *Irish Television: A Political and Social History* (1996). He has published a number of scholarly articles on twentieth-century Irish history, media, and visual arts. His current book project explores the politics of broadcasting in Ireland in the 1960s.

JOHN WALSH is pursuing postgraduate research with the Centre for Contemporary Irish History, Trinity College, Dublin. He has recently completed his PhD thesis on 'The politics of expansion: a study of educational policy in the Republic of Ireland 1957–1971'.

CHAPTER ONE

Whose Ireland? The Lemass era

BRIAN GIRVIN
GARY MURPHY

—

Seán Lemass is one of the most impressive figures in Irish politics during the twentieth century. More so than Eamon de Valera, contemporary Ireland bears the stamp of Lemass. In less than a decade he achieved more than his predecessor did in forty years. A veteran of the 1916 Rebellion at the age of 16, he played an active role in the War of Independence and supported the anti-Treaty forces in the Civil War. Earlier than many in the republican opposition, he recognised the importance of political activity, yet though a founder member of Fianna Fáil he like many others retained an ambivalent attitude to democracy for some time. At the age of 32 he became Minister for Industry and Commerce in de Valera's first government in 1932, a position he held until the outbreak of war in 1939. He then took the post of Minister for Supplies, but in 1941 took over the Industry and Commerce portfolio in addition. In 1945, a month short of his 46th birthday, Lemass was appointed Tánaiste after Seán T. O'Kelly was elected President. A sympathetic observer of Fianna Fáil, Frank Skinner, wrote in 1946 that Lemass 'was only beginning his career', adding that '[t]he appointment may be regarded as a pointer to the future'.[1] This suggests that Lemass's succession as leader of Fianna Fáil and Taoiseach was inevitable, though it was not to occur until 1959. For most of this time, despite his formidable success in government and politics, Lemass like many others remained in de Valera's shadow.

It is with some of these thoughts in mind that the editors decided to call this volume of essays a study in the Lemass era and to focus primarily on the period from 1945 to 1973. If de Valera's shadow remains potent for most of this period, it is also true to say that in retrospect the most significant contribution to Irish public life was that made by Lemass and not de Valera after 1945. The year 1945 is the beginning of a new era in Europe and it is with this era that Lemass's contribution is most closely associated, whereas that new world was increasingly out of sympathy with the Ireland created by de Valera. Although we decided to

end with 1973, this is clearly not the end of an era. In 1973 Ireland finally joins the EEC with a strong commitment to European integration and a commitment to economic modernisation. It is also the moment when significant sections of the Irish elite and its population seriously come to question de Valera's Ireland. Although Lemass was present at the creation of de Valera's Ireland and indeed contributed to it in a substantial fashion, he also presided over the redesign of that policy as a consequence of his actions after 1945. The contributors to this volume seek to assess this contribution and to emphasise various turning points on the road to a new Ireland. The editors are of the view that Lemass largely reforged Ireland after he came to office in 1959 but his influence outlived him after his death in 1971. Lemass did not openly challenge de Valera's Ireland, but he cultivated forces and individuals that would not be constrained by the limitations imposed by that earlier vision.[2]

Perhaps some justification is required for this claim. It is true that there is no clear break with the past in Ireland in 1945, as was the case in Britain, France or Germany. Ireland is similar to the United States, where the radicalism of the New Deal had been exhausted, but the Democrats remained the dominant party. Fianna Fáil was in an analogous position, defending what it had achieved against critics inside and outside the party. In both countries there was a wide-ranging consensus on most issues, but this was increasingly conservative in form. In similar fashion to the Democrats, Fianna Fáil had achieved much since 1932 but the future was not clear after the war. Despite his appointment as Tánaiste, 1945 was a year of failure for Lemass. Though some of his policy initiatives may have been ill judged, he remained committed to change. In this he was thwarted by the inertia and conservatism of his own party and colleagues. The appointment of Frank Aiken as Minister for Finance might have produced an ally, yet Aiken was ill equipped for the role of innovator and there is little evidence that he recognised the need for change as Lemass did. In any event, de Valera did not appoint Aiken because he recognised his commitment to unorthodox economic policies, but as a reward for his steadfast support on neutrality throughout the Emergency. De Valera's own vision of Ireland was already a traditional one, best expressed in his 1943 St Patrick's Day message to the United States, but reflected also in other statements and policies. Lemass's ambitious plans for economic growth, full employment and an active trade policy all foundered in the years after 1945, while his attempts to incorporate the trade union movement were plagued by inertia and obstruction.

Lemass's failures in the immediate post-war world reflected a wider malaise in Ireland at this time. The country had stabilised and settled into a period of self-imposed isolation that obstructed further change. By this time the power-ful nationalist forces that had driven Ireland since the beginning of the century had largely been exhausted. Fianna Fáil had achieved much in its own terms since 1932. Some of this achievement was positive other less so, yet the party and the country had no clear direction in which to go by 1945. Was it to be more of the same or could it move in a more radical direction? To adopt more of the same entailed emphasising the restoration of the Irish language and creating the conditions to unite the island into a single nationalist state. Language revival seemed increasingly elusive in a society that was now predominantly English speaking. The campaign proved attractive to nationalists and to those sections of the professional middle classes who used it for self-promotion in the public sector. The commitment to Irish unity was reduced to anti-partitionism (which is a very different matter) and, when it was not merely ritualistic, served to mobilise activists during elections or when Fianna Fáil was out of office after 1948. Indeed, the very policies that made Fianna Fáil popular were the ones that alienated Northern Unionists the most. Political success between 1932 and 1945 made Fianna Fáil more conservative. De Valera's governments had estab-lished a new institutional architecture, which had been broadly accepted by the opposition and the general public. Fianna Fáil was now committed to pre-serving what it had created. This overlapped and gave expression to more general trends in Irish society, making Ireland after the war the most conservative state in Western Europe. Erskine Childers's remarked on this tendency within the Fianna Fáil party when he reported on the state of the party during the post-war period.[3]

Despite these conservative trends, it is possible to make the case that 1945 is an appropriate point of departure for considering this period an era especially associated with Lemass. It is the moment when Ireland began to fall behind the European norm. The country becomes poor in comparative terms after 1945 and continued to be so until the late 1980s. The question for Ireland (but especially for Lemass) after 1945 was how could an independent Ireland improve the economic and social welfare of its population. Irish nationalists had assumed that political independence would significantly improve Ireland's economic position and that the state could provide employment opportunities for an increased population. However, much of this confidence was misplaced, especially after 1932. If Cumann na nGaedheal had been conservative during the 1920s, this had been based on a realistic if cautious assessment of the economy's strength. Fianna Fáil's policies were more radical in intention, but frequently ill-judged in terms of what was best for Ireland's future. By the end

of the Emergency, therefore, the Irish economy was heavily subsidised, inten-
sively protected and largely controlled by the state. In addition, the strength of
the economy was heavily dependent on privileged access to the British market
and the success of British policy making. The economic consequences of this
were severe, but the crisis that Ireland faced was more dangerous than this.
Ireland's weakness was compounded by other social patterns, not all of them
linked to the economy. Mass emigration returned after the war ended, especially
of women and the young to an expanding Britain. Economic growth and living
standards grew slowly throughout the 1950s, if at all. This reinforced the tendency to emigrate, as did the virtual collapse of the traditional farming sector,
especially in the West of Ireland. Nor did Ireland develop a successful export
sector, as most successful European states did at this time.[4] All of this took place
in a political framework that was isolationist, cutting Ireland off from outside
influence. These trends also provided a justification for a moral tyranny exercised
by the Catholic Church, moral vigilantes and at times the political authorities.
While much of this was implicit in the inter-war political culture of independent
Ireland, these trends came to dominate the two decades after 1945.

The very desperation of the situation provided the opportunity as well as a
challenge for the Irish political elite. In this basic sense it was a point of departure from the high point of de Valera's Ireland and the beginning of a journey
that led to the EU and the so-called Celtic Tiger. This is the period when
Lemass made his most important long-term contribution to Irish politics. It
was also his opportunity to shape Ireland for the foreseeable future and this he
did in a number of ways. While there is a surprising amount of continuity,
what set Lemass apart is that he questioned many certainties and challenged his
colleagues to think in a different fashion. Thus while Lemass remained a
nationalist, in contrast to de Valera his nationalism was promoted as an active
commitment to change and development. Closely linked to this was an expansionary vision, one that provided an optimistic assessment of Ireland's strengths.
Despite failures, setbacks and political obstruction he never quite lost the view
that if Ireland was to survive it had to change. Unlike most of Fianna Fáil and
indeed most of the country, Lemass sensed that de Valera's Ireland was no
longer sufficient in the changing world. The dead hand of de Valera is recog-
nisable in many ways, but perhaps most disastrously on Northern Ireland and
on the economy. De Valera seems to have had little interest in the economy or
in the conditions under which Irish people had to live. His call to Irish
emigrants in Britain to return home, as their living conditions in British cities
were often poor, demonstrated a lack of understanding about the underlying

state of Ireland. In contrast Lemass recognised that conditions in Ireland were pushing young men and women out of the country and his various policy suggestions during the 1940s and 1950s attempted explicitly to address this. Likewise on Northern Ireland, de Valera seemed content to reiterate old platitudes about unity, yet when Lemass suggested a new departure in 1955 de Valera vetoed his initiative. What can be seen in the 1950s is Lemass developing a set of ideas that challenged the existing certainties of de Valera and Fianna Fáil. In a more general sense, Lemass appreciated that the world outside had changed, that it did not owe Ireland a living and that Ireland had to change to meet the challenge of this new environment. In this sense he promoted the modernisation of Irish society, as did others such as T. K. Whitaker, the secretary of the Department of Finance and Garret FitzGerald, later to be a modernising Taoiseach in his own right.

De Valera remained a constraint until he retired as Taoiseach and leader of Fianna Fáil in 1959. The years between 1945 and 1959 were to all intents and purposes lost years for Ireland. During this time the crisis got worse and the introduction of new policies was postponed. Indeed it was the depth of the crisis that provided Lemass with his opportunity in 1959 when he succeeded de Valera. In his poem 'The Siege of Mullingar' published in 1972, John Montague declaimed that:

> Puritan Ireland's dead and gone,
> A myth of O'Connor and Ó Faoláin

It may be that Montague was premature in his description, but he recognised the changes were already in train. By the time this was written Seán Lemass was dead (in 1971). De Valera outlived his deputy by four years, but it was Lemass's vision of Ireland that came to dominate the following decades rather than that of de Valera. It is our contention that the Ireland that has evolved since 1973 is primarily a product of Lemass and that this new Ireland has emerged through conflict with that of the de Valera vision. This conflict has frequently been a subtle one of accommodation, but also on some issues the conflict has deeply divided the society and political culture (Northern Ireland and moral issues such as abortion and divorce). John Horgan in his important biography of Lemass calls him the 'Enigmatic patriot', and this draws attention to the continuing importance of nationalism in the thinking of Lemass. T. K. Whitaker has described Lemass as a 'pragmatic nationalist', noting that he was probably not opposed to the Ireland that de Valera had created but 'he simply had some impatience with it in so far as it might be a hindrance to change, the change he wanted'.[5] There is considerable strength in both these comments but perhaps both underestimate the destabilising impact of Lemass's brief tenure as Taoiseach between 1959 and 1966. In some senses at least Lemass challenged most of the features of the society that de Valera had put in place, although he did not always do so directly.

If 1945 was the highpoint of de Valera's Ireland, it was nearly all down hill after that. Irish neutrality during the war, although understandable, was handled in such a narrow way as to alienate both the British and American governments. More importantly it increased Ireland's isolationism (both in practical and intellectual terms) after the war, making it more difficult for a small state in a period of change and uncertainty to adapt to the new circumstances. Ireland was in crisis at the time of the 1957 general election, but as yet there was no clear vision for the future. We now know from the archives that Lemass was thinking about a new economic policy and he was certainly prepared to be creative on Northern Ireland. But beyond that there is little evidence that he had recognised the changing nature of the world economy or the balance of power in Europe. He remained opposed to European integration, though no longer ideologically opposed in the way he had been during the 1930s. He increasingly recognised the value of free trade, but was not clear how that could be achieved without widespread disruption of the Irish economy.

It is probable that de Valera remained in office too long. If he had resigned in 1945 there would have been some turmoil but surely a new (and possibly younger) leader would have proved to be more innovative. We can only speculate, but the evidence from the 1950s suggests that de Valera was paralysed politically, without any clear understanding of what was happening to his society. This is not to maintain that there was a groundswell for change after 1945. Indeed it is probable that emigration reinforced the stability of the system, because those who remained had a stake in the society.[6] However, the political elite could not ignore the crisis of emigration, unemployment and the widening gap in the standard of living between Ireland and Britain and most sensitively with Northern Ireland. What emerges after 1957, but is more crucially consolidated in 1959 when Lemass becomes Taoiseach, is a modernising coalition that recognises the need to pull Ireland out of the slump it is in and share in the prosperity apparent in Europe (and not just the EEC).

There are two decisive moments in this process. The first is 1959 when Lemass becomes Taoiseach. He exercises full power for the first time and uses it to promote an active expansion of the economy. He not only recognises the need for state intervention but also accepts Whitaker's position that state investment should be for expansionist purposes. Furthermore, he accepts that Ireland had to be reintegrated into the global economy if it were to benefit from the worldwide expansion then under way. The second is the British decision to apply for membership of the European Community in 1961. This had two consequences of long-term importance. In the short run it made Ireland very dependent on Britain, because without the United Kingdom's good will Ireland could and would not have gained entry. But it also shifted policy outwards in a more fundamental fashion than had previously been the case. Policy makers now recognised that Europe was the object of policy and this was quickly internalised. In this respect Ireland had been more pro-European than Britain because in the 1960s it had limited options, but Irish diplomats and Ministers gained in confidence during the negotiating process and learnt to be good Europeans.

The decision on Europe had another indirect effect on policy. Ireland now became committed to free trade, but also to multilateral trading arrangements. The Anglo-Irish Free Trade Agreement 1965 was bilateral in nature, but the message it sent was that Ireland was prepared to leave behind the narrowly protectionist policies dictated by de Valera's commitment to economic nationalism and isolationism. This commitment to multilateralism has been maintained ever since and open markets have been a keystone of Irish policy since 1966 (indeed in recent surveys the Republic of Ireland was considered to have the most open economy in the world – ahead of the United States and Singapore). This was a startling departure from previous Fianna Fáil policies. Indeed we have a situation where the very person who introduced the original economic policies now removed them from the statute book. The contrast between de Valera and Lemass is quite striking here. When Lemass recognised that the policies were not working, he changed them. He may have been reluctant to do so, but his incisiveness permitted him to change at short notice. Furthermore, Lemass reinforced this when he recognised that native Irish industry could not achieve the growth, export or employment levels required for prosperity. He and his successors then jettisoned the protected sector and devised a sophisticated package of incentives to attract foreign industry to locate in Ireland.

By the time of his death, the economic environment created by Lemass during the 1930s had largely disappeared and a drastically different one put in its place. But more significantly, Ireland had begun to move away from the certainties of de Valera's Ireland. The road from 1959 leads to the application for European Community entry and then on to membership. In turn this leads to a different economic policy, one that integrates Ireland into the wider world economically and increasingly politically. Lemass would have been willing to give up Irish neutrality if that had been necessary to join the European Community, though that did not prove to be the case. By the time Ireland joined the EEC in 1973, Lemass's Ireland was coming into being. It had already proved successful on the economic front and there was a view that the worst was over. However, that did not prove to be the case. For most of the next 20 years Irish political life was divisive and in some cases lethal. This was not only a result of the conflict in Northern Ireland, but also reflected deepening division within the party system and in public opinion. Lemass could not have predicted this and he would have been taken aback by many of the changes, especially in terms of personal behaviour and attitudes now evident. However, the Ireland that has emerged is a consequence of his actions. He was the political catalyst for the changes and without him the world that we have inherited would have been a very different one.

In different ways the essays in this collection address Lemass's contribution to Irish political life between 1945 and 1973. As noted above Lemass died in 1971, yet his legacy continued long after this. This is not a self-contained period but it does mark a decisive break with the past. As various contributors show, the past often hung heavy over the changes, nowhere more so than in Northern Ireland. Lemass's most immediate and long-term impact was on the economy. Economics may be the dismal science and not everything should be reduced to it, but when a population is deserting the state because of lack of employment then it becomes a political imperative to improve this area of policy making. As Gary Murphy shows this was indeed a priority for Lemass once he returned to office in 1957 and especially after he became Taoiseach in 1959. It is during this time that Ireland ceases to be an inward-looking protectionist state, breaks with economic nationalism and adopts free trade and European integration as a developmental strategy. Ireland also ceases to be a primarily agricultural economy, but does not quite become an industrial one. What is significant is the decision to use state resources to attract foreign investment and to base policy on an export strategy. This chapter also charts the emergence of a corporatist consensus in respect of industrial policy and EU membership, drawing together the political and economic elites. This has remained an important policy dimension in Irish institutional history since then, though as Murphy reminds us this has never been unproblematic. Peter Murray's contribution focuses on the issue of productivity and the tortuous efforts to establish a national productivity centre. This had its origins in the Marshall Plan and the American view that productivity growth was the key to economic success in the post-war era. Early plans foundered due to opposition and possibly shortsighted-ness. It is telling that the centre was finally established shortly after Lemass became Taoiseach. In a sense it could be seen as a symbol of his commitment to the modernisation of the Irish economy. It is also as Murray points out an early example of social partnership that came to characterise Irish economic policy in the late 1980s.

Maurice FitzGerald addresses the issue of how Irish foreign policy was 'mainstreamed' under Lemass. The most dramatic example of this was the decision to apply for membership of the EEC in 1961. While this was originally prompted by the surprise decision of the UK to apply, successive Irish governments subsequently pursued the goal of membership as an independent objective. Irish foreign policy was transformed as a consequence. The diplomatic service became more professionalised and sophisticated, while foreign policy became more outgoing and multilateral. As well as abandoning de Valera's isolationism, Lemass questioned the continuing value of Irish neutrality. Lemass's commitment to European policy was decisive, as this was an aspect of Ireland's developmental strategy, but it was also a remarkably successful one. Ireland was the first poor country to join the EU and its experience demonstrates both the difficulties and opportunities associated with membership. Michael Kennedy examines Lemass's dramatic initiative on Northern Ireland. When Lemass met Terence O'Neill in January 1965, it seemed that the decades of enmity between nationalist and unionist could be left behind. It initiated a brief period of dialogue and promised much. Lemass had recognised earlier than most that traditional anti-partitionism had failed, but his action came too late to prevent the return to violence in Northern Ireland soon after he left office. Kennedy identifies the opportunities available as a result of these exchanges between north and south, but he also demonstrates clearly the very real obstacles to dialogue as well as the mistrust and misunderstandings that quickly undermined what good will existed.

In some areas continuity was much stronger. Enda Delaney shows how emigration was a central feature of the Lemass era, though as his and other contributions argue Lemass was committed to removing the causes of emigration. Lemass, Whitaker and others were motivated by a genuine fear that emigration would weaken Irish morale or even destroy its sovereignty. The new economic policies promoted by Lemass did not eliminate Irish emigration but they did provide some hope and opportunity that employment could be found in Ireland. The shortfall between the number who wanted to work in Ireland and the employment available continued into the 1990s to push a percentage of Irish people out of the country. Though emigration was a long-term pattern for Ireland, Lemass recognised that successful policies could remove the worst aspects of this. Niamh Puirséil also examines an aspect of continuity. Her chapter reinforces the view that little changes for the political parties and party competition by the time Ireland joined the EEC. Indeed, the most significant change in Irish politics by this time was Fianna Fáil's success in consolidating its dominant position in the political system. Fianna Fáil remained in office from 1957 to 1973, due in part to the opposition's weakness but also as a result of successful policy implementation. What seems remarkable is that the political party that had been most closely identified with the previous policies of stagnancy could prove so successful in electoral terms while jettisoning them. Puirséil suggests that this outcome was not inevitable, especially when the history of party competition between 1945 and 1957 is considered. Alternatives were available, yet it was Lemass and Fianna Fáil that was able to maintain (or re-establish) its dominance during a period of rapid change.

Change of course is a matter of perception. As Brian Girvin notes, Church–state relations remained remarkably stable for virtually all of this period. Liberal initiatives can be seen towards the end of the 1960s and debate becomes more lively and open by the early 1970s. Nevertheless, it might be argued that the moral community reflected in the 1937 Constitution and the influence of the Church on policy and society remains largely intact. What can be seen is the beginning of a re-evaluation of traditional Ireland rather than a confrontation with it. John Walsh highlights some of the pitfalls for Irish policy making in the sphere of education. It was also one that overlapped with Church–state relations. The modernising elite considered educational reform necessary if Ireland was to develop its economy and society. Yet the Catholic Church, the main establishment force in this sector, opposed radical change in education. Walsh traces the various policy initiatives and records some of the objections and responses to them. Though a policy area with the potential for considerable conflict, Lemass and his government negotiated this troublesome policy area with some skill and without open confrontation with the church. Robert Savage recounts how television provides the most public symbol of change during the 1960s. There was no television service in Ireland during the 1950s but the British influence was not far off. The introduction of television was novel and its consequences could be debated, but what was significant was the extent to which Lemass attempted to control its introduction and its operation. Despite a growing liberalism in the decade, it is possible to see aspects of Fianna Fáil authoritarianism in Lemass's thinking here. He recognised how powerful television could be in creating images and sought to control the impact of them on his government and party. In the short run this proved successful, but over a longer period effective government control proved to be more elusive. Roddy Flynn examines the impact of state policy on the film industry. Flynn discusses Lemass's active interest in this field, while emphasising its industrial rather than its cultural value for him. What is most striking about Flynn's study is Lemass's close interest in the field over a number of decades. What this also shows is the lingering influence of protectionism and the use of the semi-state model to make up for the failure of private enterprise in Ireland.

In essence what this volume shows is a Lemass struggling to overcome the constraints of both his own past and that of his party. It paints him not so much enigmatic as pragmatic in his attempts at providing leadership of both his party and his country. It shows how he in essence transformed the state in his too short a period as Taoiseach, a transformation that he had been planning in all but name since the immediate post-war period. The important point about Lemass was that he was willing to give the leadership that de Valera so patently did not. In that, the years between 1945 and 1973 are without any doubt the Lemass era.

CHAPTER TWO

Political and party competition in post-war Ireland

NIAMH PUIRSÉIL

—

Politics after the Emergency

Once the Second World War came to an end, elections were held throughout Western Europe with voters going to the polls for the first time since before the war.[1] The conflict had created an impetus for change and post-war reconstruction focused minds on the need for social and economic reform. This was not the case in Ireland, however, where the political scene was one of consistency bordering on rigor mortis. Success in the 1944 general election meant that Fianna Fáil, which had been in government since 1932, held office with a secure majority and the prospect of a further four years before it would have to face another election. Its 'position in the party system appeared unassailable'.[2] But the apparent unassailability of Fianna Fáil's position was less the result of the party's popularity among the electorate per se, than the inadequacy of the opposition. Fianna Fáil's main rival, Fine Gael, appeared to be in inexorable decline; it had lost seats at almost every election since 1932 and the 1943 contest saw its parliamentary party reduced by one third, with several senior members included in the cull. The general election held the following year saw it make an implicit admission of its status as a party of opposition by failing to field sufficient candidates to form a majority government. Nor did there appear to be any immediate threat to the government's position from the left. Wartime privations and a wages standstill had seen the Labour Party make significant gains in terms of membership and votes in the first couple of years of the 1940s; in the 1943 general election it increased its number of seats from nine to 17, each one gained at the expense of Fianna Fáil.[3] Labour's advance came to an abrupt end, however, as the party was sundered by personality-driven splits which saw five of the party's ITGWU deputies break away to form the

National Labour Party, on the specious excuse that Labour had been 'infested by communists', and for the rest of the decade schism, fear of a protracted red scare and lack of resources combined to see Labour operate as a shadow of its former self.

Fianna Fáil's overall majority in 1944 belied a slip in the party's support. For one thing the election had been won on a fairly low turnout, indicating a lack of active support for the regime, while the fall off of transfers from other parties, and from Labour in particular,[4] indicated that antipathy towards Fianna Fáil was in fact crystallising, a trend confirmed at the presidential election the following year.[5] Nor did the new government do very much to increase its popularity with the electorate at large. Its most significant projects, in particular Seán Lemass's plans for post-war development in the areas of electricity, turf, aviation and industry,[6] were for the long term and although important pieces of social legislation were drawn up, of which the 1947 Health Act was probably the most notable, the benefits were not felt immediately. In practical day-to-day terms the bad outweighed the good. Rationing not only continued after the war, but after a particularly bad winter, it was actually extended to cover bread in 1947. There was increasing industrial discontent, of which the 1946 teachers' strike in Dublin is probably the best remembered, and resentment towards the government grew. After so many years in office it looked tired and uninspiring, dominated by the same old faces and offering nothing of the post-war excitement that people could see elsewhere. There was a sense, as Erskine Childers wrote in 1948, that it had ceased to be the poor man's government, and 'even our supporters believe we have got above ourselves'.[7]

The foundation in the summer of 1946 of Clann na Poblachta, a coalition of republicans and social progressives which had much of the appearance of Fianna Fáil in its early more radical days, was somewhat symptomatic of the party's malaise. It was widely regarded as filling the vacuum created by Fianna Fáil's steady decline into respectability and it attracted not only disillusioned members from that party but also many previously unaffiliated people who had found all existing parties deficient in vision or energy. The appearance of the Clann had a powerful effect on the mood in the country; to a political scene which had become rather flat it lent excitement and to an electorate and an opposition which had come to see Fianna Fáil as invincible it gave confidence that an alternative government was possible.[8] When its first outings at the polls in a series of by-elections at the end of 1947 saw Clann na Poblachta win two of three seats, de Valera determined it was time to arrest its growth before it established too strong a foothold, and called a snap election for February 1948.

Fianna Fáil conducted a very poor campaign. Rather than promote any of its future plans it ran on its record, which still included the success of maintaining neutrality.[9] It was a very negative campaign. The opposition parties ran on a ticket of 'put them out' while the contest saw Seán MacEntee in especially vitriolic form as he accused both the Labour Party and Clann na Poblachta of communism.[10] Lemass complained during the campaign that if he could 'just get MacEntee to shut up and get the Chief to come out fighting we'd win',[11] but it was not to be. Fianna Fáil's vote dropped by seven per cent to its 1943 level and the party lost eight seats while the opposition parties (with the exception of the western farmers' party Clann na Talmhan) all made gains: Fine Gael one, Labour and National Labour six and one respectively, independents one, while Clann na Poblachta although it did not sweep the boards as anticipated won ten seats.[12] As it became apparent that no party had an overall majority talks began between Fine Gael, Labour, Clann na Talmhan, Clann na Poblachata and a number of independents about the possibility of putting together a coalition, but Fianna Fáil remained the largest party and confidently expected to be returned to office with the support of the six National Labour party deputies who had voted for de Valera as Taoiseach in 1944. This faith in National Labour turned out to be misplaced, however, when its five deputies decided at the eleventh hour that a seat at an inter-party cabinet table outweighed the honour of putting Dev back in office once again.[13]

Fianna Fáil's response to the 1948 election

Out of office for the first time in 16 years, Fianna Fáil felt hard done by. It saw its removal from office as ill recompense for its careful guidance of the country through the worst of the war years and the manner of its removal added to the sense of grievance. Had the party suffered a more ignominious defeat, its response to the election might have been quite different but, as it was, it attributed its loss of votes to factors such as Clann na Poblachta's 'unscrupulous campaign' against its leaders and the effect of the 1947 supplementary budget, and its loss of power due to the opportunism of various parties,[14] not least the duplicitous National Labour Party. Since the election had not been contested on policies, with most of the Fianna Fáil candidates contenting themselves with 'talking up Dev and down coalition',[15] the widely held belief within Fianna Fáil was that its policies had played no part in its defeat and so did not require any significant revision. Instead the party focused on its machine.[16] Believing the diverse and potentially volatile make-up of the new administration would militate against its longevity, it was felt that all that the party needed to do was keep the cogs of its electoral organisation well oiled and sit back and wait for the government to collapse, which was bound to happen sooner rather than later.

There was some improvement in the state of the party around the country but little was done in the way of serious systematic reorganisation.[17] Even if this had been undertaken, however, it is questionable whether it would have yielded any significant result on its own, for while the new threat of coalitionism might have been enough to rouse existing activists back to life nothing was done to attract new members, or more importantly new supporters, into the Fianna Fáil fold. The party had grown stale. Years in government had seen most of its early radicalism dissipate and the party had become increasingly aged and conservative at every level. As Tom Garvin has noted, many of those who had joined Clann na Poblachta had done so having found Fianna Fáil unreceptive to 'new blood or ideas', it being dominated by an ageing leadership 'determined to prevent younger men replacing them'.[18] The place for athletic youths was on the football pitch rather than near the corridors of power. Some younger people were joining the party, and the reports of the party's secretaries continually called for them to be encouraged, but even so they often met with a grim condescension capable of discouraging all but the most ardent young activist. Michael B. Yeats, a member of the National Executive in his late twenties at this time, recalled a suggestion he made at a committee meeting being dismissed out of hand by the chairman Frank Aiken with the words 'tá tú óg' (you are young). This attitude, Yeats observed, 'might have been understandable coming from an old man, but Aiken at the time was only 52'.[19] Fianna Fáil, apparently, was no party for young men.

1951–4

Predictions of the inter-Party government's early demise did not come to pass and the administration managed to keep going for just over three years. Over time the government had seen several deputies withdraw their allegiance to the administration over various issues. When the defection of two Clann na Poblachta deputies, Noel Browne and Jack McQuillan, over the government's shelving of the Mother and Child health proposals was followed by a revolt of a number of independents over the price of milk in April 1951, the administration found itself in a very precarious position, prompting Costello to call a general election. As such, when the government broke up it was because it had lost its working majority rather than because of any significant dispute between the constituent parties. The outgoing government's decision to contest the election as a unit meant for the first time the electorate was faced with an explicit choice of two blocs, Fianna Fáil or 'the rest'. There was no difference between the Fianna Fáil that went before the electorate in 1951 and that of 1948, and the contest saw the party run on a negative campaign encouraging voters to choose it and strong government, rather than seek a mandate for any specific policies – a variation on the theme of 'put them out' which had worked so well for the outgoing government the last time around. The result was inconclusive with very little change in the parties' strength in the new Dáil. The exception to this was Clann na Poblachta, whose behaviour in government – particularly the way in which it turned on its Health Minister Noël Browne when his Mother and Child scheme began to founder on the rock of ecclesiastical damnation – had exposed the hollow nature of its early promise. This time the party won only two seats. Fianna Fáil returned with only one extra seat but was able to secure the support of enough independents to give it a slender working majority.

Years later Lemass recalled how he had not welcomed the 'prospect of coming back into government in the conditions of 1951 at all . . . we had not really got down to clearing our minds on post-war development'.[20] In fact, the cause of economic development within Fianna Fáil had, if anything, declined during the years in opposition. Post-war boom, high capital expenditure by the inter-party government and stockpiling prompted by the outbreak of war in Korea combined to present the incoming government with some hefty economic problems. De Valera, a man described as being 'temperamentally disposed towards "austerity"',[21] was inclined to heed the dire warnings about inflationary pressures emanating from the Central Bank and the Department of Finance and chose his Minister for Finance accordingly.[22] Seán MacEntee's return to finance put an unequivocally conservative stamp on the new administration from the outset and signalled that Lemass's influence was on the wane: in 1939 de Valera had apparently acceded to Lemass's demand (on threat of resigna-tion) that MacEntee be removed from that post.[23] By putting MacEntee back there the Taoiseach was making it abundantly clear that economically this would not be a progressive administration.

Nevertheless, while it was anticipated that MacEntee's would be a con-servative ministry, the degree of retrenchment provided for in his first budget in 1952 was greater than anyone had bargained for. In what quickly became known as the 'famine budget' he endeavoured to tackle a worsening balance of payments deficit by abolishing or reducing food subsidies, while increasing duties on tobacco, drink and petrol.[24] The severity of the measures were a boon to the opposition parties which had lacked vigour or direction until now. Unsurprisingly there was a great deal of displeasure within Fianna Fáil itself. Some were so angered they left the party while others consciously joined forces with their colleagues in Dublin South Central (Lemass's constituency) 'in the belief that Lemass represented the authentic voice of Fianna Fáil'.[25] The public's resentment towards the government was well illustrated seven months after the budget in a by-election in Dublin North West in which the Fianna Fáil candidate was defeated by a margin of two to one. This was probably the impetus behind a demand by the parliamentary party for a meeting to review government policy[26] but while this may have given the party's representatives an opportunity to articulate their concerns it was made abundantly clear by the Taoiseach and the Minister for Finance that there would be no change in the government's economic direction.[27] The issue was not broached again within the parliamentary party for another six months.

In the meantime, the political scene was characterised by uncertainty, with the government operating on a very slim majority and extremely vulnerable in the event of a by-election. MacEntee's assurances that the balance of payments crisis had lifted counted for little amidst growing unemployment (highlighted by street protests in Dublin) and rising prices, as the heavy defeats for Fianna Fáil candidates in two by-elections held in June 1953 attested. The frantic political activity surrounding the by-elections reached its zenith with a motion of confidence tabled by de Valera. This he won (although only just) after which the fierce political fighting abated as the opposition conserved their energy for a more opportune time. After the by-election defeats, the government began to adopt a more progressive approach. Within Fianna Fáil growing disquiet prompted a number of deputies to put down a motion at a parliamentary party meeting calling for an end to financial austerity and asking the government 'to frame a progressive policy suited to the altered situation'.[28] The minutes recall that the debate was postponed to the next meeting although as Senator Michael B. Yeats recalled, animated debate on the motion went over two days before the motion was 'inevitably' defeated. As Yeats, who had been one of the instigators of the motion, left the room, Lemass said in his ear, 'never mind Senator, you were ninety-eight percent right'.[29] Only few days later, de Valera and Lemass met a deputation from the ITUC and the Labour Party to discuss the unemployment situation,[30] with the next day seeing Lemass circulate a memorandum to his cabinet colleagues recommending an increase in government spending to stimulate the economy.[31] Unsurprisingly, Lemass's suggestions prompted a damning response from MacEntee but by this time Frank Aiken had rowed into the argument, advocating the establishment of a National Development Fund. Cabinet approved the proposals in August 1953, with a committee to establish the fund put together in September.[32] It was, as Ronan Fanning has pointed out, the 'first major reversal of the deflationary policy which had been followed since the crisis of 1951–52' and indicated that the balance of power within the government had indeed swung back towards Lemass.[33]

By the end of 1953 the mood in the Fianna Fáil camp had undergone a radical reversal. The election of Fianna Fáil's candidate on the first count in a by-election in Galway South held in late August provided an immeasurable boost to the organisation's confidence. This was followed by another lift a couple of months later when three of the independent deputies supporting the government sought admission to the party. That the former Clann na Poblachta minister Noel Browne was one of the three was particularly welcome, for although he was a mercurial character with a reputation for being a difficult colleague, he was held in high standing by the Dublin working class and it seemed his decision to join Fianna Fáil would do the party some good with that constituency which had been so alienated by the government's austerity measures. It worried the Labour Party enough to issue a statement trying to dissuade Browne's supporters from following him into Fianna Fáil.[34] Indeed, such was the turnaround in the party's image over the latter half of the year that *The Irish Times* columnist Aknefton reported gossip that negotiations were taking place at the highest level between Labour and Fianna Fáil which would result in a new inter-party set-up being formed after a 'soft budget'.[35] The rumour was completely without foundation, as Aknefton indeed admitted at the time, but it is significant all the same, for such a story would have been utterly unthinkable only six months earlier.

However, two by-election successes for Fine Gael in March prompted de Valera to call an election for May. The campaign saw the opposition parties focus on the rising cost of living and promise to reduce prices, while Fianna Fáil ran once again on its platform of strong government. Despite the adverse by-election results, Fianna Fáil was relatively sanguine going into the contest, believing it would at least match its 1951 result; but the poll merely confirmed that the government had become out of touch and had underestimated the depth of residual anger about the 1952 budget. Fine Gael improved on its 1951 result by ten seats, Labour by four. Fianna Fáil not only returned with four fewer seats than in 1951, but it also lost the three independent deputies who had joined the party six month earlier, leaving it ten seats short of a majority and without sufficient independents to make up the shortfall. The onus fell on the former inter-party colleagues to form a new administration. This would be a more cohesive grouping than the first inter-party government, with only three parties – Fine Gael, Labour and Clann na Talmhan – in cabinet, relying on what was left of Clann na Poblachta for external support to give it a working majority.

The second inter-party government, 1954–7

'The future of Fianna Fáil is perhaps the most debated question in contemporary politics' noted *The Leader* after the election.[36] Fianna Fáil's ejection from office for the second time in six years was quite a blow to a party, which had until recently seen government as its natural right. Once again, first thoughts turned to the party machine. Lemass was entrusted with the task of initiating a reorganisation campaign, which he embarked upon with great vigour, selecting a team of young activists to help him in this task.[37] Logistical mastermind that he was, Lemass was acutely aware that no amount of reorganisation could bring life back to a dead horse. As he saw it, if Fianna Fáil could not offer the people an effective plan for economic development there could be no future for the party in the long run. The party's return to opposition gave it breathing space to reassess its policy away from the day-to-day problems of managing the country, and Lemass was determined that, unlike the previous time, the opportunity would not be wasted. He outlined his thesis to delegates at the Ard Fheis in October 1954, explaining that the party had to choose whether it would be a national movement – that is an organisation primarily concerned with the development of national policy and interested in elections only as means by which the organisation would receive a mandate to pursue that policy – or a political machine. Fianna Fáil, he said, had tended towards the latter and had failed to live up to the responsibilities of the former. The time had come, he told delegates, to 'get back the status and functions of the organisation which we had in mind when we started'. No one, he said, would welcome constructive comments and criticism more than the executive.[38]

It was not the first time in his life that Lemass had called for a new departure – he had identified similar shortcomings in the old Sinn Féin party before the split which led to the formation of Fianna Fáil in 1926, when he argued that the party needed to address the more pressing problems of the people if it was to succeed.[39] The most obvious sign of support for Lemass's point of view among delegates came in the adoption of a proposal which stated that since the party had 'already achieved many of the objectives set forth at the time of its foundation' the National Executive should 'publish a statement of the Party's future programme, with particular emphasis on the social ideas enshrined in the Democratic Programme of the first Dáil'.[40] But yet, while Lemass and his supporters were anxious that the party should re-orient itself towards a more practical agenda, the old guard appeared unchanged, with de Valera devoting his president's address to the problem of partition.

The Ard Fheis had seen Lemass appeal for change through the members of the organisation. It is clear that Lemass could not rely on his colleagues in the Dáil for policy ideas, and out of office he lacked the input of experienced civil servants, so he began to look elsewhere for intellectual stimulus. In September 1954 he began moves to establish an organisation whose sole purpose would be to develop and publicise Fianna Fáil policy through public discussion and which would have no role in fighting elections.[41] Full membership was to be offered to members of the party in Dublin but there was also a provision for associate membership intended to attract 'influential persons, in all walks of life' to contribute to Fianna Fáil policy without imposing on them the obligations of running the annual cumann tea dance. Comh-Comhairle Átha Cliath (Dublin consultation council), as it was called, held its inaugural meeting in January 1955 at which Lemass once again set out the task facing the party. Subject to the preservation of the aims set out in the Córú (the Fianna Fáil constitution), he said, 'every aspect of policy is open to re-examination, every plan is open to revision. There will be no idea which will not be examined, no proposal which will not be fully tested.'[42]

This lack of sacred cows led one *Irish Times* reader to remark that the party was 'causing much amusement by its ingenious and frantic search for a policy before the next general election'.[43] Such cynicism about contemporary politics was typical of the time, but chinks in this stifling fatalism were becoming evident. For instance, turned off by the apparent absence of ideas within Irish party politics, a group of middle-class bright young things formed the discussion group Tuairim in 1954 which set itself the audacious task of solving 'the social, economic, political and cultural problems of modern Ireland'.[44] Interest in economic planning was growing among academic economists (of whom Patrick Lynch was perhaps the most significant), public servants (for whom the recent launch of the journal *Administration* provided a forum for debate[45]) and trade union leaders, but within the political sphere policy development was conspicuous by its absence. A few individuals sought to provide an impetus for reform, but they found themselves easily ignored by their colleagues who were either uninterested or actively hostile to change.

Lemass was privately trying to reorient Fianna Fáil's economic policy[46] but it was not until the end of the year that he went public with his proposals. In October 1955 Lemass gave a landmark speech to a meeting of Comh-Comhairle Átha Cliath in which he laid out his proposals for economic planning which he said would create 100,000 new jobs in five years. Lemass's plan (written with some help from Todd Andrews[47]) was based on the Vanoni Plan formulated for post-war development in Italy which suffered from similar problems as Ireland, including unequal regional development and mass emigration.[48] Lemass's speech confirmed his status as an innovator and a progressive, prompting *The Irish Times* columnist Aknefton to write that 'Mr de Valera may be the romantic leader of Fianna Fáil, Mr MacEntee the senior Minister of the ex-Cabinet but Seán Lemass remains the chief executive, the guiding hand not only of the Fianna Fáil party, but of Ireland's past, present and future'.[49] In this case, Aknefton's enthusiasm had got in the way of better judgement. That Lemass was allowed make it at all, in spite of the opposition of senior party colleagues to its central tenets, was perhaps significant but it was still no more than a solo run with Lemass trying to push his agenda within Fianna Fáil. He remained far from being the 'guiding hand' within his party. In the months subsequent to the speech in Clery's Ballroom Lemass continued to answer his critics,[50] and used the *Irish Press* to disseminate his thinking[51] but as time went on there was still no sign that his policies were any closer to being taken on as the official policy of his party. Enthusiasm vanquished, Aknefton now complained that the policy initiatives of individuals such as Lemass in Fianna Fáil and Jim Larkin junior in Labour would continue to come to nothing without the support of their parties.[52] There was certainly support among the rank and file members of Fianna Fáil for change and the 1955 Ard Fheis passed a motion calling for the completion and publication of the statement of policy as a matter of urgency,[53] but this was being resisted within the higher echelons of the party where there was a refusal to accept that a fundamental rethink was vital if the country was going to get out of its morass.

And what a morass it was. A balance of payments deficit, incorrectly blamed on an increase in consumer spending after the fifth round of pay increases in 1955, had prompted the Fine Gael Minister for Finance, Gerard Sweetman, to introduce a series of austerity measures in an effort to deflate the economy which had not actually overheated, thus exacerbating the already serious unemployment problem. In the absence of an alternative policy from any of the political parties it looked as though there could be no foreseeable challenge to the negative economic approach driven by Finance. The lack of vision on the part of the Irish body politic at this point was illustrated in the choice before the electorate:

> The inter-Party Government came into power on the threat of price increases to the working man's pint. Fianna Fáil may have inflated his pint, but the inter-Party Government has blown up his tobacco. Pipes or pints – this appears to be the issue in Irish politics today. You can drink a little more under Fine Gael or smoke a little more under Fianna Fáil.[54]

The economic situation continued to deteriorate throughout 1956, the sense of crisis heightened by the publication of the interim census figures in June which showed that the population of the state had reached its lowest recorded level.[55] When Sweetman subsequently introduced a second round of levies, the trade union movement heaped criticism on the government for compounding an already disastrous state of affairs. There seemed no sign of a policy reappraisal until October, when, apparently out of nowhere (but likely in response to an incipient revolt in the Labour Party) the Taoiseach John A. Costello presented a plan for economic development to a meeting of inter-party deputies.[56] The plan, drawn up in large part by the Taoiseach's informal economic advisers Patrick Lynch and Alexis Fitzgerald, was mostly a restatement of the government's existing programme but its provision to establish a capital investment advisory committee to the government represented a significant departure.[57] Favourably received within the government's constituent parts and in the press, Costello's plan seemed as though it had stemmed the tide of criticism for the time being.[58]

Long frustrated at the party's failure to adopt a strong economic policy, the progressive section of Fianna Fáil must have been alarmed when it seemed the government was about to steal a march on its plans. The November Ard Fheis, however, provided the opportunity to demand action. Members of the National Executive approached Padraic O'Halpin, a Dublin based activist who was close to Lemass, asking him to put down a motion demanding a statement on economic policy.[59] The motion calling for the 'early publication by the National Executive of Fianna Fáil's proposals to deal with the grave economic position of the country'[60] was not in itself particularly radical, but it involved the party doing something it had heretofore avoided – that is, make a decision. There was bitter resistance from elements on the National Executive, but in the end the motion was passed, following a recount in the hall.[61] The significance of this motion lies in its illustration of the desire for change and the continued opposition of senior elements within the party to this rather than in any practical sense, for in the end no statement was actually published.

'Let's get cracking'

By the beginning of 1957 the coalition maintained that the government was no longer sustainable. Divisions were becoming more apparent both within the parties (particularly in Fine Gael where resistance to Sweetman was growing[62]) and between them (with disaffection growing in the Labour Party particularly), and from a messy break up when Clann na Poblachta's National Executive withdrew its support following a government crackdown on republicans after the IRA began attacks on the border at the end of 1956.[63] The election held in the beginning of March took place in an atmosphere of abject gloom. None of the parties ran on purposely written manifestos, but referred back to statements made prior to the election,[64] Fine Gael emphasised its policy for production enunciated by Costello the previous October, while in Fianna Fáil's case Lemass's Clery's speech from October 1955 provided the keynote. This was of little consequence, however, as policy took second place to politics. The election of 1957 was merely the latest in the series of 'put them out' elections as once again the opposition (this time Fianna Fáil) reasoned the government had done a bad job and argued it could do better. Fianna Fáil presented itself as a strong alternative to vacillating coalition and presented itself as having a sense of purpose with its distinctly Lemassian slogans: 'let's go ahead again' and 'beat the crisis – let's get cracking!'.[65] Its means of doing this were less clear – the party's emphasis was more 'can do' than 'will do', Lemass recalling later that 'the general tenor of our campaign was that the serious economic difficulties of the times were curable and that Fianna Fáil had developed ideas for effecting a comprehensive cure. We did not elaborate on these ideas on which our collective mind was not at the time, fully made up'.[66]

A national swing towards the party combined with a lower level of transfers between the outgoing coalition partners saw Fianna Fáil return with 13 more seats than 1954, giving it an effective working majority in the Dáil.[67] As Joe Lee has pointed out, the extent of Fianna Fáil's victory was deceptive, particularly because of the very low turnout, so that it 'amounted less to a vote of confidence in Fianna Fail than to a vote of no confidence in the inter-party government'.[68]

The result was conclusive in another sense nonetheless; it showed the electorate's unambiguous rejection of a government which had been characterised by its regressive economic policy, just as it had done the last time. This fact was recognised by de Valera who, listening to his inner-populist, now acceded to Lemass's demand that MacEntee not be returned to Finance,[69] and appointed Lemass's close ally Jim Ryan to the post instead.[70] This highly significant change in personnel indicated that Lemass's influence was in the ascendant, but there was otherwise little outward sign of a fundamental change in direction. The first two years of the administration had all the hallmarks of an interregnum except the king, or chief in this case, was stubbornly refusing to let go of the reins of office. De Valera, who had seemed out of touch with the lives of most people for some time, now looked increasingly anachronistic. The 1957 Ard Fheis was a case in point. It had been a sober affair dominated by the question of how to end the country's economic malaise, but yet again he failed to address the concerns of the assembled delegates preferring, as he had done the previous year, to recapitulate the evils of partition. If this had been a case of Dev simply playing to an audience his choice of theme might have been acceptable but he was regularly treating his colleagues on the National Executive and parliamentary party to similar performances. 'It won't do', complained a dejected Oscar Traynor after one such occasion, 'the young people need jobs.'[71] Despite the growing sense of impatience at all levels at the need to inject more dynamism into the government, with Lemass in particular growing increasingly irritated by what he saw as de Valera's passive leadership,[72] the Chief remained in situ until the summer of 1959 when, somewhat grudgingly, he allowed himself to be translated to the presidency.

The politics of consensus

A number of commentators wondered if there could be a future for Fianna Fáil without de Valera at the helm – the party's attempt to replace proportional representation with a straight vote electoral system was seen as a sign of its own anxiety on the matter – but for many within the organisation the prospect of Lemass's leadership was a cause for rejoicing. Michael Yeats recalled an air of exhilaration on the day of Lemass's election as Taoiseach, 'For years the Fianna Fáil organisation, particularly the younger people, had been waiting and hoping for this day.'[73] Perhaps in the short term his election was more significant in lending an appearance of modernisation rather than any actual policy departure, for the fact was that by the time Lemass's long awaited accession had come to pass he had already won the policy battle. The government's approval for the endeavours of the secretary of the Department of Finance, T. K. Whitaker, to draw up a plan for national development in 1957, was a victory for Lemass. Published as *Economic Development* in May 1958 under Whitaker's own name, this was then used as the basis of the programme for economic expansion, which would constitute the blueprint for Irish economic development between 1959 and 1963.

By the time Lemass became Taoiseach, the rest of the political world had finally caught up with his thinking. As Joe Lee has pointed out, while there are many laments that he did not come to that office earlier, it is likely that he would not have achieved the same kind of success for he would still have had to battle the conservative mindsets that did so much to slow down the nation's progress.[74] Perhaps it was a case of cometh the hour, cometh the man. It had taken, as T. D. Williams had argued in 1953, a 'severe jolt' to shake the country out of its political and economic stagnation and once this had happened all Lemass could do was say 'I told you so', and get on with it.[75] The depression of the fifties was the hinge on which all political activity turned for almost the next two decades. Lemass had been a voice in the wilderness before, but now, after the Irish economy's dire performance through the 1950s, it would have been difficult to find anyone who would argue that a fundamental change in approach was not necessary. Planning in general was universally accepted, and Whitaker's plan in particular attracted little in the way of serious criticism. By deliberately identifying the work with a civil servant rather than the government, the first plan never became a political issue. In the year the programme went into effect Patrick Lynch lamented that 'Irish political economy, unfortunately, sometimes tends to be more political than economic'.[76] It is a comment largely borne out by the dreadful performance of the Irish economy up to that point but, on the other hand, if the politicians had been more political and less economic in 1952 or 1956, then the respective parties might not have lost both subsequent elections and the decade would not have become the political equivalent of Lannigan's ball. Nevertheless, it can be said of the first programme, as it later became known, that it took the economics out of Irish politics. In effect it did not matter which party was in office, economic policy would be largely determined by a group of civil servants, most of whom were in the Department of Finance and, following the setting up of the neo-corporatist National Industrial and Economic Council in 1963, representatives of industry and the trade union movement as well.

The mid-1950s crisis had another effect, which had greater practical impact on Irish politics than the absence of policy competition between the parties. The breakdown in the relationship between the former inter-party colleagues had been total. For Labour the trauma of being in government during those dark days, and the electorate's desertion of the party in 1957 as a result, was so great that even the most enthusiastic coalitionists now determined that Labour would never find itself the junior partner in government again. The result of Labour's anti-coalition stance was that, unless either it or Fine Gael managed a major breakthrough, Fianna Fáil was the only party capable of forming a government. Lemass used this to very good effect at the 1965 general election, and was returned with a majority government for the first time since 1944. Gerard Sweetman once told Declan Costello that the country needed alternative governments rather than alternative policies,[77] but the consensus on planning and Labour's anti-coalitionism meant that the electorate in effect had neither.

This was the case for most of the 1960s. There may have been differences in emphasis, ethos and style,[78] but nothing of substance. All the parties leaned slightly to the left of centre, although they switched positions within this area at different times, often leapfrogging over each other to give the impression of being furthest to the left. Lemass's 1963 statement that the party was moving to the left is one such example, Fine Gael's 1965 *Just Society* document another. Labour which should, in theory, have been the furthest to the left found itself hopelessly outmanoeuvred so that, as Basil Chubb put it, 'at a time when planning and state-inspired development were advocated by everyone' Labour could be found 'complaining feebly . . . that the clothes they could never quite bring themselves to put on had been stolen from their wardrobe'.[79] As the dapper young gentleman in a *Business and Finance* cartoon told his glamorous lady companion, 'darling, it's tragic, but I just can't find a party whose capitalist ideals measure up to my own'.[80] The irony of this lack of ideological or governmental choice was that the electorate did not appear to mind. In the early sixties David Thornley had warned that 'a condition of rigor mortis is reached with public acceptance that since government is expert and bi-partisan, and party conflict irrelevant to it, parties are themselves superfluous',[81] but in fact as the cynicism of the 1950s was replaced by a new optimism people actually returned to politics once again with voter turnout and party membership increasing across the board.

When Lemass stepped down as Taoiseach in 1966 there was a slight shift in emphasis although not necessarily in policy. His successor, Jack Lynch, was less inclined towards Lemass's leftist posturing and there was also a diminution of the dynamism which had characterised his predecessor's governments. Nevertheless, despite predictions to the contrary, Lynch was able to guide his party to victory once again on a combination of personal charm and alarmist attacks on the Labour Party, which had adopted some unnecessarily radical language and policies in an effort to distinguish itself from the other two parties. It was only in 1973, after a further 16 uninterrupted years in office, that the opposition parties managed to join forces and eject Fianna Fáil from office once again.

The 1960s were the age of Lemass by luck rather than design. Despite the sense of destiny that surrounds Lemass's period as Taoiseach it ought to be borne in mind that there was nothing inevitable about either his coming to power, or indeed the continued dominance of Fianna Fáil. As Richard Dunphy observed: 'from 1948 to 1957 Irish politics were in a state of flux; cracks were beginning to appear in Fianna Fáil's hegemony, but the very paucity of responses of the other political forces to the severe economic crisis eventually permitted the re-creation of Fianna Fáil dominance on a new basis'.[82] Had the second inter-party government survived long enough for the political storm clouds to dissipate and give Costello's plan for recovery the chance to get going, it is possible that Fianna Fáil might not have been returned to power so quickly and Lemass might never have had the chance to lead either his party or his country.[83] But it did, and Lemass took the opportunity to firmly establish his economic agenda which remained dominant throughout the 1960s 'not because of the dominance of the government party, but because of the permissiveness of the two opposition parties'.[84]

CHAPTER THREE

From economic nationalism to European Union

GARY MURPHY

—

Introduction

Of all the changes that took place in Ireland between 1945 and 1973, economic ones were among the most important. During this timeframe Ireland moved from being a largely agricultural economy to one increasingly involved in a complex global framework. Two features of this process are fundamental. The first was the recognition that Ireland could attract mobile capital from trans-national companies intending to invest in Europe and the other was the decision to join the EEC. This chapter will focus mainly on the policy-making process within Irish government from the late 1950s and trace the evolution of thinking in the economic field. It will suggest that one of the major difficulties for Lemass when he became Taoiseach was that the agrarian economy could not provide additional exports nor could it generate further employment (in fact it was discarding labour). Additionally, Irish industry proved unable to sustain growth and in particular could not break into export markets. This is the background for the dramatic change in policy that accompanied Lemass's period of leadership. Intertwined with this was Lemass's decision to incorporate the various social actors, particularly, the trade unions, business interests and farmers' groups into the economic policy-making process. The reasoning behind this revolves around Lemass's belief that he had no option but to bring these groups into the charmed circle of power if his attempt to move both the Irish economy and Irish society from economic nationalism to European union was going to be successful.

From protectionism to economic development

Protectionism, the mantra of Fianna Fáil's economic policy since coming to power in 1932 and which can described as the primordial symbol of economic nationalism, was reinforced during the 1950s. The crisis in the Irish economy in the 1950s lay not so much within industry as within agriculture. However, due to the importance of agriculture for the economy as a whole, the crisis affected industry to much the same degree. Industrial employment continued to increase, though at a slower rate than before. Unlike the 1930s, however, it proved impossible for protected industry to provide enough employment for those leaving the land and for those entering the labour market for the first time. One consequence of this was the accelerating emigration, which was a feature of the decade. Moreover, Irish wage rates, which had historically remained quite close to those prevailing in Britain, fell far behind in this period. By 1960, the average British worker earned at least forty per cent more than his Irish counterpart.[1] This income gap served as a strong incentive for skilled workers to emigrate even when not threatened by unemployment. Between 1951 and 1958, Gross Domestic Product rose by less than one per cent per year. Employment fell by 12 per cent, and the unemployment rate rose. Irish Gross Domestic Product/capita fell from 75 per cent to 60 per cent of the western European average. Yet during the 1950s real product per capita grew at 2.2 per cent per year and industrial output expanded at 2.8 per cent yearly, while output per farmer grew at a respectable 3.4 per cent. While the argument has been made that these figures are only disappointing when compared with the standards of neighbouring countries and not in historical terms,[2] it is more appropriate to note that placed in a comparative perspective, Ireland after 1945 failed to maximise its opportunities in the expanding European economy and consequently did not share in the affluence that accompanied it. It was during the 1950s that Ireland went into relative decline against similar states in Western Europe. In most states the process of post-war recovery was characterised by intensive industrialisation, the development of a strong export potential (often in manufacturing) and the acceptance of a broadly multilateral and free trade environment expressed through the recognition of GATT rules.[3] Ireland clearly did not share in this experience. Economic policy making continued to be restrictive, agriculture remained in a hegemonic position, and would remain so even after the publication of *Economic Development* in 1958. In fact, if anything, *Economic Development* reinforced the belief that agriculture would remain the driving force of the Irish economy. Ultimately Ireland was still on Europe's periphery

29

in both an economic and political sense. Unlike other European states Ireland did not achieve self-sustained growth in the course of the 1950s. Serious balance of payments problems plagued policy makers during the first half of the decade, followed by recession and then a depression in 1957. This was in contrast to pretty much the rest of Western Europe.

Economic Development, the famous 1958 policy document penned by the secretary of the Department of Finance, T. K. Whitaker, emerged from this crisis. Its most critical feature was its premise to shift from protection towards free trade and from discouragement to encouragement of foreign investment in Ireland. This involved a dramatic reversal of the rhetoric, and to a large extent of the practice of all policy, but especially Fianna Fáil policy, since 1932. Whitaker argued that the government should encourage industries, which would be competitive in world markets and provide a continuing source of employment at home:

> we can no longer rely for industrial development on extensive tariff and quota protection. Foreign industrialists will bring skills and techniques we need, and continuous and widespread publicity abroad is essential to attract them. If foreign industrial investment does not rapidly increase, a more radical removal of statutory restrictions on such investments should take place.[4]

The main theme of both documents as was pointed out at the time was that 'an increase in investment and an expansion in demand – coming from agriculture – would set in motion a general expansion in the national product'.[5] In conjunction with this was the aim of attracting foreign industry. Whitaker outlined two ways to attract foreign corporations: remove restrictions and give incentives for foreign firms to establish bases in Ireland. The Control of Manufactures Acts of 1932 and 1934 were amended and a series of proposals intended to attract outside investors to Ireland were recommended. As Tom Garvin has pointed out, many local manufacturers, some of them personal friends of Lemass, would have opposed such a move reflexively. Thus Lemass, aware that many of these manufacturers had been in operation since protectionism was introduced in 1932, rescinded in 1958 only the Acts for industries that exported the bulk of their produce. He then changed the title of the new act from a 'Repeal of the Control of Manufactures Act' to an 'Act for the encouragement of exports'. Those selling on a small scale to the local market would not be concerned and would remain quiescent.[6] In many ways this summed up Lemass's problem. He was trying to reorient economic policy, but could not afford to leave his political base behind. Nevertheless the fact that a start was made in amending these acts fortified Whitaker in his efforts to modernise the Irish economy and to bring Irish society forward.

Whitaker proposed that the IDA should expand its staff, particularly in North America, in an intensification of its efforts to attract foreign capital. He further proposed increasing the capital available for outright industrial grants. This was a point echoed by one of the country's foremost public servants, well-known Fianna Fáil activist, and friend of Lemass, Todd Andrews:

> I cannot see any quick way, or indeed any way of providing these 20,000 jobs out of our own resources; the capital must be brought in from outside . . . I do not think that we have enough trained people technically and commercially to enable us to spend £100 million per annum. We must try to induce established industries to set themselves up in the country.[7]

Andrews had in mind such novel proposals as setting up casinos in the country. He was particularly worried about the poor state of Irish tourism and stated that only one new hotel had been opened since the foundation of the state. Moreover the young Garret FitzGerald, then an economic adviser to the FII, was insisting, in a comment that remains extremely prescient this day, that

> the need to maintain some margin of tax advantage over more developed countries in north-western Europe seems evident, if we are to attract foreign investment and foreign enterprise, for even if it can be argued with some reason that the level of taxation may not, perhaps have such a significant effect upon domestic investment as is sometimes suggested, it is clearly of paramount importance where foreign investors are concerned.[8]

An essential element in this new approach to economic policy was a redressing of the balance between economic and social investment in the public capital programme. This programme would gain support from a rising level of domestic savings, based on steady growth in real national income and domestic savings, and could be supplemented by reasonable recourse to foreign borrowing to promote productive home investment. Thus a decision was taken to accelerate Ireland's economic progress through an inflow of external capital directed to types of development which would increase the country's productive capacity and which would bring with it new techniques and methods. Economic policy thus became more expansionary, an appropriate Keynesian response according to Whitaker, at a time when Irish costs were competitive and world trade was buoyant.[9]

While there were some significant differences between *Economic Development* and the government's White Paper, the *Programme for Economic Expansion*, which arose out of their different parentage, such differences were for the most part cosmetic as the main thrust of both documents was the same. Where Whitaker had argued for intensive cattle production as the foundation of agricultural prosperity, the White Paper did not want to abandon completely Fianna Fáil's traditional preference for tillage. Whitaker's proposal to locate new factories in large urban centres was omitted from the White Paper owing to Fianna Fáil's policy of decentralisation of industry, despite Lemass's own doubts about his party's line. While the political document did advance a firm commitment to a two per cent annual growth in Gross National Product over each of the ensuing five years, *Economic Development* was, in time honoured civil service fashion, suitably vague about targets. Yet on the whole the two documents were remarkably similar.

Economic Development did not, however, impinge on the consciousness of the body politic immediately. The major newspapers gave it only cursory treatment while the political parties showed a similar lack of interest. The Fianna Fáil parliamentary party minutes of the period are fascinating for their discussion, or rather lack of it, of *Economic Development*. In its first discussion of the document it was recorded that 'the Party be given a directive on the implications of the recent White Paper on Economic Expansion'. The Minister for Finance, Dr James Ryan gave this meeting, at which Lemass was not present, a general resume of the contents of the paper which was then followed by the rather bizarre spectacle of a discussion 'in which arterial drainage and of certain very necessary drainage schemes was stressed by several members'.[10] A planned session devoted to the White Paper on 6 January 1959 was deferred to 28 January, when Lemass 'explained that the proposals in the White Paper were to be regarded as an outline of minimum requirements for the future and do not exclude further proposals'.[11] The agricultural effects of *Economic Development* were not discussed until March. While this seems to have occupied the party somewhat more as the debate ran into April, the minutes of these discussions are even more sparse than usual although they state that the debate continued with contributions from various deputies.[12] It would appear, however, that few politicians, whether in Fianna Fáil, or elsewhere were greatly struck by the attempt to modernise national economic policy making.

Seán Lemass and the remoulding of economic policy

The one politician interested in such modernisation was of course Seán Lemass. He told a correspondent in July 1959:

> It is of course true that the Irish economy at its present state of development is not producing enough resources to maintain all our population at the standard of living we desire them to enjoy. The fundamental task facing this country is to expand its total production so that this situation will be brought quickly to an end. This cannot be done, however, by just wishing for it but by sustained hard work in support of an intelligent development programme. The Programme for Economic Expansion provides one element and we are now trying to generate the other.[13]

This second element was to enter a free trading body in an attempt to develop Irish industry and subsequently Irish exports. It went hand in hand with bringing new industry to Ireland. The protectionists of the Department of Industry and Commerce, under their acerbic secretary, J. C. B. MacCarthy, still made their protests known to the government and continued to advance caution in any potential upcoming negotiations with an existing trading bloc.

There is, of course, an inconsistency between the dynamic Lemass grasping the nettle of free trade as Taoiseach and that of his old department providing the main opposition to the somewhat inevitable outcome of membership of a European trading bloc. In December 1959 Whitaker and MacCarthy engaged in a very forceful correspondence on the usefulness of protection for the Irish economy. It began with a memo written by Whitaker arguing that

> a closer degree of association with the international economy, through reduced protection and participation in a free trade arrangement, would help to compensate for the narrowness of the domestic market, more especially if it also promised a surer and better market for agricultural exports. It is only by gearing ourselves for a growing trade with the rest of the world that we can tackle, with real prospect of success, the problems of unemployment and emigration.[14]

For MacCarthy, however, protectionism had served Ireland well. Where Whitaker stressed the point that industrialisation, under protection, had not solved the unemployment problem and that the continuation of such a policy would not provide the expansion the country required, MacCarthy preferred to take the view that as far as employment is concerned, if we had not had the protective policy and, even if it is not a cure for all our ills, is it logical to toss it overboard, unless it is clear that something better can be substituted which will not only maintain employment at the existing level but give the scope for expansion which is desired? All I am seeking is to get the alternatives clearly stated so that a considered choice can be recommended.[15]

There was nothing in MacCarthy's remarks that could give any solace to the thousands who had emigrated throughout the 1950s and those left without jobs as it closed. Protectionism had clearly failed them. Yet MacCarthy was insisting that it remain. His pessimism can be contrasted with the optimism of someone like Todd Andrews, who was asking the country to leave the dark days of the past behind it and begin afresh. As he told one audience:

I ask you to disabuse your minds of the pessimism so terribly expressed by Patrick Kavanagh: 'It will never be spring always autumn, after a harvest always lost, When Drake was winning seas for England, we sailed in puddles of the past, seeking the ghost of Brendan's mast'.[16]

Whitaker, however, was not seeking the complete abandonment of protection. For him the problem was that protected manufacturing for the home market offered little prospect of increased employment, and in a highly competitive world, continued protection could not guarantee the maintenance of existing employment at acceptable real wages. Thus if employment opportunities were to be created for the fresh thousands who sought work every year, industry had quickly to become more efficient so that its products could be sold on an increasing scale in export markets. This could be achieved by accepting an external commitment to reducing tariffs, accompanied by appropriate industrial incentives and aids towards industrial adaptation and modernisation.

MacCarthy's role has been much neglected by historians and he plays little or no part in any of the important studies of the period. Yet his role as secretary was hugely significant. He had entered the civil service at Finance in 1927, but had served in Industry and Commerce from 1945 and had continued that department's orthodoxy in terms of protection when he succeeded John Leydon as secretary in 1956. Moreover most of the thinking in Industry and Commerce came from the top down. Thus with Lemass's exit it was vital that the department be infused with political strength. In this context Lemass's appointment of Jack Lynch to succeed him as Minister of Industry and Commerce was an important one.[17] Appointed Minister at the Department of the Gaeltacht by de Valera in 1957, Lynch was seen as progressive on economic issues. He also had had dealings with Lemass when he was responsible for the running of the Underdeveloped Areas Act in 1951 as parliamentary secretary to the Government and to the Minister for Lands. He had evidently impressed Lemass and on his appointment was told by the Taoiseach that Industry and Commerce was now his responsibility. While Lemass would be captain of the ship, Lynch had assumed the position of trusted lieutenant. Thus Lynch to an extent took on the mantle of guiding Industry and Commerce away from a policy of protection, a policy which had been ingrained in its philosophy for a generation. In essence, though, it was Lemass who was the key figure in getting MacCarthy to accept the inevitability of tariff cuts. Once he, along with Lynch, had politically sided with the free trade position, MacCarthy was left in an administrative limbo. When Lemass was Minister for Industry and Commerce and explicitly supported the policy of protection it was easy for MacCarthy to support him from within the administrative framework. With Lemass as Taoiseach now attempting to get Ireland into a European trading bloc and supported eagerly by his own handpicked Minister for Industry and Commerce, MacCarthy was persuaded of the necessity of free trade and tariff cuts. In essence he had no choice as by this time the political machine had gained control over the administrative one and Lemass was doing the driving. Yet neither MacCarthy nor Industry and Commerce ever bought into the philosophical idea of free trade and although they agreed to tariff cuts, it was with a reluctance born out of a thirty-year commitment to the ideals of protectionism.[18]

By 1961 Ireland continued to face significant economic problems. As Brian Girvin has pointed out, to all intents and purposes it had become a marginal European economy with serious structural problems.[19] Most of these problems stemmed from the failure of protectionism. At a meeting of secretaries in April 1961, MacCarthy maintained that although 'he did not to wish to make an issue of the conflicting departmental viewpoints, . . . he was anxious that the delegation to the GATT would not be put into the position of having to enter into tariff negotiations'.[20] He was willing that tariff negotiations be settled within the context of the EEC but was insistent that no other economic body should be attempting to get the government to reduce tariffs. MacCarthy was appointed chairman of the CIO set up to examine Irish industry's suitability for entry to a European trading bloc, after Ireland had applied for membership of the EEC, and it was from this position that he finally agreed on the necessity to bring down tariffs and readapt industry to free trade conditions.[21] Professor Louden

Ryan, a member of the committee, has commented on how it became quite clear to its members, mainly economists and civil servants, that most native Irish industry was in no way ready for entry to the EEC in the then economic climate. It is also instructive to note that of the industries examined at the time, not one is still operating independently in Ireland today.[22]

When the CIO reports began to appear in the autumn of 1962 they showed the weakness of Irish industry, especially when it came to export potential. Not all industrialists were, however, in favour of entry to the EEC as the solution. Aodogan O'Rahilly, then chairman of Bord na Mona, one of the most prominent industrialists of the age and a close confidant of Lemass, was deeply worried:

> while I welcomed foreign investment, I believed that if we were going to enter the EEC then our sovereignty would be lost and in a free trade environment we would quickly go under. I drew comparisons between entry to the EEC and the passing of the Act of Union at the time as I foresaw Irish industry dying, just as what happened in the early 1800s due to the operation of economic laws. In many ways I suppose I was an old style Fianna Fáil nationalist.[23]

More typical, however, was the response of Jack Fitzpatrick of the FII who told the influential magazine *Hibernia* that Ireland would join the EEC and the result would be the 'blossoming of our economy'.[24] Officially the FII had become a supporter of Whitaker's policy of economic planning. It noted that

> in the midst of the activities in preparing for entry into the EEC it is good to see that the Government have not lost sight of their economic planning programme which will have an important bearing on our preparedness to face the challenge of the common market.[25]

The FII would become key players in Lemass's plans for an inclusive economic policy featuring industry, the trade unions and the farmers.

Shaping a corporatist agenda

The CIO was part of a continuing corporatist-style initiative by Lemass to involve the unions and industry in the policy of economic development.[26] The Employer–Labour conference came into existence in 1962 and the National Industrial and Economic Council was established a year later. These new agencies were all part of the state's commitment to economic planning. Not all observers were convinced by this rush of activity from government and its response from the economic actors. The American embassy for one was none too impressed with these developments, maintaining that:

> [The] Government sets much store by this conference as a means of working out agreements between labour and management on long-term policies . . . However the embassy has not been especially impressed by the amount of enthusiasm with which the FUE or ICTU has been approaching the conference. Both parties have been diligently preparing for it, but neither side has indicated to the embassy that it has any great prospect of success.[27]

Nevertheless, the CIO was involved in incorporating the industrial interest groups into government structures and within this framework Lemass met the FII and the ICTU in January 1962 to discuss the implications of the application for industry. Lemass told the FII that they would have only a short period of time to adapt to the new conditions and would then have to face the full brunt of competition. He recognised that some industries would not be able to make this transition easily, but said that the government were aware of this and would seek some concessions from the EEC. Colm Barnes, President of the FII, protested that Irish industry could not survive what would amount to a fifty per cent cut in tariffs. As he was to recall later:

> while we realised that the EEC would not tolerate stragglers, we thought it would be a massive act of self deception on the part of the government if they thought that industry could withstand such tariff cuts. Looking back now industry was very weak, but once you were in there was great security because you had a captive market and high tariff walls which kept out imports. If we had entered in 1963 on these grounds native industry already weak would have been decimated.[28]

Lemass, in response, noted that the Community would probably not give special concessions to Ireland and that while negotiation was possible they had to accept the principle of a broad transitional period for concluding the reduction of tariffs. It was doubtful whether the Community would agree to selective cuts, but if there was a possibility of securing a special protocol it would be necessary to specify the sensitive industries. He estimated that if Ireland joined in 1963 effective protection would be gone within three years of accession and that consequently this was the time span to be dealt with. Within that period and the longer transitional period, adjustment might be made after consultation with the Community, but he believed that the limits were well established.[29] At another level a former government official has spoken of the frustration suffered by those officials who undertook the CIO surveys:

> we would have an appointment to meet with the Managing Director of some firm down the country and we would arrive only to be told that he was gone playing golf or was off at the hunt, our experiences were literally of that kind. That was the mindset of industrialists at the time. They had no faith in the CIO, in fact they had no faith in anything.[30]

Countering this analysis, Joseph McCullough who was heavily involved in industry comments:

> I was a general manager in a tyre manufacturing firm at the time. Civil servants from Industry and Commerce came down to see us but really they were hopelessly ill equipped. The idea that these fellows could help us to organise when they were not even organised themselves was ludicrous. What happened was that civil servants were being transferred from one section of Industry and Commerce to another but they were all really of the same mindset.[31]

Another industrialist has commented on how great opportunities were lost due to the attitudes of businessmen:

> due to that lack of self confidence, which was largely within small business, and not having enough strong entrepreneurial spirit, major opportunities were lost. However, we had no business people to lead us, only politicians and civil servants. Yet there was a feeling that they did not know business, the nitty gritty of it, only the theory and as a result business people tended to try to ignore them. Their attitude to the CIO would be an example of that.[32]

Although ICTU gave only lukewarm support to the original application, its first policy statement on entry to the EEC urged caution and advised the government, rather unrealistically, to pursue alternative strategies such as searching for new markets;[33] they offered no dissension to Lemass's strategy when they met him in January 1962. Lemass urged the trade unionists to accept that changes were under way in Ireland's relationship with the wider world and that existing preferential arrangements with Britain were already weakened. He reiterated his intention to seek membership under the best terms possible, but said that they would have to operate on the assumption that tariffs would have to be removed by the beginning of 1970. He stressed that it was his view that

> state aids to industry designed to promote efficiency should be regarded as desirable . . . though the form of aid in some cases would be modified . . . In general it appeared likely that the question of adjustment to common market conditions would be a problem of the position of individual firms rather than industrial groups.[34]

This implied that even in the absence of EEC membership considerable changes in the Irish economy would be necessary. Congress issued no formal response to this meeting but there could have been no doubt in their mind but that Lemass was determined to bring Ireland into the community. Congress eventually responded to the government's stance by calling a consultative conference to debate the impact entry to the EEC would have on the union movement. It would seem that Congress were more doubtful about the EEC than EFTA owing to the political connotations associated with the former. Donal Nevin, for instance, told the 1961 annual conference that 'there is no doubt that entry to the Common Market would mean a surrender of control over economic policy', while the following year, John Carroll, of the ITGWU, told the conference that Congress had not done enough to 'point out to all of us the importance to our nation of the political ramifications of membership of the EEC'.[35] Some trade unionists, however, such as M. O'Donnell of the Irish National Union of Vintners', Grocers' and Allied Trades Assistants believed that 'the political aspect of this question is to a great extent a myth'.[36] Moreover the question of the EEC being a bulwark against communism was raised by many speakers at the 1961 conference in Cork as being a reason for entering the EEC. Irish entry to EFTA would not have the same political connotations as entry to the EEC and the Cork conference showed that there was division over this issue within Congress. Lemass realised EEC entry had political ramifications. Yet it did not deter him from pushing ahead with his proposals and there could have been no doubt in ICTU's mind but that Lemass was determined to bring Ireland into the EEC, with or without their support. After much internal debate Congress publicly responded to the proposed application by issuing a policy statement, delivered at the annual conference in Galway in July 1962. The main thrust of this response was that the conversion of the Irish economy to conditions of free trade should proceed at a pace, over a certain period of time and in such a manner that our object of securing a continuing increase in total employment shall be kept within such limits that redundant workers will be able to secure equally good employment in Ireland without adversely affecting the intake of new entrants into industry.[37]

It did concede, however, that this object might not be attainable in the context of EEC membership. What it did not point out was that there was no chance of achieving this in protective isolation. While Congress does appear here to have significant doubts about free trade, it was nevertheless willing to support the general thrust of Lemass's intentions, which were inevitably focused on the EEC. Rather inevitably some unions were intransigently opposed with J. W. Lunney of the Draughtsmen's and Allied Technicians' Association proclaiming 'we are definitely anti Common Market'.[38] Yet while a lot of individual unions, particularly in assembly and textiles, were worried about the effects of free trade, most realised that they had to face up to the fact that it was coming. In effect it was the economic rather than the political ramifications of EEC entry that worried trade unionists. Most recognised the problems inherent in Irish industry with N. Boran of the ITGWU feeling that the EEC was the answer to the country's economic problems:

> We have nothing to lose on the economic front. We have roughly 40,000 unemployed per year and 40,000 emigrate each year. Can it be very much worse than that, irrespective of what already adverse effects the Common Market have upon us? There are many protected industries in this country that refuse to install modern plant and machinery.[39]

Following on from this, P. Alexander of Congress's executive council remarked at the 1963 conference in Killarney: 'It has been made abundantly clear to us now that what sufficed in the past will not do so in the future. A state of complacency does exist at all levels of industry whether it be with management or with the workers'.[40] It was with this sense of complacency in mind that Congress were willing, however reluctantly, to join Lemass on the road to free trade as they most definitely recognised the dangers that the CIO reports painted.

ICTU held a consultative conference in March 1963 to discuss the preliminary reports issued by the CIO on the state of Irish industry. The CIO had published reports on the leather, footwear, paper and paperbond, cotton, linen and rayon, motor vehicle assembly and fertiliser industries and estimated that these could be faced with considerable redundancies if EEC rules were applied to Ireland. Unions representing workers in these industries communicated with Congress to voice their fears and to ask that consideration be given to ICTU policy in the light of these findings.[41] J. Blake, of the ITGWU, for instance noted the seriousness of the reports, proclaiming that the motor assembly industry was likely to be drastically hit by free trade:

> These reports give serious food for thought because they indicate that unless many changes are made in our industrial set up we will be unable to meet the competition of free trade conditions. That these changes must be made all agree . . . under the policy of protection many have failed to keep up with the changing times; failed to modernise; failed to introduce new techniques. Now following the CIO reports, these industries find themselves in serious difficulty. The changes that should have been made as a matter of course over the years were not made.[42]

For his part Lemass saw the CIO reports as proof positive that 'the policy of protection has been clearly and officially shown in post-war circumstances to be defective in promoting or compelling the effort needed to ensure the continuing efficiency of industry'.[43] Congress did recognise that if Irish industry was to survive it had to export; to export it had to be competitive. It would not be possible in the EEC to manufacture for export while receiving protection at home. Even if Ireland did not enter the EEC there were two good reasons why this policy should not be continued, it argued. Primarily, protected home industries tended not to export and concealed the cost of inefficiency within high priced products for the protected market. Secondly, the consumer was subsidising the cost of inefficiency through the higher prices paid and this represented a drain on the national economy. The problem Congress faced was how to ensure that heavy reductions in employment did not result from the elimination of tariffs in the process of reorganisation of Irish industry. The manpower and social affairs committee of the Organisation for Economic Co-operation and Development had accepted recommendations that member countries should make an active labour market policy an essential element in their economic policies for growth and development. Congress eventually adopted a rather catch all position. It supported the reorganisation of industry as desirable, yet said that the extent of any reorganisation should be such that redundant workers could be absorbed. To enable this to be achieved, it espoused the establishment of a planning body to gather employment information and adjust investment to overcome cyclical disturbances.[44] It is not clear, however, how Congress anticipated such a body working or if it really believed that it would solve the unemployment problems that would inevitably arise once Ireland eventually entered the EEC. Ultimately the CIO, in its final report, concluded that the sectors it examined were not adapting to the new economic environment, even though Ireland had not entered the EEC and was not likely to until 1970 at the earliest, and was offering to provide advice and finance to aid the transition. It found that most industrial sectors were not internationally competitive, that they concentrated on production for home consumption, and that unless adjustment took place there would be a considerable loss in employment.[45] As John Conroy, General President of the Irish Transport and General Workers Union, pointed out at the time: 'freer trade is coming and unless we all realise this and prepare we will find that every workshop and factory not fully and efficiently equipped will cease to produce to economic requirements and all the employees will find themselves unemployed'.[46]

The EEC is the place to be

By the early 1960s the government had decided that the future direction of the Irish economy lay in its being associated with the EEC. The trade union movement was initially lukewarm in their endorsement of this approach but were co-opted by Lemass and subsequently involved in discussions on the future development of economic policy. The Lemass governments of the early 1960s had actively sought the input of the union movement as well as other interest groups in what was effectively a realignment of government economic policy, which placed agricultural and industrial policy on an equal footing for the first time in the history of the state.[47] The government, industry and the trade unions recognised that Irish industry would have to develop rapidly to meet the rigours of free trade competition.

While the CIO was in the middle of finding out how unprepared industry would be for the transition from a protective framework to an interdependent economy, Whitaker wrote to MacCarthy advocating a unilateral all round tariff cut of between 10 and 15 per cent be implemented on 1 January 1963:

> this suggestion deserves serious consideration on a number of grounds. The most important is the need to maintain a psychological impetus towards rapid adjustment to EEC conditions during the period of uncertainty – which on present indications may be longer than we thought – about the entry of Britain

and ourselves to the EEC. We have got the preparatory work going well on the industrial side. A whole series of reports on industrial surveys will be appearing over the coming months. There will, however, be a psychological barrier – however illogical this may be – to the undertaking of effective follow-up action so long as uncertainty persists not merely about the terms of accession of Ireland but even on the question of Ireland's accession to the Community.[48]

Whether Ireland was admitted to the EEC or not, greater industrial efficiency would be necessary. Indeed this was even more urgent and necessary if Irish exports were to face additional competition from Europe without the offsetting advantages of membership of the EEC. For Whitaker, Ireland could not lose by such a reduction as they would have to get down to nil in the EEC context by 1970 and any immediate reduction would be a step in the right direction: 'procrastination in making tariff reductions merely steps up the rate of reduction to which we will have to submit on joining the Community'.[49] Even more important, perhaps, was the consideration that such a step would show the EEC the desire of the Irish government to adapt to EEC conditions and could only be advantageous in any negotiations. Moreover the other applicants, Britain, Denmark and Norway as members of EFTA, had scaled down protection, as had the existing members of the community. As all these would be Ireland's competitors there did not really seem to be any alternative to EEC entry. MacCarthy agreed with the general thrust of Whitaker's remarks, but maintained that 'we should make every effort to ensure that full credit will be given to us against the rhythm of tariff reductions for any prior reductions'.[50] Three months later, in November 1962 it was announced that 'in anticipation of our entry to the EEC, the Government has decided to make a unilateral reduction of 10% in protective duties on industrial products on 1 January next'.[51] This was described in the official announcements as an initial step in an elimination of protection, and thus it could be taken that there would be further reductions at appropriate times in the future whether Ireland joined the EEC or not.

With this statement the Irish body politic had launched the way for an export-led industrialisation policy, which was to dominate industrial and economic policy in the 1960s. *Economic Development* and the *First Programme for Economic Expansion* had both been extremely conscious of the changing nature of economic relations in the late 1950s. While neither declared an explicit aim of entering a free trade bloc, the initial steps to that outcome had been put in place. The formation of the EEC and EFTA would create two important trading blocs and could offer economic opportunity or pose new threats.

One group who saw only opportunities were the National Farmers Association (NFA). In July 1960 the NFA issued a statement asking the government to consider becoming a partner in the EEC and insisted Ireland should enter whether the British joined or not, turning the conventional wisdom that Ireland could only enter at the same time as the British, on its head. The NFA considered that the historic trading link with Britain had been weakened and that its advantage to Irish farmers had been eroded. The Common Agricultural Policy offered guaranteed high prices, access to an expanded consumer market and new trading opportunities. The NFA also suggested that Irish industry would be no worse off inside the EEC than was currently the case with respect to EFTA or the EEC.[52] For the NFA, the historic link with Britain was overstated, and it had become impracticable to get from Britain the kind of arrangement which Irish agriculture needed to survive. For them the Common Market was the place to be. Juan Greene, its first president told an Institute of Public Administration conference on higher administration studies in late 1961 that

> one is left with the impression that without becoming a partner in a larger, viable economic unit, that will seek to cater for agriculture in its wider community, there is little to be optimistic about for our agriculture over the next ten years. At all costs we must avoid the Common Market being used and becoming a fashion as the cure-all for our agricultural ills; there is no utopia for agriculture in the Common Market. All that can be said is that the Common Market will provide us with a greater opportunity . . . I think I would be right in saying that without the advent of the Common Market, the prospect facing Irish agriculture over the next ten years is pretty hopeless.[53]

For Lemass, EEC membership without a simultaneous British accession simply was not a runner. His views were echoed by Whitaker:

> We have applied for membership of the EEC because it would be economic disaster for us to be outside of the community if Britain is in it. We cannot afford to have our advantageous position in the British market turned into one of exclusion by a tariff wall, particularly as our chief competitors would be inside the wall.[54]

While the NFA disagreed with the government over the reason for applying, they were pleased once the government decided to press ahead with its application in August 1961 in response to the British application.

At this stage the key economic emphasis for the Irish government remained agriculture despite some recent commitments to industrial development. This point was made both internationally and at home. The government's formal application paper in January 1962 proclaimed that 'for Ireland agriculture will always be of major importance. We are naturally anxious that through membership of the European Economic Community, Ireland should be able to look forward to a balanced development of agriculture and industry'.[55] Lemass had similarly made this point over a year earlier when he told the Dáil:

> It is important to have it fully appreciated that the government have never treated, and do not now treat, the interests of manufacturing industry as the predominant consideration in their approach to the question of association with either of the European trading groups, or in their trading policy generally, in the sense of having failed to attach due importance to agricultural interests.[56]

While industry was constantly discussed at official level, the main objective of policy in the early 1960s was to obtain favourable membership to the EEC and to secure, if possible, continuing access to the British market for agricultural exports. This was made explicit in Lemass's statement to the Council of Ministers of the EEC in January 1962:

> Because of the close inter-relationship of the economy of Ireland and that of the United Kingdom, and the vital interest of Ireland in agricultural trade, the Irish government would wish to have the discussions for the admission of Ireland to the Community completed at the same time as those for the United Kingdom.[57]

Charles de Gaulle's veto of the British application to the EEC in January 1963, with the consequent lapsing of the Irish case for entry, brought bitter disappointment to the Irish farming community as their hopes of increasing prosperity in the larger common market were dashed. While the government did not formally withdraw its nomination, Lemass told the Dáil in February that as the six members of the EEC were unable to agree on a future procedure after the de Gaulle veto, the negotiations on enlargement of the community were 'suspended indefinitely'.[58] The government which he led responded with an extensive package of state aids which enabled industry to improve its performance substantially and would allow the government to prepare for entry in the years ahead with a stronger economy. Principally owing to its failure to gain entry to the EEC, the Irish government set about enhancing the country's trading position in its crucial British markets, as well as in its bilateral relations with other states. However, once negotiations began it became quite clear that the Irish favoured the idea of a free trade area with Britain rather than just enhancing the bilateral agreements of old. This eventually led to the Anglo-Irish Free Trade Agreement of 1965, which can be seen as a means to the end of eventual EEC membership. The aim of the government in signing the agreement was to demonstrate that it could compete on an even economic playing field with the British.[59] The new trading agreements with the British, although important in their own right, were principally intended to expedite EEC entry.

Conclusion

The Fianna Fáil government's decision to apply for membership of the EEC, and the co-option of the sectional interest groups into the policy process had opened up a new way of dealing with economic questions in contemporary Ireland. Lemass's courtship of the various economic interest groups in the late 1950s and early 1960s was driven simply by economic concerns. It was the role of government to lead these groups in a new economic partnership that could be seen as an early form of the model adopted by another Fianna Fáil government in 1987 at yet another time of economic crisis. There was a gradual maturation of relations between the emerging interest groups and the government in the policy realm. While clearly the farmers remained the most overtly selfish and sectional group, even they came to take some heed of the 'national' as distinct from the purely agricultural interest. Moreover, the vision of ICTU is really quite striking in that they were able to take a dispassionate and long-term view of the country's economic prospects in addition to attempting to advance the sectional interest of their members. In many ways the business leadership was quite similar to the unions as the debates about entry to Europe gathered pace in the late 1950s and early 1960s. While there were two distinct views about any proposed entry of a trading bloc within the business community, it is clear that they realised that the country's economic fortunes and those of their members was interlinked.

Seán Lemass, the undisputed prime economic player in government from 1957, embarked on a programme to haul the Irish economy out of the dark ages of financial austerity, mass emigration and inadequate employment once

Fianna Fáil returned to office in 1957. He did this by setting out to establish a broadly European style proto-corporatist social democracy, involving all the key players collectively in responsible decision making. He had a long-range vision for the Irish economy and realised that age-old methods, of which he had once been the main driving force, had not worked in the past and were most unlikely to do so in the future. His relations with ICTU and the NFA are categoric examples of his attempts to build such a social democracy. The emergence of both players as recognised elements in national policy making is the crucial sign in Lemass's attempts to build what we might call the broad-based church of economic interest groups. It was essential that both farmers and unions be involved as well as business. While Lemass's views did not please everyone in Fianna Fáil, as witnessed particularly by the resignation of the Minister for Agriculture, Paddy Smith, in 1964, the Fianna Fáil of the early 1960s was a distinctly different party from that which had lost power in 1948. A new generation of politicians, influenced greatly by Lemass, were comfortable with the innovative direction of economic policy that had Europe as its ultimate goal and left behind outmoded theories of self-sufficiency. By the time of the application to the EEC all the interest groups that Lemass had co-opted in his quest to make Ireland a more competitive economy were advocates of entry. Policy was to be formulated with the interest groups in mind.

The second half of the 1960s saw considerable industrial unrest, centred on demands for improved incomes and welfare for trade unionists and the demand for increased prices for their products by farmers. It could well be that Lemass was unprepared for this and decided that such grief as he was getting from the sectional interests was not what he, himself, had bought into when he brought them into the policy process. In this context, and in declining health for some months, his resignation on 10 November 1966 was unsurprising. The years between his death and ultimate Irish entry to the EEC would, however, see a significant changing of the goalposts as regards what membership meant to the Irish body politic. The CAP would come to be seen as a way of removing pressure from the government by transferring the costs of subsidising Irish farming from Dublin to Brussels. The EEC came to be seen not as part of a developmental strategy, but as a means of levering money for Irish farming and protecting the environment that was being created to attract foreign direct investment.[60] Nevertheless there can be little doubt that entry to the EEC can be firmly attributed to Lemass. Although he never lived to see the day, it was his process of involving the sectional interest groups that opened the way for entry. He believed that bringing these groups into the corridors of power was intrinsically his only option if his attempt to move both the Irish economy and Irish society from economic nationalism to European union was to be successful. In that he was proved right.

CHAPTER FOUR

Emigration, political cultures and the evolution of post-war Irish society

ENDA DELANEY

—

Introduction

According to David Fitzpatrick, Ireland under the Union (1801–1921) was 'a land which most people wanted to leave', and this continued to remain the case after the establishment of the independent Irish state in 1922.[1] From the end of the Second World War until the early 1970s nearly 700,000 people left independent Ireland.[2] Naturally this large-scale exodus had profound consequences for the evolution of Irish society after 1945. Quite apart from the psychological effects on the individuals who felt compelled to emigrate in search of a decent standard of living, mass migration had underlined the obvious shortcomings of the level of economic development since the foundation of the independent Irish state in 1921–2. Economic success or failure was measured more often than not by the number of people departing for other countries annually. Political leaders were acutely aware of this somewhat imprecise yardstick of the effectiveness of policy. In a memorandum prepared by Seán Lemass in 1929, he asserted that 'the goal of our efforts should be to keep the Irish people in Ireland and provide prosperity for them here. Everything else, even cheap living or accepted notions about efficiency, must be sacrificed to that end.'[3] For politicians in independent Ireland emigration was the source of much embarrassment, especially given that Britain, the old enemy, was the destination for the majority of people who left after 1921. The persistence of mass migration until the 1960s served to expose the illusory nature of some fundamental elements of Irish nationalist rhetoric, in particular the economic arguments for independence. For instance, Pádraic Pearse had declared in 1913 that 'Ireland has resources to feed five times her population: a free Ireland would make those resources available'.[4] For the revolutionary generation who secured Irish

49

independence in the early 1920s and governed the fledgling state until the mid-1960s, emigration was of symbolic as well as practical significance. Yet paradoxically this massive outflow had a number of obvious benefits for Irish policy makers: the unemployed left, with consequently a much reduced cost for social security to be funded from the central exchequer. Equally, the conservative nature of Irish society was maintained as emigration had a disproportionate impact on the working and lower middle-class sections of the population, or in other words, those most likely to agitate for change.

This chapter will explore the place of emigration in Irish political culture, the policy of the Irish state and how it changed over time. Politicians knew that the performance of a particular government would be judged on the level of emigration, and while solutions as such were impossible, most paid lip service to the objective of the creation of full employment and the removal of the need for people to leave independent Ireland. Unlike some other European countries, the Irish state did not regulate or control migration out of the country and official policy was neither to facilitate nor hinder the free movement of labour, with the exception of the period of the Second World War.[5] Lastly, the impact of large-scale emigration on the evolution of post-war Irish society from the late 1940s until the early 1970s will be discussed.

Emigration in Irish political culture

Irish political culture as it evolved over the first half of the twentieth century was based on a complex amalgam of Catholic, nationalist and rural values.[6] The most passionate advocate of these values in the 1930s and 1940s was Eamon de Valera.[7] Emigration sat uneasily within this schema. While de Valera famously immortalised the rural idyll, mass migration and rural depopulation undermined this aspiration towards a society based on small-scale farming, simple living and a rejection of materialism. As Lee has commented, this vision of '"traditional" Ireland relied for its survival on a human haemorrhage'.[8] The massive outflow of the 1950s even called into question the very viability of the independent Irish state, the achievement of which was the central objective of earlier nationalist ideology.

In independent Ireland all political parties viewed emigration as having a pernicious effect on Irish society, and few politicians before the 1960s dared to do anything other than declare that the reduction of the numbers leaving the country was one of the most urgent priorities.[9] More often than not discussions of emigration occurred in debates about the broader contours of economic policy. The logic here was simple enough: if economic policy proved successful in the creation of employment, the reduction of emigration would automatically follow. But whereas the job creation conjured up more pedestrian images of rows of gleaming new factory buildings, the annual departure of thousands of young Irish people was reminiscent of the much more powerful and emotive representation of exile. Involuntary exile had long been a standard metaphor in Irish nationalist memory since the Great Irish Famine (1845–52), both in Ireland itself and among Irish communities overseas, especially in the United States.[10] Irish nationalist political leaders since the second half of the nineteenth century had drawn on such emotive images to bolster arguments for self-government since 'English tyranny' had forced people to emigrate.[11] A subtle distinction was, however, made as politicians could claim that emigration to Britain was only temporary and that when conditions improved these migrants would be able to return home. Yet most recognised that while Britain was a short boat journey across the Irish Sea, there was a remote likelihood of full employment ever being achieved in independent Ireland.

In the post-war years emigration retained its centrality in nationalist political culture, even if consecutive governments could do very little to influence the numbers leaving the country. It featured prominently as an issue in a number of general elections, in particular the 1948 and 1957 elections.[12] When emigration entered into political discourse, the intention was to discredit the sitting government by exposing an embarrassing increase over a period of time. In this respect, it resembled debates about unemployment data. Whereas securing a symbolic victory in Anglo-Irish relations or other aspects of foreign policy was in part down to successful negotiation and an element of fortunate circumstances, there was no quick fix for emigration. Detailed analysis of the political discourse in the 1940s and 1950s demonstrates that despite the furore associated with emigration, this was mostly rhetoric and Irish politicians had few solutions to this 'problem'.[13] Lee has observed that this 'platform rhetoric naturally pandered to popular instincts by ritualistically denouncing the "evils" of emigration, while equally naturally failing to contribute any solution'.[14]

Practical politics also influenced the prominence attached to emigration by political groupings. Traditionally support for Fianna Fáil tended to be strongest in small farming communities in the west of Ireland, a region in which emigration had a severe impact on the working and lower middle-class sections of the population. In the early 1920s, research has found a direct link between support for Sinn Féin – out of which Fianna Fáil emerged in 1926 –

and the rate of emigration. A radical party that advocated an economic policy which 'taught that all the economic ills of Irish society could be cured by the unilateral rejection of the Treaty and the setting up of an Irish Republic' had an obvious appeal to the poorer sections of the rural community in the 1920s.[15] This pattern of support continued into the 1930s, although by the 1940s more radical groupings such as Clann na Talmhan (founded in 1938) and Clann na Poblachta (founded in 1946) usurped Fianna Fáil's position as the radical party in the short term and significantly undermined its support base in poorer farming communities in rural Ireland.[16] In the post-war period, the somewhat contradictory combination of a commitment to the maintenance of the traditional features of Irish rural life whilst at the same time an economic policy which promoted industrialisation and modernisation ensured that Fianna Fáil remained the dominant political party. Since it was in power for most of the post-war period, it was naturally most liable to criticism of its record on emigration.[17]

For Fine Gael and Labour, the other main political parties, the putative reduction of emigration was an aspiration that was designed to appeal to their respective voting bases after the Second World War. Both inter-party governments were in power in the 1950s during periods of high emigration and the Taoiseach, John A. Costello, frequently had to face embarrassing questions on the subject.[18] For Labour, its leader and Tánaiste, William Norton, could point to the establishment of the Commission on Emigration and Other Population Problems in March 1948 as hard evidence of his party's commitment to the reduction of emigration. Given the apparent appeal of Labour to farm labourers and the urban working classes, its failure to make emigration a central issue of policy is somewhat puzzling. However, its support base coincided with that of Fianna Fáil, who proved more effective at mobilising working and lower middle-class voters after 1945 as it could argue that it was the party of government. Practical politics as well as broader ideological concerns therefore combined to ensure that emigration remained one of the most contentious issues in political discourse in the post-war years.

The state, public policy and emigration

During the Second World War a range of emigration controls were imposed by the Irish government to control the flow of people leaving Ireland for wartime work in Britain: the exact numbers who left during the war is a matter for conjecture, though estimates suggest that between 100,000 and 150,000 left.[19] In the immediate post-war period, these restrictions were gradually dismantled in tandem with similar moves by the British authorities.[20] From the early 1950s young Irish men and women could emigrate without having to seek a travel permit. Between 1946 and 1951 total net migration amounted to 119,568 people, with a larger proportion of females leaving than males.[21] For the following five years until 1956 this figure rose to nearly 200,000.[22] In the late 1950s independent Ireland experienced the highest levels of emigration since the 1850s, with over 50,000 people emigrating each year. This huge exodus over three decades raised a number of significant problems for the Irish body politic. The 1960s witnessed a lower level of migration, owing to the much-changed economic context.

The first issue that generated considerable controversy in the late 1940s was the emigration of young Irish women. Statistical and impressionistic evidence demonstrated that more women than men were leaving and young women tended to migrate at a younger age than their male counterparts. Under pressure from the Catholic hierarchy, the Fianna Fáil government considered imposing a ban on the emigration of young women under the age of 22 years in August 1947.[23] In November 1948 a similar move was also contemplated by Seán McBride, the minister for external affairs in the first inter-party government.[24] For a number of reasons, not least being the practical difficulties with enforcing such a prohibition and even more significantly the negative impression that a ban of this nature would create, this radical course of action was not followed.[25] The Second World War had, however, established the principle of direct invention by the state in the movement of people. In the post-war world, it was recognised that the solution to emigration – insofar as one existed – lay in improving the wider economic and social environment. A document produced by the Department of External Affairs in December 1947 posed the often-asked question of whether government policy was to blame for emigration:

> If it is agreed that the solution of the emigration problem lies primarily in the constant creation of new employment outlets in industry, commerce and other fields of non-agricultural economic activity, what has been and is being done is as much – particularly having regard to the circumstances of the wars – as anyone could hope to do . . . Emigration could only have been prevented, therefore, if the government had succeeded not only in maintaining industrial and commercial employment at its pre-war level throughout the war years, but in increasing it over the period by creating 150,000 new employment outlets.

> To blame the government for not having been able to do that during a period
> in which, as everybody knows, raw materials and equipment were virtually
> unprocurable, is, of course ridiculous.[26]

Clearly the view expressed here was that it was the role of the state to create
employment rather than to restrict movement: a wholesale ban on emigration
of certain groups was a 'dangerous infringement of the freedom of the individual'.[27] This view was echoed by de Valera who stated in February 1948 that
'we cannot corral the people and say "you must not go out"'.[28]

On coming to power after the election of February 1948 the first inter-party
government appointed a Commission on Emigration and Other Population
Problems 'to investigate the causes and consequences of the present level and
trend in population'.[29] The commission included experts from many walks of
life and was chaired by Dr James Beddy, a distinguished public servant and
future head of the Industrial Development Authority. In the course of its
deliberations, the commission undertook rural surveys of areas throughout the
country and heard evidence from a wide range of interested parties.[30] The publication of its final reports did not take place until 1955, mainly as a consequence
of the delay resulting from a decision to take a full census in 1951.[31] The reports
were produced in stencilled form for the government in July 1954, and finally
printed for general distribution in October 1955.[32]

The published reports of the commission were based on a vast array of
statistical material as well as information provided by witnesses and public
bodies. The principal conclusion was that while 'the fundamental cause of
emigration is economic, in most cases the decision to emigrate cannot be ascribed
to any single motive but to the interplay of a number of motives'.[33] Emigration
was consequently a reflection of the poor state of the wider economic and
social environment. The report also highlighted the 'desire for improved
material standards', especially among the rural population, and the fact that
few opportunities for employment existed outside the large urban centres.[34] A
more controversial assertion was that large-scale emigration had not hindered
economic development and that 'not all emigration is bad'.[35] The practical
recommendations of the commission included a suggestion that greater efforts
should be made towards the decentralisation of government departments, that
a body be established to oversee the use of land, and that an Investment
Advisory Council be set up to provide guidance on public investment. One
official from the Department of Social Welfare, who was a member of the commission, predicted this outcome three years earlier: 'its value, in my opinion,

will be largely in the keen analysis and interpretations which it will provide, rather than in its practical recommendations'.[36]

In terms of public policy, few of the commission's recommendations were ever adopted, though it must be said that the overall tenor of the reports was cautious. At a cabinet meeting held in September 1954, each government department was instructed to prepare a response to the findings of the commission.[37] Most government departments did not seriously engage with the reports of the commission: the Department of Finance failed even to submit a consideration of the main implications of the reports. An interdepartmental committee was established in July 1956 to examine the recommendations contained in the reports, though it is unclear if it ever actually met.[38] As *The Irish Times* remarked in June 1956 after the publication of the preliminary results of the census showed a decline in the total population, the reports 'might as well have been banned by the censorship board for all the respect that the government has paid to them'.[39]

The significance of the establishment of the commission is that after 25 years of self-government it represented a tacit acknowledgement that the causes of emigration could no longer be put down to the effects of British misrule, a central theme in earlier nationalist thinking.[40] The movement of people from independent Ireland was directly related to the economic environment in which many found themselves unable to secure employment. Compared with the conditions in Britain which most prospective migrants were well aware off since many had families and friends living there, life staying at home seemed to offer a very bleak future. While *The Irish Times* argued that the setting up of such a commission was a recognition of the failure of self-government, there was perhaps an element of exaggeration in this assessment.[41] After the publication of its report, few policy makers could claim that the causes of emigration were not well documented as the reports outlined perhaps the most comprehensive investigation of Irish rural society to be undertaken in the first half of the twentieth century.

The other issue that relates to government policy was the welfare of the Irish in Britain. Historically the Irish state had refused to take any responsibility for the financial costs of establishing welfare services for Irish migrants in Britain. Notwithstanding significant pressure from both the Catholic Church in Ireland and Britain in the late 1930s and during the Second World War, this was viewed by policy makers as essentially the concern of the Catholic Church rather than the Irish state.[42] This convenient position absolved the Irish exchequer from any responsibility for services for Irish unmarried mothers and emigrants who fell on hard times, as well as more basic needs in the provision of hostels and centres for recently arrived Irish migrants who needed temporary accommodation. This was a long-standing bone of contention between the church and state, as has been extensively documented in recent research.[43]

In September 1950 the first inter-party government refused to countenance the possibility of giving financial support for an Irish centre in London, which would carry out welfare work. The scheme was a joint initiative that emanated from the Irish and English Catholic hierarchies.[44] In the event, the centre was established without any funding from the Irish government. In October 1952, the director of the Irish centre in London, Fr Ambrose Woods, again raised the issue of funding. It was agreed that the appointment of a welfare officer at the Irish embassy in London would rule out the need for official funding for the centre.[45] A decision to appoint a welfare officer at the Irish embassy in London was sanctioned by the Department of Finance in December 1953, but an appointment was never made, ostensibly because it was argued that the Catholic Church was already heavily involved in this type of work.[46] Even if financial support were not forthcoming from the Irish state, it did however closely observe the position of its citizens in Britain, mainly through officials based at the London embassy. In one well-known controversy de Valera stated in a speech at Galway in August 1951 that the Irish in Birmingham, Coventry and Wolverhampton were 'living in conditions of absolute degradation'.[47] This strategy of highlighting the shortcomings of life in Britain for Irish migrants paid few dividends as the obvious question that it raised was why the migrants were there in the first place. It was disingenuous to complain about the conditions of the Irish in Britain, while at the same time failing to create the employment which would reduce the need for people to seek work in Britain in the first instance.[48]

In the early 1960s the issue was again raised both publicly in the Dáil and also with the relevant ministers and officials. During the debate on the estimates for the Department of External Affairs in July 1961, Frank Aiken was asked if his department would give financial assistance to welfare organisations working with the Irish in London. His reply summed up official policy for the previous forty years.

> It would be impossible to do it financially. There would be no end to it. We cannot take that responsibility. We cannot do it as a voluntary organisation could do it . . . There might be endless claims if we undertook to provide welfare funds for our people abroad.[49]

By laying the emphasis of the role of voluntary organisation in undertaking fund-raising, this released the Irish state from its obligations towards citizens who were, through no fault of their own, residing outside the state. In September 1965 the Catholic hierarchy approached Seán Lemass with a request for him to provide some discretionary funding to help the Irish centres in various British cities 'when they find themselves in need'.[50] Lemass acknowledged the 'excellent work' being undertaken by the Irish centres, but reiterated the long-established position relating to the provision of public money to support these activities:

> [T]he government remain of the opinion that the diversion of Irish state revenue to the support of Irish centres in England would be unsound from the point of view of state finance and would, in practice, be incapable of being kept within fixed limits. Once financial assistance was granted by the state to one particular centre, other centres and groups would claim equal treatment, even though their need might relatively be very small.[51]

Lemass also repeated the long-cherished view that voluntary organisations were more effective in this type of work.[52] While this position may well appear to be a convenient one for any government to take, the use of public funds to support a charitable organisation that was operating in a less regulated financial environment could have created problems for any state, especially if subsequently it was found that the money earmarked for such activities was misappropriated. This refusal of various governments to take any financial responsibility for its citizens living in Britain left a vacuum that was effectively filled by the Catholic Church. Its energetic and well-organised efforts starkly contrasted with the limited involvement of the state with the Irish in Britain.[53]

Only in the late 1960s was it possible for suggestions for a more realistic policy on emigration to emerge. The domestic climate had, of course, greatly changed with economic growth and the consequent reduction in the numbers leaving the country. With Ireland's application to join the EEC under consideration and 'a general trend towards greater mobility and freedom of movement' on an international level, the Minister of Labour, Patrick Hillery, proposed a fundamental reappraisal of government policy on emigration in November 1968.[54] The original document prepared by his department advocated that the employment service should make advice and placement facilities available to intending emigrants; that state aid should be given to voluntary emigration information services in Ireland; that arrangements should be made with the relevant British authorities to secure mutual recognition of educational qualifications; and finally that a board would be set up to 'promote measures to provide better services for those who intend to emigrate or have emigrated to Britain.[55] Naturally this set of proposals which would have facilitated emigration were opposed by other departments. The Department of External Affairs felt that any liaison with the British authorities could 'be employed to restrict emigration, should political pressure there build up for a total ban on immigration to protect employment for the rapidly-expanding coloured population or in the event of a continuing high level of unemployment'.[56] The argument here was that the British government had justified the exclusion of Irish citizens from immigration restrictions introduced in 1962 because of the land border with Northern Ireland and that any element of control granted to the British authorities could in time be used on a selective basis. This department also opposed the use of exchequer finance for welfare work in Britain on the basis of the large burden this would impose on Irish taxpayers and that Irish migrants were the responsibility of the British authorities.[57] This view was reinforced by the Department of Finance on the basis that the state would be seen to encourage emigration and 'that it would almost certainly result in the disappearance of voluntary effort in this field of philanthropic activity'.[58]

Given the sensitivities involved in this aspect of policy, it is not altogether surprising that the discussion at cabinet level was postponed on a number of occasions. When the cabinet did eventually consider Hillery's proposals some-time later in March 1969, his far-sighted programme of measures was watered down completely. The employment service would only give advice to 'persons who wish to return to work in Ireland', a position which neatly reversed the earlier suggestion that assistance would be provided to those looking for employment in Britain.[59] In addition, the Department of Labour was authorised to seek an agreement with the relevant British authorities on mutual recognition of educational and training qualifications.[60] Shortly afterwards, Hillery secured cabinet approval for £10,000 to assist voluntary organisations who offered advice and information to potential emigrants.[61] By October 1969 Hillery's successer, Joe Brennan, announced that a national committee had been established to advise the Minister of Labour on services both for intending emigrants and those who wished to return to Ireland.[62]

Even by the late 1960s emigration was still therefore a politically sensitive issue and public policy over the previous 35 years remained virtually unchanged. The free movement of persons was the overriding element of this policy and although this was driven largely by ideological concerns, it was also a revealing indication of the inability of the state to control or regulate the migrate flow. At a press conference in November 1961, when Lemass was asked to comment on the proposed British immigration legislation – and its possible effects on Irish emigration – he laid out the principles of the policy of the Irish government:

> The present absence of restrictions on travel between Ireland and Britain, and the freedom extended mutually to workers in either country to move to employment in the other is a desirable position which it would seem to be in the interests of both countries to maintain, if this is possible. While the Irish government would see some advantages in an arrangement by which Irish workers, before going to Britain, could have an offer of employment, certified as suitable and bona fide by a British government authority, it could not agree to participate in any scheme by which such offers would be made in Ireland, and which might be regarded – or in effect so operate – as to be an encouragement to emigration.[63]

Clearly an agreement to regulate the flow of labour between the two countries was out of the question and this remained the case. The benefits of such an arrangement from the British point of view would be that only people who had jobs would be allowed to travel and Irish migrants could be directed to forms of employment that needed workers. The drawback was, as indicated by Lemass, that the Irish state would be seen to actively facilitate the emigration of its citizens, a position that no Irish government, regardless of political composition, wished to be associated with. The piecemeal policy initiatives that were introduced by Hillery in the late 1960s are more significant for what they represented, rather than the practical benefits to migrants. In the first instance, the state conceded the principle of exchequer funding for migrant welfare, albeit in Ireland rather than in Britain. Secondly, even though the cabinet rejected Hillery's more radical proposals, the very discussion of issues relating to emigration indicates a degree of recognition that a much-enhanced economic climate would in itself not result in the immediate end of the outflow from independent Ireland.

Impact and consequences

Mass migration had a far-reaching impact on the history of twentieth-century Ireland. In purely demographic terms, the population of independent Ireland declined significantly and by 1961 the number of people recorded in the census was at its lowest level since the first census was taken by the Irish state in 1926. In the early 1960s nearly 1.5 million people who were born on the island of Ireland were living overseas.[64] Over the longer period since the Great Irish Famine, Ireland was the 'only country to record a significant and virtually uninterrupted decline in population', a consequence of a sustained pattern of emigration.[65] Only in the 1960s and 1970s was this trend reversed when the population begin to increase steadily as more people chose to stay in Ireland rather than emigrate to Britain or the United States.

Few contemporaries doubted the effects of sustained emigration on national morale. The 1950s were the era of *The Vanishing Irish*, an alarmist book, edited by an Irish-American priest, Fr John A. O'Brien, that was published in 1953 and articulated in a semi-serious manner the view that if emigration continued the Irish people living in Ireland would soon disappear:

> Nothing in recent centuries is so puzzling or so challenging as the strange phenomenon being enacted before our eyes: the fading away of the once great and populous nation of Ireland. If the past century's rate of decline continues for another century, the Irish will virtually disappear as a nation and will be found only as an enervated remnant in a land occupied by foreigners . . . Today Ireland is teetering perilously on the brink of near extinction as the habits of the past century persist.[66]

While O'Brien and his fellow-contributors were clearly at the extreme end of the spectrum in terms of views about the effects of emigration, the book did capture the despondent mood of the 1950s. In an early draft of what was later to become the seminal *Economic Development*, T. K. Whitaker, the secretary of the Department of Finance, recounted his reaction to a cartoon on the cover of the September 1957 issue of the satirical magazine, *Dublin Opinion*. The cartoon depicted Ireland as a mature woman who was consulting a fortune teller and admonishing her 'Get to work! They're saying I've no future'.[67] As Whitaker observed 'as so often with humorous journals, *Dublin Opinion* had caught, and vividly expressed, the mood of the moment'.[68] The effects of mass emigration in terms of population decline were most obviously demonstrated by the preliminary results of the 1956 census which became available in June of that year. The 1956 census recorded a total population of 2.9 million people, the lowest figure since 1841.[69] Emigration and the economy dominated the general election of March 1957, with the level of population decline calling into question the very viability of the independent Irish state.[70]

Large-scale emigration was an obvious indication of the limited degree of economic prosperity that was evident in independent Ireland by the mid-1950s. As a number of historians have argued, the depressing results of the 1956 also had a significant effect on Whitaker's thinking.[71] The introduction to the published version of *Economic Development* reflected the mood of the time.

After 35 years of native government people are asking whether we can achieve an acceptable degree of economic progress. The common talk among people in the towns, as in rural Ireland, is of their children having to emigrate as soon as their education is completed in order to be sure of a reasonable livelihood. To the children themselves and to many already in employment the jobs available at home look unattractive by comparison with those obtained in such variety and so readily elsewhere. All this seems to be setting up a vicious circle – of increasing emigration, resulting in a smaller domestic market depleted of initiative and skill, and a reduced incentive, whether for Irishmen or foreigners, to undertake and organise the productive enterprises which alone can provide increased employment opportunities and higher living standards.[72]

For Whitaker the economic environment had a direct relationship with Irish nationalist aspirations since the 'progressive decay of the Irish economy' would undermine political independence.[73] In addition he argued that there 'is a special obligation on the senior officials of the Irish state to do everything in their power to ensure that the state survives and prospers'.[74]

The reorientation in economic policy that occurred in the late 1950s ensured that independent Ireland was well placed to take advantage of the growth in the international economy in the 1960s. The circumstances which led to the formulation of an outward looking export-orientated economy and resulted in the creation of manufacturing and industrial employment have been extensively documented by historians.[75] Lemass emerges as a pragmatic politician who sought to redefine central elements of Irish nationalist thinking policy to achieve the 'early integration of the economy into an international trading bloc'.[76] Lemass, in sharp contrast to de Valera, 'set out to achieve his ideal instead of simply proclaiming it'.[77] While the achievements of Lemass and Whitaker were considerable and independent Ireland emerged in the 1960s as a much more 'modern' society, this economic growth was heavily reliant on the wider international economy, a dependence that was to become painfully obvious in the recession of the 1980s.[78]

The creation of employment which would reduce the need for Irish citizens to emigrate was the hallmark of the economic policy initiated by Lemass. During the early years of his period in office as Taoiseach, he made numerous statements which acknowledged the centrality of the reduction of emigration as an objective for Irish economic policy. Lemass viewed the reduction of emigration as the 'acid test' for government policy, and according to Horgan, 'the inability of many governments with which he was associated to effect any more than a temporary reduction [in emigration] was a permanent reminder of an uncompleted task'.[79] In October 1960 in a speech to the Dublin Chamber of Commerce he reminded his audience that 'the emigration rate is nevertheless evidence of the dimensions of the national problems still to be solved'.[80] He was also at pains to point out that high levels of emigration were by no means inevitable.[81] A month later in response to criticism of his government's record *vis-à-vis* emigration he declared that 'we have set ourselves the task of removing the economic causes of emigration by the promotion of a major programme of economic expansion'.[82] In January 1961 Lemass identified emigration as being 'the central problem so far as national policy is concerned'.[83]

By openly declaring that emigration was an indication of the effectiveness or otherwise of the economic policies, Lemass was merely reflecting the views of the electorate. Nevertheless, this was an inherently risky strategy and few governments prior to the 1960s wished their performance to be judged on the unpredictable index of the number of people leaving the country annually. Emigration was not solely sensitive to domestic economic conditions, but also to the availability of employment in the British economy, as was the case in 1962–3 when freak weather conditions created unemployment in Britain and fewer people left Ireland.[84] On a number of occasions, Lemass was involved in disputes with opposition deputies about annual emigration statistics.[85] Since the border with the United Kingdom was not controlled, it was impossible to measure gross emigration flows on an annual basis and the Central Statistics Office prepared data on the basis of net passenger balance statistics (the difference between the numbers leaving and entering the country in a twelve-month period). These figures were often misinterpreted as reliable estimates of net migration. In another context, that of unemployment data, a private memorandum written by Lemass to a senior civil servant, shows how sensitive he was to the untimely publication of embarrassing statistics:

The publication of depressing statistics, whatever justification there may be for it on the grounds of bringing the facts of the national economic situation to public attention, can have in itself economic effects. It is so important to sustain public confidence in the capacity of the country to achieve economic expansion that this must be the overriding consideration when deciding both the timing of publication and the method of presentation of the data.[86]

The new medium of television also served to raise the issue of emigration, much to the displeasure of Lemass. In January 1963 he heavily criticised a programme on emigration as 'thoroughly bad and depressing' and suggested that Telefís Éireann should 'take the whine out of their voice'.[87]

By the early 1960s more nuanced views were emerging in public discourse about emigration. Unequivocal condemnations of emigration as an 'evil' were a rarity, although such statements still featured in political debate. For instance, both Dublin Corporation and Dublin City Council adopted similar resolutions on emigration in late 1960 which was 'endangering the very existence of the historic Irish nation'.[88] Politicians and other influential figures sought to articulate a view that emigration was not necessarily driven by economic necessity but also by aspirations towards a better lifestyle and higher incomes. While the distinction itself is somewhat arbitrary, the point here was that even with relative economic prosperity, people would still leave in search of higher incomes. Shortly after becoming Taoiseach, Lemass argued in October 1960 that simplistic 'solutions' were of rhetorical rather than practical value. Of equal significance he urged a rethinking of the place of emigration in the Irish national psyche:

It would be a very foolish man indeed who would suggest that the factors affecting and sustaining Irish emigration are simple and capable of a simple remedy. It is time, however, that we began to think deeply about it and not merely as a political catch-cry or as a measure of our economic expansion needs. It would help, also, if we could encourage more objective thinking about it without allowing judgements to be swamped by emotionalism, although that is not easy in view of our national history and the personal problems which are often involved.[89]

This acknowledgement of the complex range of factors that lay behind emigration was a recognition that the traditional nationalist condemnation of movement out of the country as a 'bad' thing was no longer viewed as an appropriate position for political leaders to adopt by the 1960s.

Conclusion

The age of Lemass witnessed extraordinarily high levels of emigration in the 1940s and 1950s as well as a much-reduced level of movement in the 1960s. No western European society was as significantly shaped by the experience of mass migration as was post-war Ireland. The removal of the need to leave the country was a central policy objective that was articulated by leaders across the range of political parties in the post-war years. This was in part related to earlier nationalist ideology which stated that an independent state could generate enough employment which would in turn reduce the level of emigration. This proved to be an illusion and it was only in the 1960s that the opportunities offered by the creation of large-scale employment allowed for a substantial proportion of each generation coming of age to remain at home, rather than taking the well-trodden migrant pathway to Britain.

Apart from the Second World War and shortly thereafter when restrictions could be justified on the basis of exceptional circumstances, the Irish state did not directly intervene in the movement of people from independent Ireland. Quite apart from the logistical difficulties involved in introducing and regulating strict border controls, it was accepted by policy makers that restricting the free movement of labour was ideologically unsound. In any case, few obvious labour shortages existed which could necessitate such a move. On the other hand, the limited role of the state also extended to the provision of financial support for Irish citizens living in Britain. Despite significant pressure from Catholic Church leaders and other groups, politicians consistently refused to allocate public funding to centres, which assisted Irish migrants in post-war Britain.

Even though the body politic was well aware of the symbolic importance of emotive images of young people departing for other countries, there was very little that any government could do to influence the level of emigration. In fact had these migrants decided to stay in independent Ireland, the political élite may well have been forced to develop more innovative policies to counteract the significant potential for social unrest and class conflict. As the *Leader* declared in late 1953, 'if emigration were to be stopped tomorrow conditions favourable to social revolution might easily arise'.[90] In this respect, successive governments were fortunate that those most dissatisfied with the prevailing economic and social environment voted with their feet. By the late 1950s even the most conservative elements within the political and administrative élite recognised that the continuance of the large-scale emigration was raising doubts about the survival of the independent Irish state.[91] This created the wider context for the subsequent reformulations of Irish economic policy that led to the reduction of emigration in the 1960s and 1970s.

CHAPTER FIVE

Ireland and the productivity drive of post-war Europe

PETER MURRAY

—

Introduction

In June 1950 the first Inter-Party Irish government approved the setting up of a national productivity centre. The proposal was brought to cabinet not by an Irish department with a remit primarily concerned with economic development, such as Agriculture or Industry and Commerce, but by the Department of External Affairs, which acted on the prompting of a US government agency, the Economic Co-operation Administration (ECA). The ECA was responsible for running the European Recovery Programme or Marshall Plan, the source of substantial dollar loans and grants to Ireland between 1948 and 1951.[1]

'From the beginning of the Marshall Plan to its end, achievements were measured by increased output and improved productivity'[2] and the creation of national productivity centres in aid-receiving states was viewed by the ECA as an important means of mobilising broad support for the pursuit of these ends through the adoption of US methods and techniques. However, the Marshall Plan had long ended by the time an Irish productivity centre actually came into being in 1959. That centre was inaugurated during the early months of the period in which Seán Lemass held the office of Taoiseach and had as its initial focus the acquisition of technical assistance from Europe to aid newly adopted policies of planned economic expansion. Before Lemass retired in 1966 the productivity centre had, with his support, become a domestically resourced agency with a multi-faceted role in the promotion of Irish industrial adaptation and modernisation. By the end of the 1960s this agency was in crisis but a change in its composition and a narrowing of its focus enabled the oldest example of capital, labour and government collaboration from the post-1958 planning period to survive into the contemporary social partnership era. This chapter explores in turn the 1950s' delayed arrival, the 1960s' reinvention and the early 1970s' rescue through reconstitution of Ireland's national productivity centre.

1950s' delay

The approval given in June 1950 for the creation of a national productivity centre was subject to the 'understanding that specific proposals as to the steps to be taken would be submitted by the Minister for Industry and Commerce after consultation with the Industrial Development Authority'. A year later, with Fianna Fáil back in office, an External Affairs memorandum reviewed the situation. The IDA regarded the productivity centre that External Affairs had envisaged as 'far too ambitious' – in its view 'the objectives of the Productivity Programme should be achieved through the combined machinery of the I.D.A., the Institute for Industrial Research and Standards [IIRS] and the Central Statistics Office, aided by a small special staff either in the form of a separate organisation or within one of the above-mentioned Bodies, which would have the job of supplementing or co-ordinating activities in this particular field'. Moreover 'while the ECA people from Paris were very enthusiastic about the establishment of a full-scale Productivity Centre in this country this enthusiasm has not been shared by either Mr. Miller or Mr Clement of the local Mission'. To Harry Clement, 'who is primarily and enthusiastically interested in our industrial development programme', was attributed the view that 'the Productivity Programme being operated by Paris was geared to heavy industry and designed primarily to raise the marginal level of productivity in already highly industrialised countries'. In addition it was no longer clear that in geopolitical conditions changed by the Korean War the Americans in Paris attached the same priority to the productivity issue as they had previously done: 'there has been a decisive reorientation of U.S. Aid objectives – from Economic to Defence'. The recorded response of the Minister, Frank Aiken, was to suggest 'that the desirability of letting the matter [of the productivity centre] die a natural death might be considered'.[3]

However, the increased shaping of US policy by military concerns did not exclude productivity initiatives. Instead it gave them a complementary support role within a refocused set of strategies.[4] In 1952 the US Congress passed an amendment that transferred funds earmarked for productivity promotion to the Organisation for European Economic Co-operation (OEEC). Membership of OEEC had been a condition of receiving Marshall Aid: Ireland in the early

1950s was one of a small number of neutral state members alongside the NATO allies of the USA. This US funding prompted the 1953 creation within the OEEC of an autonomous European Productivity Agency (EPA).[5]

The addition of this productivity agency to existing OEEC bodies was seen by Industry and Commerce as entailing costs that would have few offsetting benefits for Ireland and the department was inclined to have nothing to do with the new body. External Affairs, on the other hand, felt that it would be impolitic of Ireland to appear reluctant to co-operate with its establishment and argued that it would be 'difficult having regard to our membership of OEEC to disassociate ourselves from the proposed agency'. Since EPA was intended 'to federate and guide the national productivity centers, as well as to service them',[6] its advent revived the issue of setting up an Irish productivity centre. In February 1954, a few months before a general election that would replace Fianna Fáil with a second Inter-Party government, an Industry and Commerce departmental conference discussed liaison with the EPA and 'concluded that it was not necessary to establish a National Productivity Agency and it was proposed that such an Agency should not be established'.[7]

In the absence of a national productivity centre, Industry and Commerce subsequently served as the EPA's Irish point of contact. This department circulated information it received regarding EPA projects to organisations that it considered likely to be interested but 'no special measures have been taken to publicise or advocate support for such Projects and the question of participating is left entirely to the interests themselves'.[8] Any participating interest had 'as a general rule' to pay out of its own resources any costs incurred through its involvement that EPA did not cover. Departmental budgets for Technical Assistance were an innovation of the Marshall Plan and were retained after the 1951 cessation of the dollar flow. However Industry and Commerce did not support EPA project participation from its Technical Assistance funds on the grounds:

> That the Projects are not initiated in this country; that they are not tailored to our particular needs; that even where there is Irish participation, it is by no means certain that any national as distinct from individual advantage is gained and that, as a general principle, it seems preferable that State funds should be applied towards the cost of technical assistance projects which are initiated in this country and which are designed to deal with specific Irish problems and conditions rather than that such funds should be used to contribute towards the cost of schemes organised by the Agency and designed to deal with more general problems of countries industrially more advanced.[9]

No Industry and Commerce representatives attended any level of EPA meeting in Paris. Nor, in the absence of interest on Industry and Commerce's part, were these covered by the Paris Embassy staff that doubled as the Irish delegation to the OEEC. With no Irish input into formative project design discussions at EPA headquarters, the assertion that the agency's projects were unsuited to Irish industrial needs became something of a self-fulfilling prophecy. The lack of an active engagement with Paris also meant that any Irish organisation potentially interested in participating in a particular EPA project was likely to learn about it too late in the day to become involved. In these circumstances, what is surprising is not that there was a minimal level of Irish involvement in EPA activities during the agency's first five years but that any participation at all took place.

Attempts to deepen Ireland's involvement in EPA were to come from three different sources. First, US officials raised the issue in the extended course of the negotiations for the 1957 sub-agreement providing for the expenditure of Marshall Aid Grant Counterpart funds on technical assistance projects. Out of a £350,000 technical assistance sub-total, £140,000 was allocated to three Industry and Commerce projects, one of which comprised 'employment of consultants by industrial firms; participation in European Productivity Agency projects; possible establishment of a National Productivity Centre'. That this was no more than a sop to the US urgings is indicated by the fact that only about £1,000 of the £54,000 provided for these purposes was actually spent on EPA-related activities.[10]

The EPA and OEEC were another source of overtures. Visiting Dublin to deliver an address to the IIRS in October 1954, Alexander King, Chairman of the OEEC Committee for Productivity and Applied Research, advocated the creation of an Irish productivity centre to the new Industry and Commerce Minister, William Norton. This resulted in the Chairman and the Director of the IIRS being asked to convene an informal committee to examine the issue. Represented on this Committee were the FUE, the FIM, the IMI, the ITUC, the ITGWU and the IDA as well as the IIRS. The approach of the IIRS was dutiful rather than enthusiastic – 'the factors affecting productivity may be economic, political, fiscal, sociological, psychological as well as technological and it is only in connection with the technological aspects in the main that the Institute could concern itself'.[11] The committee made painfully slow progress between March 1955 and November 1956 when it sent Norton a very brief draft constitution for a productivity organisation accompanied by a letter explaining that:

All the bodies invited subscribed to this document except the Federated Union of Employers. We expected that they would send us some communication saying why they were not willing to subscribe to the document but, as they have not seen fit to do so, we have thought it best to pass it on to you as an altogether unreasonable time has elapsed since you asked us to look into the matter. Whether there is any prospect of success for this organisation if the leading Employers' Association is not in favour of it, we must leave you to judge.[12]

The presentation of the informal committee's document coincided with the inauguration of an Industrial Advisory Council (IAC) to which its ministerial creator decided to refer further consideration of the question. The IAC was no more enthusiastic than the IIRS had been but its involvement with the productivity centre question was to be briefer. A general election in March 1957 saw the departure of Norton and the return of Lemass to Industry and Commerce. Lemass promptly killed off the IAC by directing that no further meetings of the body be convened and at a Departmental Conference in May he decided that no fresh action should be taken with regard to the setting up of a productivity centre.[13]

But such inaction was increasingly unacceptable to some of the member organisations of the IIRS-convened committee. The key groups here were the IMI and the trade unions. Moving from spare-time pursuit to full-time organisation, the IMI in 1957 created a Management Development Unit, with the assistance – as one of Industry and Commerce's three technical assistance projects – of Marshall Aid Grant Counterpart funding. Its first head, Norman Rimmer, had formerly worked for EPA and, 'drawing heavily on his contacts' there, 'arranged a procession of visiting management consultants and practitioners to Dublin and the larger regions' in 1957–8.[14] An IMI delegation travelled to Paris to visit EPA headquarters in January 1958 and followed this up by sending a deputation to Industry and Commerce that urged Lemass to have Ireland represented on the EPA Productivity Committee on 30 May:

The [IMI] Council felt that there was a tremendous opportunity of getting a lot of benefits out of the EPA generally . . . Ireland was virtually not represented at EPA and the country's name was not even mentioned in any of the numerous publications reflecting the activities of EPA. The Council thought that Ireland should be represented . . . everybody at the EPA was most anxious to give real help to Ireland.[15]

Lemass responded by saying that 'he had no enthusiasm for the setting up of any elaborate organisation glorifying itself as a National Productivity Centre' but admitted the shortcomings of existing EPA liaison arrangements. He suggested that the IMI might take the initiative in setting up a committee to screen EPA projects in order to identify those relevant to Ireland and said that, if this were done, he would consider having Ireland represented on the EPA Productivity Committee through this screening body.[16]

The debilitating division between the two rival union congresses produced by the 1945 split was very much in evidence when the IIRS-convened committee started meeting in the Spring of 1955 with the Congress of Irish Unions (CIU) refusing to work alongside the ITUC. The country's largest union and the CIU's core member, the ITGWU, was prevailed upon to take its place on the committee but then effectively withdrew from the work at an early stage. The committee's long drawn out proceedings stretched over a period in which congress unity moves made significant progress, with the formation of the Provisional United Trade Union Organisation (PUTUO) by the time it disbanded towards the end of 1956.[17] Direct Irish union links with Paris-based officials were also forged at EPA conferences or seminars. In November 1957 V. Agostinone of the trade union section of the EPA followed up contacts made at a seminar on productivity in ports by visiting Dublin to meet union leaders.[18] In December Alexander King, now the EPA's Deputy Director, revisited Ireland to speak at a weekend school organised by the People's College, an invitation first discussed when two ITUC delegates attended an EPA conference on automation earlier in the year. His speech called for the setting up of an Irish productivity centre and drew attention to the fact that Ireland and Portugal were the only OEEC member states without such a body.[19]

Ending the delay

During 1957 the option for inaction chosen by Lemass was almost immediately undermined and the formation of a productivity coalition facilitated by an initiative from Paris. On 3 May 1957 EPA's Director, Roger Gregoire, made 'a personal request' to the Head of the Irish Delegation to OEEC 'for your co-operation in putting into operation as quickly and efficiently as possible the Agency's programme for the human sciences and their application in industry', Project 405. The letter specifically requested 'your appropriate national authorities to constitute a joint committee in your country composed of management, trade union and government representatives as well as social scientists'.[20]

When this made its way to Dublin, Industry and Commerce officials drafted a reply to External Affairs 'indicating that we do not propose to set up the Joint Committee'.[21] However the departmental conference held on 1 July responded more positively:

> The Minister indicated that he favoured the idea of the establishment of such a Committee. He considered that the I.M.I. would probably be best qualified to examine and appraise the E.P.A. suggestion. He directed that the matter be discussed informally with Mr Hegarty, Vice Chairman of the Institute.[22]

When Hegarty, on being consulted, emphasised the need for full trade union co-operation and questioned whether this would be forthcoming if IMI were to take the initiative,[23] Lemass decided on a direct personal approach through John Swift of the Bakers' Union, from whom Industry and Commerce had recently received a detailed report on an EPA seminar in Berlin that he had attended.

> The Minister directed that a letter be prepared for his personal signature to Mr Swift. This letter should be linked to the preceding correspondence. It should inform Mr Swift of the proposal under consideration; should ask him to explore the proposal with his colleagues in the Trade Union Movement and should say that before taking any steps the Minister would require to be satisfied that the trade unions were prepared to support the idea in principle.[24]

With leading IMI figures like Hegarty positively engaged with productivity promotion in a way the IIRS had not been, and with Industry and Commerce more actively supportive, the sounding out of potential participants continued over several months.[25] When Alexander King stayed on in Ireland for an extra day after the People's College weekend school, IMI hosted a reception in his honour whose invitees included 'representatives of organisations which might be represented on the proposed committee to study Human Sciences in Industry'.[26] In March 1958 a first preliminary meeting 'to consider the establishment of a Joint Committee to implement E.P.A. Project 405' was convened by IMI. In addition to employer, manufacturer and trade union representatives those invited comprised educational institutions (the two Dublin universities and the capital city's Vocational Education Committee) as well as a number of the large semi-state companies.[27]

Apart from their stated purpose, the preliminary meetings increased Irish contact with EPA, whose Director came to Dublin to attend one in June, and provided a forum in which the national productivity centre issue was revisited. Here the halfway house of a screening panel, as suggested by Lemass to the IMI deputation on 30 May, lost out to the 'formation of a Body with wider functions in relation to Productivity, as well as the function of liaison with E.P.A.'. The functions not specifically linked to EPA liaison encompassed advising the Irish government 'on matters relating to the stimulation of productivity in Ireland', engaging in productivity propaganda aimed at all sections of the Irish community, disseminating productivity information, facilitating information exchange within and across industries as well as assisting or encouraging the adoption of productivity schemes.[28] What was in essence a resurrection of the 1956 IIRS-convened committee's constitution for a national productivity organisation did not on this occasion encounter the stumbling block of obdurate FUE objection.[29] When Hegarty headed a deputation that met Lemass on 11 July the stage was set for the establishment of two new bodies – a National Joint Committee on the Human Sciences and Their Application to Industry (HSC), which would have to create from scratch the expertise it was supposed to apply,[30] and the Irish National Productivity Committee (INPC), the centre for which government approval had been given eight years earlier.

Table 5.1 **Representation on Committee 'to promote productivity and to advise the Government in connection with liaison with the EPA' as agreed at the Fourth Preliminary Meeting to Consider the Establishment of a Joint Committee to Implement EPA Project 405 (1 July 1958)**

Organisation	Number of Representatives
Provisional United Trade Union Organisation	8
Federation of Irish Industries	2
Federated Union of Employers	2
Irish Management Institute	2
Industrial Development Authority	1
Institute for Industrial Research and Standards	1
Universities	1
City of Dublin Vocational Education Committee	1
State Sponsored Companies	2

Working with EPA and setting out productivity principles

The two sides of INPC's self-defined remit – collaboration with EPA and independent domestic initiatives – were to be in evidence over its first three years of existence (1959–62). Writing to Industry and Commerce in April 1962, Hegarty, who had become the Chairman of INPC on its formation, stated:

> The productivity work hitherto carried on by the Committee and which has introduced so much new thinking into the Country was enormously helped by E.P.A. which made possible the flow of propagandists and experts to this Country and the flow of people from this Country to Europe so that they might be influenced by the new outlooks and techniques.[31]

Elsewhere INPC estimated that there had been a six-fold increase in the number of EPA projects with Irish involvement in the three years after 1959 compared with the two years preceding it.[32]

Domestically the initial focus of the new body's work was on defining a basis upon which the productivity drive could secure broad acceptance. To this end, work began, at the unions' prompting, on drafting a general Statement of Productivity Principles. Agreed in September 1961, the principles associated increased productivity with improvement of living standards and the elimination of unemployment. Benefits from increased productivity 'should be enjoyed by all contributing thereto i.e. by the owners and the workers (as well as the consumer) having due regard to the necessity to strengthen the financial structure of industry and bearing in mind the interests of the community in general'. Employer-union consultation centred on safeguards for the worker that should precede the introduction of productivity schemes. Such safeguards might take the form of 'assuring as far as possible the continuation of his present employment, developing a new job or finding suitable work for him'. Here 'the initial responsibility should rest with the Employer, the Trade Unions and the industry directly concerned, but where necessary, the help of the State should be sought for the provision of re-training and redeployment schemes or special compensation'. A separation should be maintained between productivity co-operation in the common interest and 'normal industrial negotiations with regard to wages and conditions of employment'.[33]

Agreement on the principles was not easily reached. A draft circulated in November 1960 ran into FUE opposition. Lemass wrote to FUE supporting the concept of a principles statement on 29 December and suggesting that he meet an FUE deputation with Hegarty present to try to resolve the difficulties. FUE responded by seeking a private meeting and circulating a memorandum detailing its objections to the principles draft. These centred on the issues of benefit sharing and prior consultation. Both Hegarty and the Taoiseach's Department were unimpressed and both urged Lemass to press the FUE to accept the principles. The latter pointed out that practical work such as joint missions abroad was being held up by the dispute and that failure to agree 'would almost certainly contribute to a worsening of industrial relations and to mutual recrimination between employers and workers'. The former commented: 'so many of them [FUE members] are unenlightened as to the value of this new approach'. At his meeting with the FUE deputation on 23 January 1961 Lemass followed the line suggested. With regard to sharing, 'I said that in view of my own public statements in the matter I could not press unions to drop their insistence on this word'. The difficulty with consultation, construed by FUE as 'a written-in right of veto', Lemass characterised as 'a very theoretical objection', querying whether productivity change would actually be attempted in the absence of agreement.[34]

The FUE was unmoved and subsequently sent Hegarty amendments to the draft that were based upon the January memorandum. When Hegarty in April tabled his own revised draft, rather than the FUE amendments, for discussion by INPC, the protest that followed also referred to 'instances which have occurred at factory level which reinforce very clearly the misgivings which have been expressed by many concerning the possibilities for contention inherent in the publication of any document of this nature'. A continuation of these occurrences might, it was threatened, force FUE to review its participation in INPC.[35] The standoff was eventually resolved by the INPC setting up a sub-committee of its FUE and ICTU members that hammered out an agreed document.[36] FUE was not alone in its misgivings about the productivity principles. Industry and Commerce regarded the reference to possible state compensation for redundant workers they contained as undesirable, illustrating the way in which the productivity drive provided a forum for raising important issues that agreement on the general need for industrial adaptation left unresolved.[37]

1960s' reinvention

As the statement of principles was being agreed at home, the international dimension of the productivity drive was coming to an end. With the strength of Europe's economic recovery, the OEEC had lost much of its original rationale by the end of the 1950s. Through its own successes in technical areas such as currency convertibility mechanisms it had partly worked itself out of a job. Europe's big integration and liberalisation issues had been taken over by two rival blocs within the OEEC membership – the six-strong EEC and the seven-strong EFTA. In December 1959 it was decided to begin negotiations on a reorganisation that would enable the USA and Canada to become members.[38]

Without US money and advocacy no EPA would have come into existence but the US view of how a Western or 'free world' economic co-operation and development body of which it would itself be a member should be structured had no place for the productivity agency.[39] Thus, as OEEC was transformed into the Organisation for Economic Co-operation and Development (OECD), EPA was disbanded. It ceased to exist at the end of September 1961, although some programmes and projects ongoing at that date had until June 1962 to wind up. With EPA killed off, OECD emerged as an organisation oriented towards analytical studies rather than the provision of support services. Ireland pressed for services related to management development to be retained but this was done only for areas in the process of economic development, a status Ireland was unwilling to embrace.[40]

A mix of EPA funding support and a more liberal provision of departmental technical assistance grants had been the basis upon which Irish interaction with the agency had expanded since 1959. Both INPC and HSC were provided with secretarial support by Industry and Commerce but neither body had a budget of its own. Technical assistance funding had to be sought on a project-by-project basis. Against the background of the changes taking place in Paris, Hegarty embarked on a campaign in late 1961 to establish a national productivity body with a greatly widened range of activities supported by a secure source of domestic funding. The revamped INPC, it was proposed, would operate an advisory service targeted at small and medium enterprises, provide general information services, engage in promotional activities through a network of productivity committees organised on both an industrial and a regional basis, support educational activities and promote research.[41] Over the next two years the ongoing support of Lemass was drawn upon by Hegarty and by his successor as INPC Chairman, trade unionist Ruadhri Roberts, to overcome Industry and Commerce's reservations and have a multi-faceted INPC established as an independent company limited by guarantee in receipt of an annual grant-in-aid from Industry and Commerce's budget.[42] Throughout the process the importance of retaining trade union support for productivity initiatives was the key concern expressed privately by Lemass who was seeking in public speeches to counter expressed disquiet about a rising wage trend by pointing to increased productivity as the counteracting means by which economic expansion should be sustained.[43]

Late 1960s' crisis

The revamped INPC was publicly launched at its annual conference in Skerries in September 1963. In a passage of his speech welcoming the merging of the HSC into the INPC, Lemass made an observation prophetic of the difficulty the INPC would experience in retaining the role it appeared to have succeeded in carving out for itself:

> There are many organisations concerned with aspects of these problems of national efficiency – perhaps too many . . . As we go on with the campaign and see the problem becoming clearer we can consider the possibility of advantage in a greater concentration of effort.[44]

In the mid-1960s many of the principal characters in the story of the Irish productivity centre's establishment departed the scene. Lemass retired as Taoiseach in November 1966. In the following month Adrianus Vermuelen, a senior EPA official with a Dutch trade union background brought to Ireland by Hegarty as Technical Consultant to the post-EPA INPC in 1962, died suddenly. When a new term of office for INPC members began in January 1965, the IMI decided that its two representatives would be the Chairman and the Director *ex officio*, thus excluding Hegarty from the executive of an organisation in which he had served as Chairman and Vice-Chairman and which was to a very considerable extent his personal creation. This ousting of Hegarty, which led to bitter division within the IMI itself, was prompted mainly by the inclusion within INPC's remit of advisory services to firms, a field of activity coveted for the IMI by some of its leading figures.[45] Further turf wars broke out with other bodies spawned by the economic planning system of 1960s Ireland, precipitating new divisions within the interests represented on INPC – 'the FII maintain the productivity committees [for individual industries] interfere in matters that are the sole concern of management. The ICTU . . . resists this approach generally.'[46]

As a private limited company receiving a government grant-in-aid, the INPC was obliged to submit audited accounts and an annual report to its sponsoring department for presentation to the Houses of the Oireachtas. When its

1967/68 report and accounts were circulated in the spring of 1969, the Minister for Finance revived the issue of overlaps and duplications which had been central to Industry and Commerce's reservations regarding the INPC's plans in 1961–3. The areas of alleged overlap singled out were, first, with 'such bodies as the Irish Management Institute, the Institute for Industrial Research and Standards . . . and the expanding Small Industries Division of the I.D.A.' in advisory services provision and, second, with the Economic and Social Research Institute and government departments, especially the Department of Labour, in the field of human sciences research. This attack was broadened out by the observation: 'In general there is a fairly common impression that this organisation is not functioning successfully. For the last two or three years it has been largely stultified by the tug-o-war between employer and employee interests.'

Finance's observations concluded by calling for a review of INPC's operations and future 'if possible in the light of the plans which the IMI are understood to be formulating for its own [advisory] service'.[47] Prompted by Industry and Commerce, INPC proceeded to review its activities and objectives – and to provide support for Finance's critique when it was not possible to achieve agreement between the constituent members of the Committee. Assistance from abroad was turned to in the form of Svein Dalen and Tony Hubert of the European Association of National Productivity Centres, a network created in the early 1960s to fill a void left by EPA's demise. These consultants, whose conclusions found their way onto the front page of *The Irish Times* on 27 October 1970, encountered an unhappy organisation where 'at times we had almost the feeling by the furtive looks around, and speaking softly, that we were in less than a free society'.[48]

The agreement that had previously eluded the INPC was now to be attained on the basis of a course of action that flew in the face of the recommendations made by Dalen and Hubert and was accompanied by the departure of many of the hitherto represented interests:

> The main proposal is to restructure the Committee by substituting . . . a Council which would be composed of six representatives of the Federated Union of Employers and six representatives from the Irish Congress of Trade Unions, with an observer from the Department of Industry and Commerce. Bodies like the Irish Management Institute, the Institute for Industrial Research and Standards, the Universities etc. which had previously been represented on the Committee will be asked by the Council to provide expert advice on appropriate subjects from time to time. The Confederation of Irish Industry [formerly FII]

and the Federation of Trade Associations withdrew from the Committee because the recommendations of Dalen/Hubert that the Advisory Service be transferred elsewhere was not implemented . . . The Chairmanship would alternate between F.U.E. and I.C.T.U. . . .[49]

This restructuring secured continuance (into the 1990s) of state grant-in-aid to the renamed Irish Productivity Centre, an organisation that has survived with essentially the same constitution into the present day and currently defines its mission as 'to help Irish businesses to significantly improve productivity and competitiveness through the provision of high quality and relevant consultancy, facilitation, training and research services, supporting adoption to structural change and establishing an environment favourable to initiative and innovation'.[50]

Conclusion

In his book *Preventing the Future: Why Was Ireland So Poor for So Long?* Tom Garvin highlights an interview Lemass gave in retirement in 1969 to Michael Mills of the *Irish Press*:

> He [Lemass] gave unstinting praise to the American aid agencies that gave Irish economic planners and leaders advice on development strategies after 1945. He also burst out, with an emotional fervour evidently born of an intensely remembered sense of political and psychological isolation, 'After the war when international agencies were set up, it was almost inconceivable to us that high quality American personnel could be made available free to advise us on our resources and development plans'. With great emphasis he remembered not being able to believe his luck and was enthused retrospectively by the extra-ordinary open-handedness of the Americans and the OECD. Coming from an experience of Irish impoverishment and concomitant mean-mindedness combined with British superciliousness, he was stunned by the generosity, practicality and egalitarianism of the Americans.[51]

This study of Irish involvement in the European productivity drive presents the response of Lemass to a key post-war developmental initiative of US origin as being somewhat less euphoric. Industry and Commerce's negative line had been set while Lemass was out of office and local US officials were not singing from the same productivity hymn sheet as their Paris and Washington superiors. But Lemass instigated no change in the departmental line when he was back in office from 1951 to 1954 and on his return in 1957 was disposed to take no action on the setting up of a national productivity centre. Positive engagement with the international productivity scene came from the IMI and from the leadership of a trade union movement sometimes characterised in studies of Ireland's strategy shift as a vested interest wedded to the status quo, veto group or change-blocking coalition member.

Moves to set up a national committee on the human sciences and their application to industry opened up the way for a national productivity centre to be formed. Why the prevailing Industry and Commerce negativity was set aside in this instance is not clear. That External Affairs was happy enough while a modicum of appearances were kept up through the most minimal Irish involvement in EPA but would certainly have been unhappy with the delivery of a direct snub to a personal request it had received from the director of an international organisation of which Ireland was a member may have been a factor. It may also have been significant that a senior Industry and Commerce figure involved in dealing with the request, Thekla Beere, was also a leading member of the Statistical and Social Inquiry Society of Ireland.[52]

What is clear is that the bringing together in 1957 of Lemass and Denis Hegarty, and the perception that these two men shared that securing trade union support for an Irish productivity drive was vital, shaped the Irish productivity movement into the mid-1960s. As Taoiseach, Lemass remained notably accessible and responsive to the INPC's first chairman. The rebuff from Lemass to the FUE's attempt to enlist his support for the watering down of the productivity principles did not settle the issue but it set the parameters within which agreement between FUE and ICTU was subsequently reached. The blueprint for a post-EPA INPC would hardly have overcome Industry and Commerce's reservations about overlaps with the functions of other organisation and have secured the level of funding it required by late 1963 without repeated interventions from the Taoiseach.

This blueprint could not be sustained in the face of internal division and external criticism. But the role shrinkage that accompanied INPC's transformation into the IPC is less striking than the fact that the productivity centre survived at all. When a short history of the European Association of National Productivity Centres was written to mark its thirtieth anniversary in 1996, the IPC was one of only four of the 13 centres represented at the inaugural meeting that still existed 'in more or less the same form'.[53] National centres had been left dependent on national resources with the end of US sponsorship of and funding for the productivity drive. General decline set in with the public spending cuts that followed the end of the long post-war boom in the early 1970s. With the rise of neo-liberal New Right thinking, vice rather than virtue has been attached to employer-union joint approach bodies in many states. In its revival of social partnership since 1987 Ireland has gone against this trend. This partnership environment accounts to a considerable extent for present day Ireland still having, despite many vicissitudes, the productivity centre that was conceived while Marshall Aid dollars were flowing and created while Lemass presided over a new departure in economic planning and expansion.[54]

CHAPTER SIX

The 'mainstreaming' of Irish foreign policy

MAURICE FITZGERALD

—

Introduction

Lauded as a moderniser by most commentators, the majority view regarding Seán Lemass, his contribution to and the conduct of foreign policy during his premiership, is a relatively positive one. There is no denying that once Fianna Fáil returned to power in 1957, just over a decade into the post-Second World War era, and certainly once Lemass took office as Taoiseach two years later, he began to have a profound impact upon this particular policy area. This process continued not only throughout his tenure as premier, but also after he left office, and even beyond his death. Indeed, it is possible to argue that his legacy in Irish foreign policy continues to be felt right up to the present day, that he helped to engender a more outward, and undoubtedly less parochial approach to how Ireland saw itself, and how it in turn was viewed by others. Joe Lee has argued that, in terms of Ireland's historical development, Lemass was 'attempting to divert the mainstream'.[1] To be brutally frank, in comparison to its European neighbours, the mainstream was not where Ireland was located, but Lemass helped to haul the country out of a backwater. Indeed, upon his retirement, it no longer languished forgotten on the European periphery.

Background

This chapter examines a variety of policy decisions made under and positions reached by Lemass, whether in opposition or in government, in his time as industry and commerce minister, as well as Tánaiste, or subsequently as Taoiseach. It concentrates on the post-war years when Fianna Fáil were in power. In doing so, it shows how and why he made such a difference when in office. Ranging from its role within the United Nations (UN) to European integration, it touches on subjects such as foreign direct investment (FDI) and Irish-American ties, while also referring to the Cold War, decolonisation, and nuclear proliferation, as well as examining Anglo-Irish relations and neutrality in some detail. The years between 1945 and 1973 had enormous repercussions for Ireland in general, and the foreign policy conducted out of the Department of External Affairs based at Iveagh House in particular. On occasion, the decisions that were reached were affirming and reflective, showing how small states can coherently pursue their objectives; at other times, they were reactive and weak, demonstrating just how inadequate and lacking influence states such as these can truly be. In essence, the developments that took place in Irish foreign policy during this period have increasingly led to its mainstreaming, with Lemass reining in a maverick and independent actor on the global stage, allowing it certain eccentricities while concurrently maintaining, and perhaps even increasing, its limited European and world influence. In sum, it holds that Lemass had a considerable impact upon the conduct of Irish foreign policy, making it more western and less radical.

I am focusing here on his time as Taoiseach, which ran from 1959 to 1966, because that is when the most significant foreign policy changes took place, and when Lemass had his greatest input into decision making. Obviously, the chapter is not completely limited to that period. During his time as a senior minister in various post-war governments, there was less opportunity for him to influence foreign policy unduly, even if it saw periodic excursions to cities such as Paris, London and Washington. With this focus, I concentrate on the Europeanisation of Irish foreign policy, simply because that is one of the more significant legacies of the Lemass era, although it also examines his pro-American inclinations, and growing aversion to Anglophobia. But, most of all, it shows how Ireland slowly matured and began to appreciate the realities of the present and prospects for the future rather than simply yearning for the past. It reflects how the desire for independence of action was increasingly tempered when faced with the realities of interdependence. A proponent of economic autarky during the 1930s, Lemass was to become an apostate of trade liberalisation before the 1960s. It thus argues that the ability to adapt a course of action, or even to change direction completely, is what truly defines the age of Lemass.

Divided into three main parts after this background section, I first examine the economic choices made in eschewing dependence on Ireland's nearest neighbour for interdependence with the countries of Western Europe. Secondly, I investigate the acts and efforts undertaken to switch the focus of Irish foreign policy away from the UN at New York to the rapidly developing EEC centred in Brussels. Finally, I argue that foreign policy moved away from an emphasis on the singular, or otherwise peculiar, to the western mainstream, demonstrating how the heretofore sacrosanct policy of military neutrality was readily sacrificed for the future promise of collective defence, before explaining why signing up to the Anglo-Irish Free Trade Area (AIFTA) agreement not only recognised economic realities but mirrored an increased maturity in bilateral ties. The order of these three sections is not accidental. It becomes clear that Lemass was primarily concerned with Ireland's economic development and growth rather than foreign policy activism or in sustaining outdated policies, and that his impact was based upon the ability to make decisions readily and to utilise power effectively.

When Éamon de Valera left party politics in 1959, due in part to increasing pressure from a new crop of Fianna Fáil politicians, as well as his age and ill health, he was elevated after the requisite election to the symbolic position of president. Lemass quickly set about modernising Ireland, certainly in economic terms, but also in other policy areas as well. It has since been remarked that Lemass quickly 'shattered' Frank Aiken's even-handed policy by instigating a more pragmatic approach to foreign relations, that the new Taoiseach quickly gave 'praise for the USA as the guardian of all we stood for against the Eastern hordes'.[2] To be fair, the worldview of Lemass can be divided under two headings: Atlanticist and European. The Atlanticist side of his nature viewed western defence and security considerations in generally supportive terms, in essence supporting the US-backed North Atlantic Treaty Organisation (NATO) of which Ireland was not a part. Meanwhile, his European side saw the economic future of the country located in a multilateral trading bloc, partly as an escape from British domination and dependence, partly because such a development was becoming increasingly inevitable and necessary. However, on the surface, Ireland's global policy continued to strive for three central goals, listed by authors such as Patrick Keatinge as: (i) decolonisation; (ii) disarmament; and (iii) peace-keeping.[3] In reality, however, economic considerations had taken over from politics as the main impetus behind Irish foreign policy. EEC membership effectively became the foreign policy priority, and Irish activism at the UN slipped from the central focus. In addition, oft-repeated political concerns and positions were being quietly relegated to the past, or at least were being couched in less absolutist terms.

From dependence to interdependence

The ability of a nation – particularly a small state – to assert its independence and to express its sovereignty can manifest itself in various forms but, for a country to maintain or improve its relative position, it normally needs to operate within the rules of the game, as well as knowing how and when to bend them. It must realise that there are times when it is necessary to take the initiative, while at other stages demonstrating that it knows how to react, when to shape or to make the best of the inevitable, and most of all to realise that there are periods where adaptability may be the key, especially when developments are beyond its immediate control. Indeed, the conscious appreciation of the relative strengths and weaknesses of a position, whether in domestic or foreign policy terms, and especially with regard to how change will impact, demands an understanding of how foreign policy is made and carried out. For a country like Ireland, this will often require rapid responses to a developing situation, the ability to persuade and to take decisive action, as well as no small measure of good fortune. Most of all, it requires pragmatism ahead of idealism if it is to prosper and to make the global system work for it.

It can be persuasively argued that the first half century after the birth of the state saw Irish foreign policy slowly move away from serious and understandable concerns regarding the establishment and enhancement of independence to a more nuanced awareness of the twin dangers and desirability of internationalism. At the same time, Ireland's protracted dependence on its ex-colonial master was evidenced in so many ways, certainly in pure economic terms, that it is beyond the realms of this chapter to explore more than a limited number in any detail. For example, the Irish punt's reliance on sterling would continue virtually unquestioned throughout the Lemass years – was this the way for a sovereign state to assert its individuality?[4] Of course, Anglo-Irish financial arrangements are not the only prism through which to view Irish foreign policy in this era. There are other means as well, such as realignments in its foreign economic orientation, participation in international organisations, and the ability to reconfigure inherited positions. In truth, there was strong evidence of systematic change taking place during the Lemass era.

Having railed against it on various occasions when in opposition and cautiously in favour of it during the Fianna Fáil government of the early 1950s, Lemass gradually articulated a more mature approach, first as industry and commerce minister and then as Taoiseach in the late 1950s. Where previous de Valera governments had exhibited a rather backward orthodoxy, there were signs that Lemass favoured a more progressive approach.[5] Back in 1953, during a visit to the United States, he tentatively outlined Irish government attempts to remedy the country's economic woes by more actively welcoming FDI.[6] When the opportunity finally arose to implement his ideas, firstly as the most senior minister in de Valera's last cabinet from 1957 and then as Taoiseach from 1959, he became a strong proponent of FDI as just one of the means to modernise Ireland's stale and struggling economy, thereby shifting government emphasis and support away from indigenous and/or financially unviable industries by encouraging more international and/or income producing firms. Taking his cue from T. K. Whitaker, the senior Department of Finance civil servant who had called for the dramatic overhaul of both policy and outlook, Lemass embraced many of the radical plans and necessary changes prescribed by the former. He soon found himself presiding over one of the greatest development and growth periods in Irish economic history; one of the means employed 'to encourage export-oriented businesses from abroad to establish operations in Ireland' saw the government using a combination of tax incentives and other financial inducements to attract them.[7]

It is true that international conditions were also buoyant and therefore conducive to this economic upturn, and that FDI was not the only reason for Irish industrial development. But whatever elements ultimately contributed to Ireland's sustained growth, favourable emigration and unemployment statistics, increased tourism and air travel, as well as myriad other figures, soon proved that Irish economic fortunes had changed for the better, and not before time. If only trade figures are used as a measure to show how Ireland was swapping dependence for interdependence, it becomes readily apparent that the country was making considerable progress during the Lemass era (see tables 6.1 and 6.2) From table 6.1 it is possible to argue that the country was slowly moving away from dependence on the UK, while realising the potential that other markets – especially the EC – had for its economic development, both as a potential export market, and as a source for necessary imports, especially capital-intensive and other high value manufactured goods. The latter is readily apparent from table 6.2, but it also shows that manufactures had finally overtaken live animals, as well as food, drink and tobacco, in terms of importance as exported products.

At the same time, it is crucial to understand the role being played by lower trade barriers, increasing cross-border trade, and greater technological interaction. Key to this transformation of the Irish economy – from a system based on protectionism to one taking advantage of trade liberalisation – was the decision to seek out rather than to continue avoiding the new opportunities

Table 6.1 **Origin/destination of Irish trade (percentages of total), 1959 and 1966**

Irish exports				Irish imports		
UK	*US*	*EC*	*year*	*UK*	*US*	*EC*
75.2%	7.7%	5.8%	*1959*	51.7%	6.6%	12.4%
69.6%	7.1%	11.1%	*1966*	51.8%	9.3%	13.6%

Sources: Central Statistics Office, *Ireland, trade and shipping statistics* (Dublin, 1959); Central Statistics Office, *Ireland: trade and shipping statistics* (Dublin, 1966).

Table 6.2 **Composition of Irish trade (percentages of total), 1959 and 1966**

Irish exports				Irish imports		
live animals	*food, drink, etc.*	*manu- factures*	*year*	*live animals*	*food, drink, etc.*	*manu- factures*
30.1%	34.4%	27.9%	*1959*	4.5%	17.3%	72.4%
23.2%	35.7%	36.4%	*1966*	3.2%	16.0%	76.1%

Sources: Central Statistics Office, *Ireland, trade and shipping statistics* (Dublin, 1959); Central Statistics Office, *Ireland: trade and shipping statistics* (Dublin, 1966).

arising in Europe, as well as facing up to the inevitable onset of freer trade in the wider world and, in the interim, to secure more mature trading relations with the UK.[8] When it came to the actual negotiations for EEC entry, it was as much because of its lack of economic preparedness as for any other reason that Ireland failed to join at the first time of asking. However, by applying for entry in 1961, just as the UK was about to do the same, the Dublin government was reacting to developments. And, by not making any substantial progress in its negotiations over the next 18 months, despite having begun a process of tariff reductions as part of a 'carefully phased affair',[9] this left the Irish facing up to the realities and implications of the UK's veto by France in early 1963. Ireland would have to wait a decade for entry, but this did not stop its focus gradually turning from the Anglo-Irish and the global to the European in the enforced interim. The 1960s would be used to further Irish economic preparations for entry, with the Departments of the Taoiseach, Industry and Commerce, and Finance playing as active a role as the Department of External Affairs, and efforts would also continue to allay any remaining fears regarding Ireland's political propensities. The country, which had spent half a century looking inwards, was more and more inclined to look at the external as an opportunity for freer trade and rapid economic development rather than as a safety-valve for the unemployed and a forum to rail against partition.

Apart from Ireland's European integration efforts during the Lemass premiership, another significant impact on its global understanding at the beginning of the 1960s was the presence of an Irish-American in the White House. A decade earlier, Lemass had spoken openly and admiringly of the world role played by the US, and how Ireland viewed it:

> The Irish people feel a more intimate relationship with the United States than with any other country . . . We have watched with sympathy and understanding the efforts of the American Government and people to secure for all mankind the same freedoms and privileges which American citizens enjoy . . . To a far greater extent than ever before the fate of the world rests in American hands, and we for our part would not wish it differently.

It was not just to US audiences that Lemass made such statements.[10] Indeed, his views did not change upon becoming Taoiseach. He argued in favour of US 'leader[ship]' of the free world'. In his opinion, it was the US government which should take on the mantle of spokesperson for the western world, whether other western powers liked it or not, the basic reason being that the USSR had taken on this role of speaker for the communist world. In this regard, Lemass gave his uncategorical support for an expanded US role.[11] It was clear which camp Ireland was in, and it was not that of the USSR.

The visit by US president John Kennedy to Ireland in the summer of 1963 gave Lemass an ideal opportunity to cement this relationship. At the same time, it injected and reflected the enthusiasm and hope that this decade was bringing. In his address to Dáil Éireann, as well as in other speeches he delivered, Kennedy's approval of Ireland's active role in international affairs was allied to his considerable support for Anglo-Irish rapprochement, as well as his enthusiasm for European integration, seen as one of the elements required for western defence during the Cold War. In addition, he praised the Lemass government's promotion of economic modernisation and self-development through the use of FDI.[12] From the US perspective, the Irish premier was viewed as 'intelligent and shrewd', as well as 'efficient and hard-working'; indeed, they noted that his 'managerial temperament has been described as the antithesis of de Valera's professional type'.[13] He symbolised a new and vibrant Ireland. In addition, the US understood that the meeting between Lemass and Kennedy was being interpreted as a real 'political highlight', and a clear 'indication that Ireland is in the mainstream of international affairs'.[14] In fact, their discussions centred on issues such as Irish participation in UN peacekeeping and the control of nuclear weapons, as well as the performance of the Irish economy.[15] It was clear where Lemass had his priorities that national self-interest needed to balance its international role.

From New York to Brussels

Without wanting to delve into huge detail regarding the exact nature of Ireland's evolving role in the UN, this has been done in-depth elsewhere,[16] it is possible to illustrate how the nature of this relationship was changing, how economics was gradually triumphing over politics. At a meeting between Kennedy and Lemass in late 1963, during which the latter had been detailing the extent of Irish-American trade, it was apparently pointed out that the majority of Irish exports to the US were comprised of agricultural goods, mostly meat 'and a little bit of sugar'. At that time, it looked as if Ireland was going to miss out on a new round of sugar quotas that the US was allowing, but Ireland's ambassador in the US, T. J. Kiernan, had made Kenny O'Donnell, a Kennedy aide, aware of this situation. Thus when the Irish ambassador received a telephone call from Kennedy asking for support over the Kashmir crisis, the US president remarked that O'Donnell had 'mentioned something' and that he would 'look after that'. The question of any quid pro quo for a sugar quota, if indeed there was one, was not mentioned to the Irish External Affairs minister, it was felt that this would have prejudiced him against the US request. In turn, when informed of the US president's desire for this resolution, Aiken duly acceded despite his delegation at the UN having initially turned down lower level efforts by the Kennedy administration to persuade them to this course of action. However, Con Cremin, the senior civil servant in the Department of External Affairs in this period, was fully aware of the wider elements involved in this arrangement. Ireland tabled the resolution at the UN that the US were seeking, and, in addition, received improved access to US markets once an executive order specifically included it in their sugar quota arrangement.[17]

Clearly, one anecdote does not prove the radical overhaul of policy. Nevertheless, when considering the foreign policy developments, which took place in the Lemass years, one of the most significant and constant undercurrents saw a shift in the role and authority of the External Affairs minister. Irish prime ministers have regularly played an important part in shaping foreign policy, whether by design or accident – de Valera's coupling of the post before, during and after the war with the office of Taoiseach, and the rather premature announcement regarding the Commonwealth by John A. Costello, provide ample evidence of both phenomena. As with other countries, it is not necessarily the foreign minister who is 'called on to articulate new visions of . . . interests and policy, even if they wanted to'.[18] Increasingly, this task falls within the purview of premiers. In truth, Lemass did not show himself to be unnecessarily reluctant to assume this increase in his influence over policy, especially when his foreign minister clearly had his priorities focused elsewhere.

Throughout the Lemass premiership, the External Affairs portfolio was continuously held by Aiken – in fact, he held this post from 1951 to 1954 and again from 1957 to 1969 – and was to be the last of the old guard to give way to the 'young turks' taking political office across the 1960s. But there was also a marked change in the orientation of Irish foreign policy at this time, as it was increasingly channelled away from activism at the UN towards better relations with the UK and an accommodation of the developments taking place in western Europe. The latter only truly began with the protracted efforts by the OEEC to create a Free Trade Area, but was mainly concentrated on the EEC, and to a much lesser extent EFTA. As early as the return of Fianna Fáil to office in 1957, it was Lemass, rather than Aiken, who acted as the Irish 'government's principal spokesman on European affairs and handled all questions of Ireland's relations with EFTA and the EEC'.[19] In fact, as Brian Farrell goes on to argue:

> Following the 1961 general election he answered a question about the conduct of the Irish application to the EEC explicitly: 'I think the main responsibility for these negotiations must rest on myself as Taoiseach', and he continued to exercise that responsibility. But, with Aiken mainly concerned with Irish representation at the United Nations, Lemass took on a wider role. Starting from his original special interest in the economic and trading aspects of foreign policy, 'he became considerably involved in the evolution of policies' and, in the extended absences of the Minister in New York, even in the administration of the department.[20]

Of course, what this actually means is that the decision by Aiken to spend so much time at the UN impacted upon the influence that he would then have back home regarding other areas of Irish foreign policy, none more so than support for full EEC entry.

In fact, Aiken's extended periods away from Ireland, and crucially from cabinet meetings not only facilitated the prime minister's ability to shape foreign policy, they necessitated it. In many ways, Lemass was only filling the vacuum left by the extensive absences of his foreign minister but, in other respects, the shift in emphasis away from New York to Brussels reflected changing realities and priorities as much as it does any extension of prime ministerial power. Indeed, this 'decline in diplomatic activity at the UN and an intensification of interest in Europe' as the 1960s progressed has been much commented upon, demonstrating exactly where Aiken's emphasis lay and how that impacted on his ability to conduct foreign policy.[21] He had clearly presided over an exciting period in Irish diplomatic activity at the end of the 1950s and even the beginning of the 1960s, but EEC membership by 1970 was to become the refrain and central focus of Irish foreign policy as the decade advanced. As John A. Murphy has argued:

> an independent foreign policy, after all, was a luxury for a small and poor nation, increasingly vulnerable in a world of ever-more interdependent trading blocs and communities. So it was that an anxiety not to offend the most powerful nations of the West had already become evident by 1961, as Ireland turned her eyes towards the European fleshpots . . . an adventurous and exciting foreign policy was going to be considerably modified.[22]

The praise heaped by Lemass on the US as the 'guardian of the "free world"' was only matched by his unequivocal condemnation of the 'communist bloc'; in turn, tolerance rather than approval of Aiken's 'internationalism' meant that pragmatism triumphed over wide-eyed optimism, that a pro-American and pro-EEC Taoiseach had impressed upon Irish foreign policy makers where the future lay.[23] On the surface, it did appear as if Aiken had 'greater freedom in formulating foreign policy under Lemass than he did under de Valera, even though Aiken and Lemass are not cordial friends',[24] but the reality was that Ireland's foreign policy was shifting from an emphasis on the idealistic to the realistic, away from the altruistic and more towards the self-interested.

The UN forum had meant that a small state such as Ireland was able to play a significant part, whether in administrative terms – through, for instance, the work of Frederick Boland as General Assembly president, the efforts of Conor Cruise O'Brien in the Congo, or Ireland's term on the Security Council – or indeed through policy development – for example, by advancing the cause of decolonisation, promoting peace-keeping activities, or advocating the nonproliferation of nuclear weapons. This worthy altruism would bear fruit and was widely acclaimed, but it was also to be superseded by more self-interested, and increasingly concerted, efforts to accede to the EEC. And, even if the 1961–3 effort to negotiate entry failed, this would only encourage Jack Lynch, successor as Taoiseach to Lemass, and in certain respects a continuation of what had gone just before, to instigate further attempts in 1967 and 1970–2, the latter effort ultimately proving to be successful. Viewed simply in terms of diplomatic presence, never mind the energy and focus employed in carrying out Irish foreign policy, the establishment of a diplomatic mission in 1959 and creation of a Permanent Representation to the EC in 1966 first matched and then surpassed the setting up of a Permanent Mission to the UN in 1956, indicating firmly where Ireland's destiny lay.

One of the main features inherent in this shift of emphasis from New York to Brussels was that certain Irish leaders were finally cottoning on to the fact that more subtlety was going to be required if partition – the mainstay of Irish diplomatic activity – was ever going to be brought to a satisfactory conclusion. Lemass had also been one of those people who had slavishly regurgitated the official line that partition was affecting the country domestically and internationally, economically and politically. On one visit to the US, for instance, he argued that the economic and social situation, not just in Ireland, but in Northern Ireland as well, was being badly hampered by partition; in addition, he said that bilateral relations with the UK were also being seriously affected by this situation.[25] Nevertheless, under his stewardship, Dublin's position on partition noticeably changed. It was becoming increasingly obvious that the traditional policies of active diplomacy and creative propaganda were never going to change official US or wider world attitudes towards the situation in Northern Ireland, never mind the substantive issue of the actual partitioning itself. Therefore, the actual Irish government position was modified under Lemass to a more conciliatory line towards the de facto state of Northern Ireland. After all, this position only reflected the reality of the situation, and was just one example of a shift away from the more individual aspects of Irish foreign policy to the European mainstream. Of course, this move was in marked contrast to the views espoused by entrenched advocates like Aiken, who regularly emphasised Ireland's position on partition to international audiences, whether they wanted to listen or not. Although Aiken stated that he felt that Ireland was not in a position to force a satisfactory resolution of the issue, he maintained, however, that a hard-nosed government attitude would be rewarded in time.[26] The Lemass view was rather more subtle, even if equally transparent.

By the early 1960s, even if he publicly hoped that full EEC membership would help to bring partition to an end, essentially by raising living standards so that they were comparable with those of their northern brethren, Lemass was making it readily apparent that he preferred cooperation with the Northern Irish government when and if possible. He thus began to move away from the traditional line on partition, a policy which had attracted little response from other governments and organisations except ire and boredom. Although he tried this different tack, it had no real impact on international opinion, the official US government position, for instance, remaining very consistent and essentially non-interventionist.[27] Lemass appears to have taken the hint, even if other Irish leaders, such as de Valera in a meeting around that time with Dean Rusk, the US Secretary of State, had not.[28] In effect, partition had been dropped by Lemass from the diplomatic portfolio of topics, one of many other issues which would find themselves lower down the list of speaking subjects.

From the peculiar to the mainstream

If the considerable shift in economic outlook away from dependence to inter-dependence or the steady transition in foreign policy orientation away from the UN to the EEC are not evidence enough of the substantial developments taking place under Lemass, a brief examination of some of the peculiarities of Irish foreign policy is all that is required in order to understand the scale of the changes that were taking place. This begins with an examination of the relatively limited interaction that Lemass had with the formation and execution of Irish foreign policy before he became Taoiseach. Thereafter, the two main policies that are examined in this section are neutrality, in particular the future promise made regarding an Irish contribution towards western Europe's capacity to defend itself, and economic relations with the UK, especially concentrating on the signing of the AIFTA agreement. In each of these two cases, a policy which was rather peculiar to Ireland was tempered by other exigencies, so much so that the particular became more common, and the different more diffident. Irish foreign policy slowly entered the mainstream, edging away from the singular, a transformation that Lemass himself underwent in the immediate aftermath of the Second World War.

As early as 1947, reflecting his fears regarding a possible return to pre-war protectionism, Lemass indicated that Ireland should orientate itself towards the European mainstream. At that time, he spoke of the country's 'vital interests in European recovery',[29] attended meetings of the Committee on European Economic Cooperation, the precursor necessary for Marshall Aid, and made public statements regarding the government's participation in studies considering European economic rehabilitation.[30] This indicated that there were individuals capable of thinking outside the normal insular boundaries limiting most Irish politicians, even if partition and varying degrees of Anglophobia often ran through their contributions. Recognised as the 'economic brain' of Fianna Fáil, Lemass was said in one Central Intelligence Agency report dating from 1948 to be someone with 'administrative ability and general competence', as well as 'something of a *bon vivant*'.[31] He was marked out as one for the future. At least their participation in the Council of Europe and OEEC demonstrated to the world that the Irish possessed an international consciousness, while their efforts to join the UN did the same.[32] At the same time, this showed the Irish people that there might also be an alternative, or at least parallel arrangements, to the Anglo-Irish obsession. By 1957, Ireland would also join the International Monetary Fund and the World Bank, while the government finally decided to seek accession to the General Agreement on Tariffs and Trade. Thus, when the opportunity, or indeed threat, of substantial European economic co-operation eventually came along in the guise of the EEC, and despite having voiced some earlier prejudices and fears regarding its implications, Lemass was pragmatic and realistic enough to recognise where Ireland's future lay.

Having given public vent to changes in foreign economic policy such as support for the funds made available through Marshall Aid in the late 1940s, Lemass was also capable of taking other momentous, if rather more muted, decisions in the development of Irish foreign policy. This was to become possible to decipher in the case of neutrality. Unlike any of the other European countries at the beginning of the 1960s who held themselves to be neutral, Ireland was not in a position to defend itself from attack nor was the Dublin government doctrinally attached to its declared policy of military neutrality. Lemass said so himself in 1962, though the implications of this statement appear to have been largely played down by successive governments, certainly when Fianna Fáil are in opposition. With the country on the UN Security Council at that time,[33] he found himself obliged to tell the *New York Times* that:

> We recognise that a military commitment will be an inevitable consequence of our joining the Common Market and ultimately we would be prepared to yield even the technical label of neutrality. We are prepared to go into this integrated

Europe without any reservations as to how far this will take us in the field of foreign policy and defence.[34]

There was little room for ambiguity in this statement, even if the Irish public continues to show an attachment to neutrality. This policy, which had been – at least relatively – strictly observed during the course of the Second World War, and erroneously linked to partition thereafter, will be sacrificed as soon as a viable European alternative becomes available, an undoubted legacy of the Lemass era.

This shift in policy must also be seen in the Cold War context, as Lemass made it clear to both the US and the USSR exactly where Ireland stood, claiming that:

> [the Irish people and government] do not profess or pretend to be indifferent to the outcome of an East–West conflict, nor present ourselves as neutral on the ideological issues. Nobody who knows our people, their deep religious convictions and love of freedom, could ever think of us as neutral or negative. We are clearly on the democratic side, and everyone, East or West, knows that is where we belong.[35]

Thus he sought to engender stronger relations with the US. In terms of Irish foreign policy, despite being virulently anti-communist, this did not mean that it would necessarily join NATO, a position which remained virtually unchanged for successive Irish governments throughout the second half of the twentieth century. But, even here, Lemass maintaining that he was not antipathetic towards NATO is a truer reflection of government policy since the 1960s. He was, however, particularly concerned that any question regarding Ireland's relationship with NATO and Irish efforts to attain EC membership should not become entwined. Indeed, at a press conference in 1962, the Taoiseach observed:

> nor would we wish to receive an invitation [regarding NATO membership] at this time, because it would, I think, create misunderstanding in the mind of the Irish public as to the aims and purposes of the European Economic Community and be a further complication for us in the consideration of the problems which membership of the Community must necessarily involve for us.[36]

Full EEC membership was one of Ireland's main foreign policy objectives, if not the most crucial, and in this Lemass had the support of the US government, which did not show the same attitude towards other European neutrals. In effect, Irish government policy on neutrality changed under the leadership of Lemass, and has arguably not retained the same significance since this era despite irregular flickers of interest.

Another relationship where there was a considerable shift in foreign policy approach was with regard to the UK. At first glance, the AIFTA agreement is evidence of increased economic dependence on London rather than proof that Ireland had other options open to it. In fact, the decision by the Lemass government to ally itself more closely to the UK was a decisive change in policy, marking as it did further evidence of the end of protectionism and the embracing of free-trade and economic liberalisation. As much as the 1960 Anglo-Irish trade agreement demonstrated a relationship of dependency, as well as Dublin's lack of influence over London, the FTA created five years later was proof that interdependence was what Ireland now sought. The creation of the AIFTA would help to prepare Ireland – in advance of its EEC entry alongside the UK – for the harsher realities of European integration, especially as the lowering of economic barriers between EEC member states was well on schedule, and due to be completed by 1968. In essence, the AIFTA offered Ireland a similar relationship with the UK and, crucially, access to its markets, but its full impact on the Irish market would be staggered well into the mid-1970s. Thus, the AIFTA offered some – even if diminishing – shelter for up to a decade.

It is worth noting that there were significant improvements in other aspects of bilateral Anglo-Irish relations during the first half of the 1960s, particularly with regard to Northern Ireland, but it was the increased normalisation of relations through a shared interest in EEC membership that brought Dublin and London closer together at this time. The thawing of relations with the Stormont government, especially the meetings with Northern Irish prime minister Terence O'Neill, were not just symbolic changes, they were symptomatic of something much more substantial. The Anglophobia – particularly with regard to partition – inherent in post-war Irish foreign policy, most especially from the likes of Aiken and his attachment to 'emotional baggage of the past', has been commented upon.[37] Indeed, it was resurrected at various junctures by Irish government ministers after the departure of Lemass from office in 1966. Regressive rather than progressive, Anglophobia, which was often coupled with aspirations for some mythical and self-sufficient past, was tackled – even if only subtly – in the Lemass years as part of the ongoing battle between modernity and stasis, progress and the past, but it would take some considerable time for this more forward-looking approach to become the standard route taken by most Irish politicians.

Under Lemass, Irish foreign policy centred on better relations with the UK and accession to the EEC, allied to a strong and active voice in international affairs. Widely seen as the 'architect and engineer of the 'New' Ireland', and even if it was felt that the government had not seriously considered any other eventualities except EEC membership by 1970, the policy priority of the Lemass government was recognised as economic development.[38] In a speech delivered in the US during his visit in 1963, the Taoiseach affirmed that the Irish had no ambitions to influence world events, except to the extent that Ireland would remain consistent in its support of the US government's aims and principles.[39] The issues which were of central interest to Dublin remained economic, priorities such as its desire to attain EEC entry, the attraction of US industry and investment to Ireland.[40] With Lemass at the helm, Ireland remained committed to this course of assimilating to the 'mainstream of international developments', while more parochial concerns were quietly consigned to the past.[41]

Conclusion

This chapter argued that the most important contribution by Seán Lemass regarding Irish foreign policy, and by extension Ireland, has been the way in which it now views itself and the manner in which it is itself perceived. In personifying strong and pragmatic leadership at a time of rapid change, I have argued here that, certainly in terms of foreign policy, there was a major shift in emphasis away from its overly active participation at the UN to the mainstreaming of policy within a twin-pronged reorientation of improved Anglo-Irish relations and fuller support for, and participation in, European integration. The 'traditional nationalist and insular outlook' of Irish politicians in general was, according to US intelligence reports, radically altered by the dynamism of the new political elite nurtured by Lemass, and by the Dublin government's less jaundiced approach to the world and, in particular, towards Europe.[42] The Lemass approach was basically intended to engender economic growth, and it did so at the expense of political dogma, succeeding to a large extent. The attitude to foreign policy was thus marked by a significant departure because, as the 1960s passed by, the Irish government became ever more western in its orientation, less self-absorbed and less likely to be maverick. This led to some sacred foreign policy cows being challenged, negated and/or reversed, none more so than in relation to military neutrality. This did not mean that Ireland could not act in its own self-interest or that allegiances did not shift, that policy was always pursued coherently or that mistakes were not made. In truth, though, it can still be argued that Lemass helped to modernise attitudes, making them more European in essence and nature rather than just Gaelic, Anglophobic and/or Atlanticist by tradition or reaction, gearing them towards the world as it is, rather than how some would wish it to be. More than that, however, Irish foreign policy has never been the same again as a result of his time in office; his words and deeds will continue to echo long into the future.

CHAPTER SEVEN

Northern Ireland and cross-border co-operation

MICHAEL KENNEDY

—

Introduction

This chapter provides an overview of the significant changes in cross-border relations in Ireland during Seán Lemass's seven years as Taoiseach. It argues that in his redefinition of the Republic of Ireland's policy towards Northern Ireland Lemass made a significant attempt to begin restructuring political and economic relations within the island of Ireland. Bew and Patterson have argued in their *Seán Lemass and the Making of Modern Ireland* that Lemass 'contributed absolutely no new ideas in the Republic to the "debate" about the North'.[1] In one sense Bew and Patterson are correct. Unlike de Valera before him, Lemass was noticeably more silent on partition and Northern Ireland through his political career. This absence of rhetoric did not mean that Lemass was indifferent to the existence of partition or to discrimination in Northern Ireland. It simply meant that in 'the "debate on the North"' Lemass acted in a noticeably different manner towards Northern Ireland from his predecessors as Taoiseach. He had new ideas, the most important being that he dealt in realities. In a 1959 conversation with the British Ambassador to Ireland, Sir Alexander Clutterbuck, Clutterbuck reported to London that Lemass had 'said quite frankly to me that he fully realised on looking back that a great number of mistakes had been made by the government here in relation to the North; these he would work to rectify'.[2]

Lemass had shown an interest in developing good relations with Northern Ireland since first taking up a ministerial portfolio in 1932.[3] This chapter focuses on the ultimate development of that interest between 1956 and 1966. An example of his early ideas in this period was Lemass's promotion of developing neighbourly cross-border relations with the Belfast government whilst Fianna Fáil were in opposition from 1954 to 1957. A later basic but effective example occurred after Lemass became Taoiseach in 1959 when he directed that the use of 'Northern Ireland' should replace terms such as 'the Six Counties' and 'the North-East' in official Irish government documents.

What Bew and Patterson, admittedly writing eight years before state papers on both sides of the border for the Lemass years first became available, missed in their acerbic analysis is that Lemass did not contribute anything to the debate on the North in the Republic of Ireland, a debate which had become a stagnant regurgitation of rhetoric by the end of the anti-partition campaign in the early 1950s, because he simply did not enter into it. Accordingly it might be better to say that rather than 'redefine' Dublin's Northern policy, Lemass was the first Taoiseach to actively consider the realities of partition. He acknowledged the de facto existence of Northern Ireland and, though he ultimately and strongly desired the creation of a united Ireland, he realised that such a development would not occur in his lifetime. Lemass instead fashioned his own agenda for Dublin's relations with Northern Ireland, putting pragmatism before empty declaratory statements on the need for national unity. A landmark in this process was his meeting with the Prime Minister of Northern Ireland, Captain Terence O'Neill, in Belfast on 14 January 1965.

Visiting Belfast: 14 January 1965

At ten o'clock on the morning of 14 January 1965 Seán Lemass, accompanied by one of his most trusted advisers, the Secretary of the Department of Finance, T. K. Whitaker, left Dublin by car with the usual Garda escort. The Taoiseach had not told his driver in advance where he and Whitaker were ultimately bound for; Lemass merely directed that the car head north out of Dublin. In an interview over thirty years later Whitaker recalled how that morning Lemass was tense.[4] Normally adverse to small talk, the Taoiseach seemed less inclined to conversation than usual. As they continued through Balbriggan and Drogheda the two men kept up a desultory exchange on the separation of powers in the United States Constitution. Only at Dundalk was the accompanying Garda escort informed that the Taoiseach was crossing the border and Lemass told his driver to make for the customs post at Killeen. The weather had been bad the night before and the telephone lines from Belfast to Killeen were down. The Royal Ulster Constabulary (RUC) officers on duty on the border that morning were not aware until the last minute of the official Mercedes approaching from the south or the identities of its occupants.

Awaiting the southern party at Killeen was Jim Malley, Secretary to the Prime Minister of Northern Ireland, Terence O'Neill. While O'Neill waited anxiously at Stormont Castle in Belfast for his top-secret visitors, Malley told the RUC at the border post that the arrival of the southern Prime Minister was imminent and that they were not to stop Lemass's car on its arrival. At Killeen Malley joined Lemass and Whitaker and the three began the hour-long drive to Belfast where Lemass and O'Neill met for lunch at Stormont Castle. They then held an informal meeting that began to 'explore possibilities of practical co-operation in the interests of the whole of Ireland'.[5] News of the ground-breaking visit was announced in Dublin and Belfast at 1.10 p.m. The press release created a sensation: not since 1925, forty years previously, had the prime ministers of the two states in Ireland met to discuss problems of mutual concern to their jurisdictions.

Interpreting the Lemass–O'Neill meetings

The meeting between Lemass and O'Neill in Belfast on 14 January 1965, and their second meeting, on 9 February, in Dublin, were two defining moments in Lemass's seven years as Taoiseach. Generally the meetings have been interpreted positively, going some way to thaw a North–South relationship based on mutual antagonism.[6] From the collapse of the Boundary Commission in 1925 to the Lemass–O'Neill meetings North–South co-operation had inhabited a shadowy world of informal civil service contacts that circumvented the normal political processes in both capitals. Occasionally there were major agreements negotiated in public, such as the Erne Hydro-Electric scheme, the Foyle Fisheries Commission and the joint operation of the Dublin to Belfast railway by the Dublin and Belfast governments, all of which occurred in the 1950s. The ground-breaking January and February 1965 meetings created an ongoing co-operation process that replaced these one-off events. Following the 1965 meetings there was a short but effective period of North–South dialogue in fields as diverse as electricity generation and tourism. This co-operation became one of the first casualties of the Troubles after violence broke out in Northern Ireland in August 1969. Cross-border meetings were low-key to the 1990s but the agenda begun by Lemass and O'Neill was the precursor to the work undertaken by the cross-border implementation bodies of the 1998 Good Friday Agreement and the North–South Ministerial Council. The intervening Troubles in Northern Ireland understandably mask the fact that, since we are still close to their end in 1994, the process begun by Lemass and O'Neill bore successful long-term results.

Another way of interpreting the Lemass–O'Neill meetings is to say that they achieved little,[7] and further, that by his promotion of cross-border dialogue Lemass actually increased O'Neill's difficulties in Northern Ireland and hastened his downfall and the onset of the Troubles.[8] This interpretation is unhistorical as it relies strongly on hindsight and fails to take account of the widespread support for the cross-border summits in the immediate aftermath of the meetings and the fact that Prime Minister Lord Brookeborough, before O'Neill, and Chichester Clark after O'Neill, both advocated cross-border dialogue. When O'Neill called a surprise election in Northern Ireland for 25 November 1965 there was no perceivable backlash against his meeting Lemass. However, O'Neill's narrow support base and his many opponents and rivals within and without the Unionist Party, his own failed reforms and the socio-economic changes within Northern Ireland leading to the civil rights movement were together much stronger forces in bringing about O'Neill's resignation than his two meetings with Lemass in 1965 and his later meetings with Jack Lynch in 1967 and 1968.[9] Indeed, Lemass was aware of O'Neill's difficulties, and he made sure to limit his government's comments on Northern Ireland and to avoid meetings with Northern Irish politicians and civil servants at times, such as during the summer of 1966, when O'Neill was facing internal difficulties. Lynch tried to be as circumspect, but not all of his ministers followed his example.

The intention behind the meetings, as far as Lemass was concerned, has also been subject to much interpretation. In the Ireland of the 1990s Seán Lemass was refashioned as a patron saint of the 'Celtic Tiger'. Other Fianna Fáil heroes, in particular Eamon de Valera, were sidelined as unsuitable mascots for an outward looking, economically successful and newly self-confident Ireland. Lemass's pragmatism was lauded and his nationalism was downplayed in the more cosmopolitan Ireland of the 1990s. This recreation of Lemass in a modern image also suited the peace process in Northern Ireland. It could further be placed in the wider context of an ever-closer Europe that was, with fratricidal conflict in the former Yugoslavia an everyday news-item through the 1990s, increasingly uncomfortable with nationalism. In meeting O'Neill, Lemass seemed to be going beyond nationalism, accepting partition, if only in a de facto sense, and working outside its rhetoric. He thus seemed to be different from the dull anti-partitionists of de Valera's governments from 1932 to 1959. It was a suitable interpretation for the years of the Good Friday Agreement of 1998 and the subsequent referendum on the agreement which did away with the Republic of Ireland's territorial claim to Northern Ireland in articles two and three of the 1937 constitution. Lemass had taken the stance of the 'good neighbour' towards Northern Ireland and extended the hand of friendship to O'Neill, just as his successors Albert Reynolds and Bertie Ahern were doing to O'Neill's successor, David Trimble. This attitude is also unhistorical because it wrongly interprets Lemass's noted reticence towards speaking on the partition issue as indifference on partition.[10] As shown throughout this chapter, Lemass was in no way indifferent on ending the partition of Ireland.

When state papers from 1959 first became available to the public in 1990 the belief that Lemass was 'different somehow to the rest of us' began to be investigated and explained.[11] Under Lemass the business of government noticeably speeded up; after the ailing de Valera there was now vision and scope in a wide field of action by a forward-looking Taoiseach. Yet by 1997 the Irish media had caricatured this view of Lemass and re-engineered him in the mould of the 1990s.[12] The process had the result of separating Lemass from the mindset of Ireland of the 1950s and the 1960s and also from his own mindset of the independence struggle, partition, civil war and the foundation of Fianna Fáil. This resulted in a simplistic analysis, which could not take account of Lemass as a multifaceted and complex politician. When this analysis came to dealing with relations with Northern Ireland, Lemass's hopes for neighbourly relations between the Republic of Ireland and Northern Ireland, cross-border co-operation, and dialogue between politicians north and south of the border were reformulated to suggest an agreement with the existence of Northern Ireland. After thirty years of violence in Northern Ireland it became popular to suggest that Lemass, being after all a maker of modern Ireland, could not hold views suggestive of latter-day Irish Republicans. Lemass was a republican and, though eschewing violence as a way to solve partition, he never lost his belief in the need to end partition or his dream of ultimate Irish unity.

Lemass's views on cross-border relations: 1956–9

Lemass's views on partition notwithstanding, it was in his overall attitude towards Irish unity that Seán Lemass differed most strongly from his Fianna Fáil cabinet colleagues. This was not so much in terms of his belief in the ultimate necessity for Irish unity, but rather in the practicalities of achieving unity. An example of this can be seen when de Valera returned to government for the last time in March 1957. Lemass became Tánaiste and returned to the

Department of Industry and Commerce. At a meeting of the cabinet on 16
April 1957 de Valera asked his ministers to prepare 'specific detailed proposals
for the reintegration of the national territory'.[13] Reminiscent of an exercise
carried out by Cumann na nGaedheal in the autumn of 1925 when it expected
to receive large swathes of territory from Northern Ireland following the award
of the Boundary Commission, de Valera called for 'an intensive study of all the
practical problems that may be expected to arise' in the event of Dublin taking
over the government and administration of Northern Ireland.[14] Preferring
realities to aspirations, Lemass took the initiative in bursting de Valera's dreams.
A week after the cabinet meeting, Industry and Commerce politely sent a note
to the Department of the Taoiseach that Lemass considered that 'further work
on the study at this stage would not be justifiable [and] the study should be
deferred'.[15] Just why de Valera felt the study was necessary in 1957 is unclear,
but, following Lemass's attack on the Taoiseach's policy, the cabinet down-
graded the priority of the study and departments of state were instead
instructed to examine 'whether there would be any value . . . in pursuing, in the
present circumstances, the study'.[16]

Lemass regarded de Valera's proposals as a waste of time and resources.
He was looking elsewhere for a more realistic policy on Northern Ireland. An
early indication of this new direction was seen during a speech in Belfast on
12 December 1956 where he called for closer economic co-operation between
North and South regardless of political differences.[17] The sub-text of this was
that he would not compromise on his own political principles regarding Irish
unity. But his main message was that increased economic activity across the
border would benefit Northern Ireland as much as it would the Republic of
Ireland. Lemass wished to remove the tariff barrier that had been put in place
between North and South in April 1923 and which had been undermining
economic activity on both sides of the border, in particular cutting border
towns off from their natural economic hinterlands on both sides of the frontier.

Using a call in the Seanad by Belfast-born senator William B. Stanford for a
government commission to promote cross-border co-operation, Lemass brought
plans for cross-border economic co-operation to cabinet on 22 October 1957.
The results were disappointing: there was merely agreement that North and
South faced similar economic problems and that consideration should be given
to inter-governmental discussions. The Seanad debate on Stanford's motion
also made little progress. Addressing the chamber, de Valera saw only problems.
Concluding that he would 'welcome such a coming together' he despaired that
'how to start it or get it going is the question'.[18]

In one sense de Valera was correct, the Prime Minister of Northern Ireland, Lord Brookeborough, was against co-operation with Dublin until North and South countered the threat from the IRA, which had been resurgent since the beginning of their border campaign in the winter of 1956. Brookeborough demanded that Dublin recognise the status of Northern Ireland before Belfast could contemplate furthering cross-border co-operation.

Following the successes of the Lough Erne hydro-electric scheme and the Foyle Fisheries Commission and the partial success of the Great Northern Railways Board it was hard now to see from where the next move for cross-border co-operation would come.

The move came from an unlikely source. Furniture manufacturers in the Republic of Ireland had developed a strong market in Northern Ireland while their counterparts in Northern Ireland were prevented, because of Irish tariffs, from developing a market in the South. Accordingly, the Northern Irish manufacturers felt that the southern firms were 'dumping' goods in their market. Representatives of the Northern Irish furniture manufacturers had attempted to raise their concerns with the Stormont government. Despite the attempts of Northern Ireland Minister of Commerce, Lord Glentoran, to interest his cabinet colleagues in talks with Dublin to open cross-border trade, the Northern Ireland government, fearing that such a move 'might be seen as the first step towards turning all Ireland into an economic unit', sought refuge in proposing retaliatory measures against southern exports to Northern Ireland.[19] They decided that limited free trade with the Republic of Ireland 'could not be supported on political grounds'.[20]

Limited cross-border contact could be developed through addressing the concerns of the Northern Ireland furniture manufacturers. The problem was that there was no co-ordinating force to bring the various sides together. In this problematic situation Lemass's accession to power, replacing de Valera on 23 June 1959, was a crucial turning point, not only for the immediate issue of furniture imports and exports, but also for the wider context of overall relations between North and South.

Beginning to dismantle the barriers to cross-border trade

In the Dáil on 21 July 1959 during his first major speech as Taoiseach, Lemass called for an improvement in relations with Northern Ireland. He hoped that he could meet with Brookeborough, partition and the political differences

between the two men notwithstanding. Lemass spoke of many opportunities for cross-border relations, not only in freeing up North–South trade but broader areas such as a shared merchant shipping fleet, a cross-border electricity link-up and even a joint nuclear power station. The Taoiseach specifically referred to the concerns of the Northern furniture manufacturers by mentioning 'economic difficulties in the North in some trade sectors' and hoping 'that if we can promote the growth of co-operation . . . it can contribute to the economic development of both parts of the country'.[21]

The speech had an immediate impact. John E. Sayers, the editor of the *Belfast Telegraph*, wrote to his friend J. J. Horgan in Cork that Lemass had 'begun something that, properly fostered, may lead to a definite improvement in relations of all kinds'.[22] Horgan passed the letter on confidentially to Lemass telling him that 'you are on the right road towards the North, but it will be a long one'.[23] The problem facing Lemass was how to overcome the objection of the Northern government that it was only willing to co-operate as a quid pro quo for an explicit recognition of Northern Ireland by Dublin.

When Brookeborough replied to Lemass's Dáil speech he made it clear that 'nothing I have said rules out co-operative efforts with the Republic where mutual advantages can be demonstrated, as they have been in electricity, drainage, fisheries and transport'. However, as always he added that 'in none of these schemes did we sacrifice any part of our attachment to Great Britain'.[24] In a meeting with the British Chargé d'Affaires in Dublin, Gurth Kimber, Lemass said he was aware when making the July speech that little would result because Brookeborough had to keep his supporters in mind. Not to be discouraged Lemass spent September 1959 looking at existing North–South co-operation. It covered very limited areas: the Foyle and Erne fisheries, water, drainage and electricity supplies and even fire protection for parts of Donegal was provided by the Northern Irish fire service through arrangement with Donegal County Council. It was, however, clear that North–South trade had increased significantly over the past five years. Lemass anticipated that this would be the window of opportunity for increased cross-border co-operation.

An indication of the increased importance of cross-border co-operation for Lemass was his 15 October 1959 address to the Oxford Union. In the speech he unveiled his new approach towards Northern Ireland to a high-profile British audience calling for 'practical co-operation . . . even in advance of any political arrangement'.[25] Lemass forcefully argued that it was 'plain common sense that the two existing political communities in our small island should seek every opportunity of working together in practical matters for their mutual and common good'. 'For a long time', Lemass argued, 'our attitude towards the solution of the partition problem was influenced by the conviction that it would eventually collapse of its own inherent weakness and artificiality'. Lemass purposely used the past tense to suggest that a new outlook was in the offing. Though the address was couched in many familiar anti-partitionist terms and called for eventual unity by agreement, there was an undeniable sense of movement away from the old agenda of Irish unity as the total of what had previously passed for Dublin's Northern Ireland policy.

It was clear from the Oxford Union address that Lemass also saw economic co-operation between North and South as a means towards a wider end. 'Ireland', he said, 'is too small a country not to be seriously handicapped in its economic development by its division into two areas separated by a customs barrier.' This taken alone was a standard attitude, but Lemass followed it by linking North–South co-operation into a greater plan: 'the fact that [Ireland's] progress has fallen behind that of other countries of Western Europe is certainly due in some measure to this cause'. Whereas de Valera saw North–South co-operation, if it were possible, only as a means to ending partition, Lemass additionally saw it as a step on the road to Irish entry into the EEC and as a means to end partition in the much longer run.

When Lemass returned to Dublin he indicated that steps be taken at official level to begin the freeing up of North–South trade. In the conclusion to his Oxford speech Lemass had spoken of developing 'contacts which will tend to build goodwill and to strive for concerted action in particular fields where early practical advantages can be obtained'. It was to be, 'a policy of good sense and good neighbourliness'. In a memorandum to the heads of the senior government departments Lemass took up the most immediate cross-border concern and 'directed that the possibility of giving tariff concessions for six county furniture should be examined'.[26] Lemass saw the proposed reductions in furniture tariffs as progress on the road to Irish involvement in a European free trade regime: 'as an advance instalment of tariff reduction it would help industry and workers to gauge the possible consequences, should we join EFTA'. Though Taoiseach for less than four months, a major overhaul of Northern Ireland policy was taking place under Lemass's guidance.

At the November 1959 Fianna Fáil Ard Fheis, Lemass continued to press his new line on cross-border co-operation. During the debate on partition he became more explicit: 'we are ready, without imposing any prior conditions, to explore any promising prospect of developing useful co-operation for the sake of the practical benefits it may yield to the ordinary people in the North and the South'.[27] But he would not recognise Northern Ireland, saying instead that he recognised that partition existed and that it was Dublin's 'desire to see our people and country reunited'.[28] Hugh McCann commented on the favourable British press response to the speech.[29] However, it failed to move its primary target. Brookeborough would not budge. Economic co-operation was, in Brookeborough's eyes, a soft way towards a united Ireland.

An Anglo-Irish trade agreement was signed on 13 April 1960. Addressing the Dáil, Lemass reminded the deputies that the Northern government had rejected his calls for a trade co-operation body as part of the agreement. He argued that it was 'foolish in the extreme . . . that there should be no procedure for consultation or even direct communication' with Stormont. Instead of working towards co-operation, the Northern members at Westminster had urged 'the British government not to make, or at least to minimise trade concessions to us'. This had irked the British who 'have been made aware of our desire to promote greater trade and encourage commercial contacts between the two areas'. The British agreed with the Irish policy, and, in an explicit reference to the furniture manufacturers, Lemass made clear that there were:

> many business interests in the North who will share our view that, regardless of any differences of opinion between the governments on the question of the future of partition it is sensible to try to minimise its economic consequences for the benefit of the people of both areas.[30]

Stormont's lack of action on cross-border trade forced the suffering Northern Irish industries to take action on their own. On 28 November 1960, prompted by the Northern authorities' refusal to take up Lemass's offers, the Ulster Furniture Federation began informal contacts with the Department of Industry and Commerce. A meeting between Minister for Industry and Commerce, Jack Lynch, and a deputation from the Ulster Furniture Federation took place in Dublin in mid-February 1961. The delegates said that 'the people in their trade were very anxious to take advantage of the Taoiseach's offer for 32-county free trade. They were suffering severe competition not only from the 26 counties but also from Britain.' The businessmen explained that they had tried to interest Belfast in Lemass's ideas, but to no avail and hoped for a unilateral gesture. The Federation said they did not expect resentment in the North at their move and hoped 'to raise even one small corner of the "iron curtain" which existed between the two countries.' They expected that this would lead to increased pressure for co-operation and that the Northern authorities would eventually give in. Their objective in meeting the Southern government was to make the first move.

At a further meeting on 14 March the Northern furniture manufacturers mentioned that they had met the Brookeborough and Glentoran and discussed their proposed meetings with the Dublin government. The reply was very significant when compared to the Northern Irish government's previous discussions on cross-border trade. The Northern Irish government assured the delegation that 'any arrangement which they proposed to make with the southern authorities was entirely a matter for themselves and that there would be no government interference with it.' Even more remarkable was that 'the ministers added off the record "we wish you good luck"'.[31] Cross-border free trade returned to the Southern cabinet agenda in March and April 1961 when Ministers were asked to consider the substantive issue of according free entry to Northern Ireland furniture exports to Ireland. There was no meeting of minds and Lynch was instructed to explore the matter further.[32] Lynch then met representatives of the Federation of Irish Industry and the Federated Union of Employers and explained the government's proposed policy but, though the industry representatives welcomed the move, their final line was to draw attention to the 'practical difficulties'.[33]

The Northern businessmen were more forthcoming. The meetings with the furniture representatives were a catalyst that created conditions allowing other Northern Irish industries to venture in the direction of Government Buildings in Dublin. The July holidays in Northern Ireland brought representatives of the linen, paint, cardboard boxes, carpet and electric motor industries south to see Jack Lynch. The Irish government remained 'disposed to favourable action on trade'.[34] The summer of 1961 had seen other reasons why Lemass's administration should be so inclined to favourable action on free trade. Lemass was steering Ireland towards the Europe with a white paper on Europe followed by Ireland's first application for EEC membership and an Industry and Commerce memorandum considered how North–South free trade would be 'a very useful exercise in anticipation of membership of the EEC'.[35]

Lemass's first general election as Taoiseach was pending for the autumn of 1961.[36] An improvement in relations with Belfast, increased economic growth and prosperity and the prospect of membership of the EEC would be a good record with which to face the electorate. But progress had slowed on liberalising cross-border trade and the Southern manufacturers were reported by Lynch to be 'dragging their feet', whilst their Northern counterparts had 'some difficulty . . . making themselves available for meetings'.[37] Lemass and Lynch saw that most obstacles were being overcome through joint North–South meetings chaired by officials from Industry and Commerce. By early July 1962

Dublin was ready to move on freeing cross-border trade. Lynch aimed to confine concessions to goods 'which are bona-fide owned within the six counties'. Lemass favoured zero tariffs in the case of electric motors and paint, and a new lower preferential of duty as regards furniture. Lemass hoped these specific reductions would lead to further enquiries from other interested industries.

The divisions in the Southern cabinet over cross-border trade liberalisation emerged again during the summer of 1962. Significantly it was the Minister for Agriculture, Paddy Smith, who was to resign from the Lemass government in October 1964, who first broke ranks with the cabinet policy. Smith did not trust Lemass and Lynch's policy, fearing a backlash from Belfast, annoyance from London and a breach of existing trading agreements.[38] Minister for External Affairs, Frank Aiken, threw his weight behind Lemass, and argued 'that the existing economic situation in the six counties provides a particularly appropriate opportunity for a gesture of this kind'.[39] When James Ryan, the Minister for Finance, rowed in behind Smith and opposed the tariff reduction Lemass was faced with a division amongst the senior members of his cabinet over the practical operation of his new Northern Ireland policy. Whilst Lemass pondered how to deal with this cabinet discord, many in the North were getting 'cold feet'. The delays in implementing the tariff reduction led to feelings 'that the suggestion for closer economic co-operation between North and South was not genuine.'[40] To overcome internal cabinet differences and increased suspicion from industry sources on both sides of the border Lynch was instructed to steamroll proposals for cross-border trade liberalisation decision through cabinet on 11 September 1962.

Duty free licences would be introduced immediately for electric motors and paint, implementing the reduced duties for linen and furniture would take longer. The announcement on 21 September 1962 recounted how Lemass's statements had led to approaches from interests in the six counties and these had led to the decision to reduce or remove certain duties and tariffs. The *Derry Journal* welcomed the move, referring to the 'six county manufacturers [who] felt that this was an offer not to be missed' and attacking Brookeborough who was 'bypassed' and left 'to sulk in his sash'.[41]

The Northern Irish records show little immediate reaction to the reduction. Though 'there was general agreement that actions beneficial to Northern Ireland trade and employment deserved appropriation' the Northern Irish Ministry of Commerce refused to take an active part in the tariff reductions; the channel would be between the Dublin government and the manufacturers.[42] However, as a Taoiseach's Department memorandum made clear, the Ministry of

Commerce was involved 'to the extent of advising their manufacturers to make their case in Dublin'.[43]

Lemass waited some time before asking Jack Lynch if the unilateral action had resulted in any further industries approaching the Dublin government. Lynch wrote back with a long list: handbags, shop fittings, joinery shirts, flowerpots, watch strings and silencer exhausts.[44] All of these cases were being examined by Industry and Commerce and the representatives of the six counties were meeting departmental and Southern interests. A significant step forward in developing North–South trade, so badly hit by partition and the subsequent lowering of commercial contact, was under way. In December 1962 Lynch announced a further reduction, linen imports from Northern Ireland into the Republic were to have their duty reduced to 25 per cent.[45] By the beginning of 1963 Lemass's new initiatives in Northern Ireland were bearing fruit. Businessmen in Northern Ireland were increasingly accepting cross-border economic co-operation. Lemass's next move was to endeavour to set up a series of official-level meetings between civil servants from Dublin and Belfast

New plans for cross-border relations

On 25 March 1963 Captain Terence O'Neill replaced Lord Brookeborough as Prime Minister of Northern Ireland. Here was a younger man, formerly Brookeborough's Minister of Home Affairs and his Minister of Finance, who was a capable administrator with some idea of the direction in which he wanted Northern Ireland to develop economically and politically.[46] Compared to Lemass, O'Neill was a political neophyte. He had been chosen as Brookeborough's successor without a vote and this annoyed many in the Unionist Party, especially Brian Faulkner, who was to be O'Neill's main rival through the 1960s. Through 1963 Lemass began to court O'Neill with ideas for closer North–South relations, but though O'Neill appeared to warm to the suggestions he, like Brookeborough, prefaced them with the precondition that Dublin should first recognise Northern Ireland's de jure existence as a political entity. But O'Neill was also drawn to Lemass; he was fascinated by how the Taoiseach had succeeded in promoting Irish economic growth, a success he hoped to emulate in Northern Ireland. O'Neill was also intrigued by T. K. Whitaker. He had met Whitaker at meetings of the World Bank and he longed to have officials of a similar calibre at his own disposal to promote economic development in Northern Ireland. O'Neill's meetings with Whitaker at World Bank meetings were later to be an important personal channel in facilitating the Lemass–O'Neill meetings of 1965. Simply, O'Neill wanted to meet the men who had undertaken in the Republic of Ireland the transformation he wished to undertake in Northern Ireland.

Visits by members of the Young Unionists to Dublin in April 1963, with the unofficial backing of O'Neill, to meet representatives of Fianna Fáil and Fine Gael were evidence of what *The Irish Times* called a 'wind of change' in Northern Ireland in the aftermath of Brookeborough's resignation.[47] One of the Young Unionist visitors to Dublin, Robin Baillie, whose father was chairman of the Unionist Party organisation in O'Neill's constituency, concluded his speech to a combined Unionist Party and Fianna Fáil audience at the Shelbourne Hotel in Dublin[48] that the 'time is now ripe for a meeting [between the two prime ministers], now is the accepted hour'.[49] O'Neill was starting to put out significant feelers to Dublin less a month after becoming Prime Minister of Northern Ireland. On 23 July 1963 Lemass made a major speech at Tralee in an attempt to kick-start the co-operation process. In one of the most significant speeches on a Northern Ireland theme of his years as Taoiseach, Lemass stated that Ireland had 'never failed to recognise the genuineness of the fears which have influenced the religious minority in the North'.[50] He continued by dealing with the constitutional status of Northern Ireland, significantly recognising 'that the Government and Parliament there exist with the support of the majority in the Six County area – artificial though that area is . . . recognition of the realities of the situation has never been a difficulty with us'. This was deeply significant and was seized upon as the first time a Taoiseach had, as the *Irish Independent* put it 'admitted the facts of Partition'.[51] This was an overstatement as the facts of partition had been often commented upon in the past, but the speech used more tolerant language towards Northern Ireland, recognised the principle of consent written into the 1949 Ireland Act at Westminster, and continued to nurture the feeling that there were new options for developing cross-border relations.

On cross-border co-operation Lemass said that it was 'foolish in the extreme . . . that there should persist a desire to avoid contacts even in respect of matters where concerted action is clearly seen to be beneficial'. He hoped that by extending contacts at all levels 'a new situation would develop which would permit of wider possibilities in accord with our desires'. Much as co-operation had developed in Europe since the Second World War, Lemass argued for 'rolling co-operation' in functional matters. Here was a further statement of intent for the development of a new Northern Irish policy. However, within the speech, for all its newness, the standard Fianna Fáil line on unity remained as Lemass called for 'the solution of the problem of partition . . . to be found in Ireland by Irishmen', it was clear that beyond the medium term gains to North and South by closer cross-border relations, co-operation was for Lemass the starting point of a longer term process towards ultimate Irish unity.

Despite an initially cool Northern Irish response, Lemass sensed an opportunity after the Tralee speech for North–South discussions at 'civil service level on cross-border co-operation . . . in the early future'.[52] He lowered his objectives away from an immediate meeting with O'Neill and aimed at a longer-term strategy of building on the ongoing tariff reductions. Lemass called for discussions 'at whatever level is likely to be most fruitful' to accelerate co-operation.[53] In a more helpful tone, O'Neill released a statement 'expressing the hope for the development of a more friendly spirit' and continuing that 'there is no bar to specific co-operative measures provided that these are of clear mutual benefit, have no political or constitutional undertones'.[54] In the autumn of 1963 O'Neill seemed to be moving towards favouring cross-border co-operation. Perhaps talks about co-operation rather than talks on co-operation were in the offing. There was a lukewarm response from government departments in Dublin to Lemass's request for possible topics for civil service level talks on co-operation. When departments were instructed to inform the Department of the Taoiseach of their existing cross-border links, most departments instead submitted a list of areas for future co-operation, the subtext being that existing co-operation was best left the way it was. Since such official level co-operation was already taking place smoothly, government departments were loath to endanger those links through the politically inspired plans of the Taoiseach. Tadhg Ó Cearbhaill, assistant secretary at the Department of the Taoiseach, wondered whether 'overtures for a meeting on a wide range of topics would produce resistance at political level in the North [and] the behaviour of officials would be negative'.[55] However, Lemass departed for the United States leaving his senior officials to draw up a short list of topics for further discussion. Lemass hoped that the process would develop to create a regular system of official level talks on cross-border co-operation.

Whilst in the United States two of Lemass's speeches brought his Northern Irish policy into conflict with his American policy. In a combative mood at the Washington Press Club on 16 October he told his audience that the British government had no long-term interest in maintaining partition and called for a clear statement of intent 'by British political leaders that there would be no British interest in maintaining partition when Irishmen want to get rid of it'.[56]

Lemass was overtly playing to his American audience and saying what they expected to hear from the leader of Nationalist Ireland. Lemass spoke of his wishes for Irish unity and of Ireland's 'right to sovereignty over all the national territory, and the right to have our national destiny decided by the democratic process of the majority decision'.[57] Though Lemass did not call overtly on Britain to end partition, as, for example, Minister for External Affairs from 1949 to 1951 Seán MacBride was prone to do on all conceivable occasions, when reports of the Washington speech together with reference to ending partition during a speech to the United Nations General Assembly filtered back to Northern Ireland O'Neill reacted harshly to Lemass's comments: 'where is the Tralee speech now?' he mockingly asked Lemass.[58] Still unsure of his position in the Unionist Party O'Neill again backed away from meeting Lemass. The Washington Press Club speech left North–South relations at their lowest ebb since Lemass had taken office in 1959. Lemass's policy of co-operation with Northern Ireland was in tatters. The timely conclusion of a cross-border extra-dition agreement for ordinary crime in December 1963 and a series of judicious interviews that portrayed Lemass as the pragmatic politician attempted to woo O'Neill and his wary Unionist government towards a warmer relationship with Dublin as 1963 ended. But O'Neill would not budge, telling a Unionist Party rally that the United States speeches had 'wiped out all those remarks which he [Lemass] made in Tralee last July'.[59] *The Irish Times* 'Letter from Belfast' commented that 'gone now, and probably for a long time to come, is the courteous tone that marked some earlier exchanges between the two Prime Ministers'.[60] Though by the summer of 1964, with the memory of Washington receding, the mood seemed to be changing and O'Neill, in an interview in the *Guardian* newspaper, said that co-operation was now 'quite possible',[61] a point Lemass and O'Neill both reiterated in separate interviews to the *Irish Times Review of Industry and Technology* in late August when they told journalists that 'they would wish closer economic co-operation with each other.[62]

Little did Lemass and O'Neill know it, but they had just missed their last chance of meeting in a relatively stable climate in Northern Ireland. Throughout 1964 pressure for reform in the province grew as discrimination in employ-ment, housing and education were publicly criticised by backbench Nationalists Party MPs in Northern Ireland and by Labour MPs at Westminster, the latter breaking the taboo that Northern Ireland affairs were not discussed at the London parliament. The October 1964 election, which brought Harold Wilson and Labour to power in the United Kingdom, had been particularly hard fought in Northern Ireland, with the hard-line Unionism of the Reverend Ian Paisley coming to widespread popular notice for the first time. In this climate Wilson began to put pressure on O'Neill to introduce reforms to end all forms of discrimination in Northern Ireland, which resulted in O'Neill realising that he had to adopt a more traditionalist approach and put cross-border co-operation further out of reach to appease hardliners in the Unionist Party.

Through these years O'Neill was also coming continually under pressure from Brian Faulkner who was still trying to outmanoeuvre him politically. Following the 1964 Westminster general election Faulkner had been the first Northern Irish minister to meet a member of the new Labour government in Britain and he had a high profile media position because of his work in bringing new industries and employment into Northern Ireland. Faulkner was openly being spoken of as O'Neill's successor, but he refused to enter the fray. As 1964 drew to a close press reports indicated that Faulkner was going to take the unheard of step of travelling to Dublin to meet Jack Lynch to discuss cross-border co-operation in trade and tourism. Of particular importance to Faulkner was closing the £21 million trade deficit that Northern Ireland had with the Republic of Ireland.

The Lemass-O'Neill meetings January–February 1965

O'Neill had been losing public support in Northern Ireland and political support in London since taking office in 1963 and he moved quickly to counter Faulkner's threatened visit to Dublin, and in order to show Wilson that he was implementing reforms in Northern Ireland.[63] He needed a publicity coup to restore his flagging image in Northern Ireland. Lemass was planning to visit Belfast in February 1965, but O'Neill had already stated that he would not meet him. An editorial in the *Belfast Telegraph* on 20 November had concluded that 'no danger to the Unionist cause would be involved' if O'Neill and Lemass met.

There was no prior indication in December 1964 or January 1965 that Lemass and O'Neill were about to meet, except perhaps under pressure from Wilson, himself under pressure from pro-Irish backbench Labour MPs. Fearing Faulkner would outmanoeuvre him, O'Neill sent his private secretary, Jim Malley, to Dublin to meet T. K. Whitaker, the Secretary of the Department of Finance, to convey an official invitation to Lemass to come to Belfast. Whitaker sent Malley to the National Gallery, a few hundred yards from Lemass's office in Government Buildings and then hurried to find Lemass. Whitaker briefed Lemass on Malley's visit and the invitation he carried with him. According to

Whitaker, Lemass had been expecting that a meeting with O'Neill would eventually come about, but he was unsure as to how the initiative and eventual date of the meeting would emerge.[64] Lemass immediately decided that he should accept the invitation and rang the Minister for External Affairs, Frank Aiken, to inform him officially of the invitation and to seek his advice. Aiken agreed with the Taoiseach that the invitation should be accepted. Malley was then brought to meet the Taoiseach and Lemass told him that he accepted O'Neill's invitation to meet him in Belfast on 13 or 14 January 1965.

The most suitable date for Lemass to travel north was finally selected as 14 January. Plans for the visit were kept secret to the last minute. Department of the Taoiseach files record only a few scribbled notes in Lemass's blue biro on setting up the meeting. Though Aiken knew of the meeting in advance, Lemass only informed his entire cabinet the night before the meeting; O'Neill, less certain, told only the Governor of Northern Ireland, his Minister of Finance, Ivan Neill, and the Chief Constable of the RUC. The Faulkner–Lynch story went strangely quiet, but in Belfast Faulkner continued to work on drafts of a memo to be circulated to the Stormont cabinet on cross-border tourism in advance of his projected meeting with Lynch.

Lemass arrived in Stormont at 1.00 p.m. on 14 January where O'Neill welcomed him. Any initial nerves disappeared over lunchtime conversation and following the meal Lemass and O'Neill sat at the fire in O'Neill's office and began to sketch out how North–South co-operation in non-political fields might be developed. There was no pre-arranged agenda, the meeting was merely exploratory, but the most important fact was that it had finally occurred. The promotion of tourism, trade liberalisation, improvements in information exchange in agriculture, health and education and the interconnection of electricity grids were all discussed in what Belfast officials called 'a preliminary "tour d'horizon"'.[65] Overtly political issues were not discussed. The meeting only covered 'areas of practical co-operation in matters of common interest'.[66]

Lemass and Whitaker had returned to Dublin by seven o'clock on the evening of 14 January. The lunch and meeting with O'Neill had lasted less than four hours. Described as 'one of the most sensational events in Irish politics since the establishment of the border', it marked a significant thaw in the 40-year-long Dublin–Belfast cold war.[67] Harold Wilson sent a personal telegram to O'Neill that the visit was 'well prepared and made just the right public impact'.[68] Nationalist Party leader Eddie McAteer, to whom Lemass later explained that because of circumstances he could not tell in advance of the meeting with O'Neill, welcomed the visit to Belfast as 'a significant step forward'.[69] Indeed the Lemass–O'Neill meeting was a significant factor in persuading the Nationalist Party to return to Stormont as the official opposition on 2 February. Bolstered by largely favourable press comment and a vote of confidence in favour of his policy towards the Republic, and the unanimous approval of the Grand Orange Lodge of Ireland, O'Neill travelled to Dublin on 9 February 1965 to continue the summit level discussions with Lemass. It was the first time a Northern Ireland Prime Minister had been in Dublin since Sir James Craig met Michael Collins in 1922.

In the period between the 14 January meeting and O'Neill's return trip a structure for cross-border co-operation had been prepared in Dublin and Belfast. A 17-point plan for cross-border co-operation was sent to O'Neill on 3 February. As well as covering existing areas of co-operation – transport, electricity and agriculture – the plan encompassed new areas which had arisen over the past few years – trade, justice and civil defence – and added to them new areas such as economic co-operation, planning and construction, health, education and consultation on administrative issues.

The second North–South Prime Ministerial meeting took place at Iveagh House and involved a 'general review of the scope for mutually beneficial co-operation in matters of common interest'.[70] The attendance of Frank Aiken at the meeting led to speculation that overtly political issues had been raised, but his participation was instead due to his role as Lemass's confidant in developing cross-border relations. There was general agreement on the Northern side in the 17-point list sent to O'Neill, the only exception being that trade negotiations were an area reserved for Westminster. In addition co-operation between Northern and Southern Public Record Offices, fisheries co-operation and co-operation in the detection of ordinary crime were suggested by O'Neill and accepted by Lemass. Jack Lynch reported progress in his discussions with Brian Faulkner on cross-border tariff reduction, but, in continuance with his insistence that such an item was a reserved matter for Westminster, O'Neill 'was neither negative nor affirmative on this question'.[71] The meeting mapped out the road ahead for future talks and planned future co-operation at ministerial level. It also cemented the relationship between Lemass and O'Neill. The lunch parties and informal summits were all very well, but now the publicity was over and it was time to do business. As Lemass joked to the press after the meeting: 'from this on the work is given to those who have the capacity to do it'.[72]

The cross-border co-operation process expands: 1965–6

Lemass and O'Neill, having set the process into operation, bowed out of the day-to-day operation of cross-border co-operation. It was down to individual ministers and their senior officials to take up the areas the two prime ministers had agreed on and to see if joint agreements could be arrived at.[73] The most important areas of co-operation were tourism co-operation, electricity inter-connection and North–South trade and joint trade promotion, but projected discussions also included civil defence co-operation, joint social welfare provisions, cross-border transport and agricultural issues. A joint committee of experts was formed to examine electricity interconnection and the Northern Irish Tourist Board and the Irish Bord Fáilte met to plan a joint promotional campaign for the American market. After the whirlwind events of the spring of 1965, the co-operation process settled down in the last half of the year as North–South ministerial meetings and meetings between civil servants in Dublin and Belfast became more normal. These meetings received considerable media attention and it seemed as if the North–South cold war of more than forty years was over. Lemass told the Dáil on 23 November that cross-border discussions had 'become such a well established practice that they would be regarded as usual and routine'.[74]

Though not an immediate concern of this chapter, it has been seen how Anglo-Irish trade and economic relations were an important influence on North–South trade relations. An Anglo-Irish Free Trade Agreement was signed in December 1965. Providing for the complete removal of tariffs and free Anglo-Irish trade by 1970, the agreement included a clause that gave an official seal of approval to the unilateral tariff reductions on Northern Irish exports to the Republic begun in the early 1960s. It allowed Ireland to give significant tariff reductions to Northern Irish exports to the South in excess of those given to British exports to Ireland. Because this clause was officially negotiated in an Anglo-Irish agreement it allowed Faulkner to use it to become officially involved in the North–South trade liberalisation process on behalf of the Northern Irish government.

It seemed that by 1966 a significant change in the relationship between Dublin and Belfast was under way. Teams of ministers and civil servants were working to conclude agreements that would allow both states in Ireland to work together for the good of the entire population of the island. However, the year was to be a dangerous one as it saw the 50th anniversary of two politically charged events: the Easter 1916 Rising for nationalists and the Battle of the

Somme in July 1916 for unionists. These two events and an upsurge in sectarian killing in Northern Ireland in the summer of 1966 gravely destabilised the ongoing co-operation process. T. K. Whitaker, who, as a relatively anonymous civil servant, undertook secret trips to Belfast to meet his Northern Irish counterparts and their ministers, considered it too dangerous to travel across the border that summer.

Trade concessions, electricity interconnection and joint tourism promotion continued to set the pace for cross-border relations into the autumn of 1966.[75] Discussions were also ongoing on joint civil defence fallout and radiation monitoring, co-operation in social welfare provisions, in areas of health, education and transport and to smooth tensions between Southern and Northern fishing fleets over herring catches off the south-east coast of Ireland.[76] When on 4 November Whitaker travelled to Belfast to meet Northern Ireland cabinet secretary, Sir Cecil Bateman, Lemass asked Whitaker to convey to O'Neill via Bateman an 'assurance of our continuing interest in promoting co-operation on the themes on which it has been proceeding'.[77] A quiet but healthy level of co-operation was taking place and was expected to continue into the future.

Lemass's legacy for cross-border relations

Seán Lemass retired as Taoiseach on 10 November 1966 and was replaced by his Minister for Finance, Jack Lynch. Lemass seemed to leave a strong immediate legacy in cross-border contact and in providing Dublin with a realistic and coherent Northern Ireland policy based elsewhere than in the rhetoric of anti-partitionism. Yet Lynch ultimately found it hard to capitalise on Lemass's achievements. Partly this was due to the climate in Northern Ireland as O'Neill underwent another period of political instability, seeing out another backbench plot that again implicated Faulkner as a rival. Though destabilised, the co-operation process continued; it simply shifted down a gear as ministerial meetings were set aside and replaced by civil service level contacts. But Lemass's replacement by Lynch also ushered in a fundamental change in Dublin's Northern Ireland policy that was to become more obvious over the next three years. Lynch's Northern policy was much more nationalistic than Lemass's pragmatic approach. In part this was due to Lynch's own background, but the more nationalistic members of his cabinet such as Neil Blaney also pushed him into adopting this policy.

From his first day in office Lynch was asked when he would meet O'Neill, but given the events of the summer of 1966 such a meeting was far off. Lynch countered such questions with the stock answer that whilst ministers were developing co-operation plans there was no need for a summit meeting. So 1967 progressed quietly as Lynch settled in as Taoiseach and O'Neill seemed to have seen off the storms of 1966. In October 1967 Brian Faulkner and the Irish Minister for Transport and Power, Erskine Childers, signed an agreement for a North–South electricity interconnector to provide standby power in cases of emergency for the Northern and Southern grids. It was the most important cross-border agreement to be signed since the Lemass–O'Neill meetings in 1965 and was a visible sign of North–South co-operation. Faulkner commented after the signature that 'the significance of today's signing is that it represents a firm decision to translate theory into practice'. He reiterated that 'we in the Northern Ireland Government are very anxious to co-operate economically in every possible way with the South' and concluded that the electricity link-up was 'co-operation at its best'.[78]

Tragically for Northern Ireland, violence and the political instability of the Troubles would undermine the province's development for the next quarter of a century. Though the Republic of Ireland remained peaceful through the Troubles, it did not escape the influence of events over the border. Lemass's Northern Ireland policy was interpreted in light of the subsequent events in the island of Ireland. The Lemass–O'Neill meetings were seen as symbolic of their time, an important short-lived episode in the modernisation of Ireland in the 1960s. They were also held up as a sign of what might have been had Northern Ireland not descended into violence.

Lemass's role in improving North–South relations suitably fits that of the man stylised as the 'Managing Director of Ireland Inc.'. What this chapter has illustrated is that he came up with the overall ideas for better relations with Northern Ireland, continually developed and publicised them, seeing them through to fruition in his two meetings with O'Neill. In this sense it is also interesting to look where Lemass was not involved by focusing on the way in which he delegated responsibility for policy development to ministers and civil servants. Whitaker's role was, of course, central, particularly as a personal conduit to O'Neill, through Jim Malley and later Sir Cecil Bateman, to Lemass and it has often been highlighted. But this chapter has also shown how Lemass relied on his cabinet colleagues at strategic moments in the development of his relations with Northern Ireland from 1959 to 1966 in particular Jack Lynch to get the initial trade liberalisation programme through cabinet and Frank Aiken as a confidant in his first meeting with O'Neill.

As befitted a successful chief executive, Lemass led from the front in the change in attitudes towards Northern Ireland in the Republic. But he also delegated the responsibility for developing the agenda he had drawn up between 1959 and 1965 for improved cross-border relations to the members of his cabinet. Drawing on their strengths and abilities he watched carefully as the multi-faceted cross-border co-operation process developed. The outbreak of the Troubles and the internal crisis in Fianna Fáil over dealing with Northern Ireland after August 1969 leading to the Arms Trial of 1970 and chaotic scenes at the Fianna Fáil Ard Fheis of January 1971 may have suggested to Lemass before his death in May 1971 that in trying to adopt a pragmatic approach to the North he had achieved little other than to divide Fianna Fáil over Northern Ireland. However, the seeds sown by Lemass between 1956 and 1966, the themes and topics he and O'Neill and their respective cabinets discussed in the expectant years before Northern Ireland was engulfed in thirty years of Troubles were those that Dublin, Belfast and London would return to again and again and which were finally codified in the British-Irish Agreement Act of 1999 which along with establishing the North–South Ministerial Council and the British Irish Council established six cross-border implementation bodies covering waterways, food safety, trade, languages, contacts with the European Union and the Foyle, Carlingford and Irish Lights Commission. Despite the suspension of the Northern Ireland Executive, the implementation bodies continue in operation, a fitting legacy to the form of cross-border co-operation that Lemass did so much to initiate.

CHAPTER EIGHT

Church, state and the moral community

BRIAN GIRVIN

—

Seán Lemass remains an ambiguous figure in twentieth-century Ireland. So closely identified was he with the changes that occurred after he became Taoiseach in 1959, that he is widely applauded as the father figure of Irish modernity. He can also indirectly be considered the architect of the changes that led to the economic success that Ireland has experienced since the early 1990s. Yet, he was also a 1916 veteran, a key figure in Fianna Fáil from its foundation and for 25 years he promoted a narrow economic nationalist policy framework that condemned the country to stagnation and emigration.[1] At the very least Lemass was a complex figure and much of his private thoughts and views remain hidden. Nowhere is this better exemplified than in his attitude to Church and state and to the moral community that dominated much of nationalist Ireland during the twentieth century. In many respects Lemass was a representative figure of the political generation that took power after the Sinn Féin victory at the 1918 election. Yet, unlike most of those he associated with, he seems to have been sceptical concerning religion. His biographer records some disquiet among his fellow internees during the Civil War when he refused to attend mass, reporting also impious remarks on his part. Despite this evidence, and Horgan provides some additional examples of Lemass's scepticism at later stages in his career, the public image was entirely in conformity with the dominant ethos and values of Catholic-nationalist Ireland. In a speech in 1961, Lemass endorsed the common Irish view of the time, identifying Catholicism with Irish identity. Indeed in this respect there is little difference between Lemass's published statements and those of his predecessor de Valera. The difference may be that de Valera believed them, and it is possible that Lemass did not. It is telling that an independent and intelligent figure at the heart of the Irish political process could disguise his views in this way.[2]

How are we to account for this? In other matters, Lemass was quick to engage in debate on issues that concerned him. However, there is no evidence that he objected to those articles in the 1937 Constitution which reflected the teaching of the Catholic Church or provided them with a special place in the life of the country. Nor was this because there was no opposition to the draft Constitution. His colleague Gerald Boland threatened to leave the country if the Constitution was enacted in its original form, complaining that it reflected too closely the teachings of one church.[3] Nor was Lemass above using the Church for political advantage. When Fianna Fáil was accused of communism during the 1932 election, Lemass retorted that 'A Fianna Fáil government will endeavour to manage the affairs of the nation in the spirit of Cardinal McRory'. While this may have been a defensive reaction to a political challenge, the actions and behaviour of successive Fianna Fáil governments suggest a partiality to the demands of the Catholic Church reflecting more deeply rooted concerns and attitudes. Paradoxically, at the end of his career, Lemass wanted to suggest that the overall relationship between Church and state in Ireland was cordial. When asked if the influence of the Catholic Church was exaggerated he replied:

Oh, yes, As Taoiseach I never had the slightest problem in this regard, nor do I recollect any occasion when the Church tried to pressurise me in an area affecting government policy. Once or twice members of the hierarchy came to me to express anxiety about certain minor developments that were taking place, mainly in the context of the appointments of individuals in whom they had not much confidence, but never to the extent of pressing for change.

Lemass wanted to assure his interviewer that the representations of the Church had been proper in every respect, insisting that:

I felt they were expressing their concern as citizens with certain things that were happening but they never made any attempt to impose their views on me. Once or twice I was in doubt as to what the reaction of the Church might be to some proposals and I went along to discuss them with members of the hierarchy; but this was merely to clarify my own mind.[4]

This was a fairly representative view at the time and one shared by the hierarchy when its members commented on the issue of Church–state relations. It suggests that the Catholic Church is just another interest group, one with special interests that would be listened to in the same fashion as the Irish Congress of Trade Unions or the National Farmers Association. It contrasts sharply with the view expressed in *The Irish Times* immediately after the resignation of Noel Browne as Minister for Health in 1951, when it concluded that 'The most serious revelation, however, is that the Roman Catholic Church would seem to be the effective Government of the country'. Likewise author Seán O'Faoláin's cutting comment that 'The Dáil proposes; Maynooth disposes' was one that was shared by many in Ireland then and later. The American author, Paul Blanshard, concluded that 'The Irish Republic is a clerical state', though he distinguished it from other Catholic states such as Franco's Spain or Salazar's Portugal. Blanshard acknowledged that:

> Its political democracy is genuine, and it grants complete freedom to opposi-
> tion political parties and opposition religious groups. In Ireland the Catholic
> church has no official share in government, which is officially democratic.

Despite this, he charged that there was an unofficial Church–state alliance, providing considerable evidence to sustain this position. He warned that political democracy in itself could not protect Ireland from a 'clerical dictatorship' when the hierarchy is so influential and effectively controls 'the organs of public opinion'. Though his argument has been dismissed as anti-Catholic by Irish critics, the evidence he produces is formidable and all the more remarkable when it is recognised that he was writing without the aid of government documents or private papers. The study of Archbishop Charles McQuaid, the Archbishop of Dublin, by John Cooney has done much to revive and extend the case made by Blanshard. One should not uncritically endorse Blanshard, as he underestimated the strength of the Irish democratic tradition. It is important to note that there is no established church in Ireland, nor does the state collect a church tax as is the case in many countries. Despite this, the relationship between church and state has been so intimate that the situation in Ireland cannot be compared to those countries, such as the United States, where church and state are formally separated.[5] Even so, some caution is required when attempting to place Ireland within existing models of church–state relationships. Conor Cruise O'Brien warned that Blanshard's case 'may be accurate enough in detail, but leaves a false impression, excessive in darkness'. O'Brien adds however that critics of Blanshard provided a view of contemporary Ireland that was 'too bright, too sweet, too light and airy'.[6]

Whatever else might be said, the Catholic Church in Ireland during much of the twentieth century was never merely an interest group. It was far more influential than that implies, though this does not mean that Ireland was a clerical state as claimed by Blanshard. As O'Brien cautions, it is necessary to appreciate the positive and negative features of the relationship of such a powerful organisation in a democratic state. But to do so, it is important to recognise the way in which power was exercised by the Church and how the state responded to this. The relationship between church and state was a complex one that requires careful evaluation. In some respects Lemass's 1969 comments reflect a significant aspect of the relationship between the two institutions. Issues concerning church and state are frequently discussed in terms of actual or potential conflict, assuming that the relationship must always be conflictual. This is not necessarily the case; indeed what is now becoming evident from the archives is that there is a high degree of consensus among these actors, considerable collusion between them and occasional conflict. Most of the conflicts were managed within the collusive/co-operative sphere, but occasionally came into the open as with the Mother and Child crisis in 1951.[7] Even then the Taoiseach John A. Costello complained that the issue should never have become public knowledge:

> All these matters should have been, and ought to have been, dealt with calmly, in quiet and in council, without the public becoming aware of the matter. The public never ought to have become aware of the matter.

At times too there are demarcation disputes over who is dominant in a specific sphere, as demonstrated in the continuing unease over the vocational education sector.[8]

At the end of the Second World War, Éire entered an isolationist phase from which it did not emerge until the 1960s at the earliest.[9] This isolationism reinforced an insularity that had been actively promoted by the Fianna Fáil government during the war itself, but was shared by many sections of Irish nationalist society by this time. This insularity closed Ireland off from developments in the outside world and affected virtually every aspect of the society, including culture, economic policy and diplomacy. Ireland became a backwater in Europe, ignoring the dramatic events occurring there while displaying a public image that was at once fearful and self-satisfied of that new world. By this time also the institutional basis for this isolationism was well established.[10] Fianna Fáil had been in government for 13 years, having won six consecutive elections. The 1937 constitution, legislation and the legal system provided a substantial basis for protecting Ireland against the outside world. Furthermore, what is sometimes described as civil society actively supported this process. The Catholic Church, the trade unions, opposition political parties and various non-political groupings shared a consensual view of Ireland's place in that world. The most explicit expression of this came when de Valera replied to Churchill's remarks on Irish neutrality in May 1945. There was no dissent from de Valera's position, while reports of its enthusiastic reception around the country reflected the collective certainty of the integrity of Ireland's cause than any more thoughtful response. *Dublin Opinion* summed up the Irish position by publishing a cartoon of Churchill listening to the reply in despondent fashion with the caption 'listen and learn' underneath it. This universal acclaim from within nationalist Ireland demonstrated not the righteousness of the cause, but the extent to which de Valera and Fianna Fáil now commanded the political high ground. Fianna Fáil had established a new consensus in nationalist Ireland, one that was dominant by 1945.[11]

The specific relationship between Church and state is a product of Fianna Fáil's dominance, extending dramatically the more limited framework established during the first decade of the Irish Free State.[12] This was a deliberate decision by de Valera to reformulate the relationship between Irish society and Catholic nationalism. Its most public expression was the 1937 Constitution, largely drafted by de Valera. The Constitution provided an institutional framework for what de Valera considered the core values of Irish political culture. However, by emphasising the Catholic and nationalist nature of Ireland, de Valera effectively ignored other major traditions in the society (Catholic, Protestant and liberal). The new constitution broke decisively with liberal constitutionalism and established a denominational framework for Irish political life. The 1922 Constitution, for example, did not mention the family, whereas de Valera's Constitution clearly incorporated the teaching of the Catholic Church on this and other sensitive matters. This was a partial view of the complex nature of Irish life in the 1930s. In contrast to the 1922 Constitution, the 1937 Constitution was illiberal, nationalistic and denominational. It reflected the certainties of Fianna Fáil, but represented them as embodying the values of an entire community. The Constitution asserted moral certainty, as well as a fixed notion of what it meant to be Irish and a rejection of alternative traditions within Ireland. It also reserved a special place for the Roman Catholic Church in the Constitution, one that privileged it over all others. This was clearly de Valera's intention, but its consequence was also to explicitly recognise the denominational nature of Irish society.[13]

By 1945 Ireland was extremely homogeneous in terms of ethnicity, religion and race. At the 1946 census, nearly 95 per cent of the population was Roman Catholic, while other religions were in decline. This homogeneity and the political success of Fianna Fáil provided the basis for the dominance of one version of an Irish moral community. Most, if not all, societies have moral communities that defend core values and articulate a distinctive culture. Moral communities can be inclusive and empowering, though more frequently they are exclusive and coercive. What they all share is a desire to protect some notion of core values or norms that most acquiesce in, though whether there is consensus on this is a more difficult question to answer. Moral communities can stretch from an open society that will be liberal and pluralistic to ones that are closed, theocratic and coercive. All social order has elements of coercion, but it is the degree of coercion that matters. Closed moral communities such as the Soviet Union or contemporary Iran are heavily dependent on coercion to maintain control, but in more open moral communities conformity and loyalty is achieved by less direct measures. One person's moral community of course can be another person's coercion. When James Deeny took up his post as Chief Medical Officer in Dublin in 1944, he could not disguise his delight at leaving Northern Ireland. As a Catholic and nationalist living in Lurgan he felt oppressed among the Unionist majority, noting that:

> Coming to Dublin was wonderful. For the first time I discovered my country. I suddenly felt a free citizen of a free country and began the process of getting the repression and bitterness of the North out of my system.[14]

Deeny left a moral community that he did not identify with and became a member of one that was more congenial to him. Thus a moral community can alienate individuals who do not share their core values, in much the same way as they can attract those who do. What occurred in Ireland under Fianna Fáil was that the content of the moral community became more limited, more authoritarian and less tolerant of those who did not share the values expressed by Fianna Fáil in its constitution. The 1937 Constitution established an institutional and normative framework for public life in post-war Ireland. It was a popular one, though initially designed along party political lines. Its intention was to consolidate the republican vision of de Valera and to promote change and development that would realise that vision (especially Irish unity and the restoration of the Irish language). The preamble to the Constitution, Articles two and three, the special position of the Roman Catholic Church as well as its social principles reflect this vision. This can be described as a Catholic constitution for a Catholic state, one with little public space for Protestants, unionists or liberals.

What the constitution also did was provide a means to extend Catholic influence and power within the state. This influence was already powerful, both directly and indirectly. The Constitution explicitly recognised this, but it was also a reality in education, medicine and social policy. This is not to say that the situation was untroubled, but as the French diplomat Jean Blanchard has written, 'There are no religious questions *per se*, public life being religious, since the nation is devoutly Christian'. He also noted that 'Irishmen continue to make no clear distinction between the religious law and the civil laws', though insisting that 'there are no official relations between the church and the State because there cannot be any, the two systems, religious and civil, being so closely intermingled in the mind of the Irish people'.[15] What Blanchard suggests is that there is a benign relationship between church and state because of the Catholic nature of the society and this gives Ireland its special feature within this relationship. However, not all of this was benign. Fianna Fáil's political success and the general acceptance of the new constitution provided a context for a popular Catholicism that was often intolerant and oppressive. Joseph Walshe, the powerful and conservative secretary of the Department of External Affairs, wrote to Archbishop McQuaid, in July 1945 pointing out 'From all sides I hear that the P's [Protestants] are very much on the run except in the higher spheres like the Bank of Ireland. So the time is right for action.' The Minister for Education Tom Derrig commended a history book to his colleagues on the grounds that it was written by Catholics, adding that 'Other histories have, of course, been written, but as they are the work of Protestants, they were not likely to be sought after.' The Department of External Affairs could reject requests for a more generous policy in respect of Jewish refugees on the grounds that:

> As Jews do not become assimilated with the native population, like other immigrants, there is a danger that any big increase in their number might create a social problem.

Nor were these unrepresentative positions adopted by individuals outside the mainstream of Irish society.[16] In the High Court Justice Gavan Duffy accepted that anti-Semitism could be used as a defence in a case where one party refused to transfer a lease to a business on the grounds that the purchaser was a Jew:

> Anti-Semitism, . . . is notoriously shared by a number of other citizens; and, if prejudice be the right word, the antagonism between Christian and Jew has its

roots in nearly 2,000 years of history and is too prevalent as a habit of mind to be dismissed off-hand, in a country where religion matters, as the eccentric extravagance of a bigot.[17]

In his ruling Gavan Duffy distinguished between the two plaintiffs, describing one as 'Irish and a Catholic' and the other as 'a Jew', despite the fact that the latter was an Irish citizen. In a number of other judgements, Gavan Duffy was anxious to reverse English precedent to establish the Catholic nationalist foundations of Irish law. In a case where a priest had been fined for not disclosing in court information that he claimed had been obtained as a result of his religious position, Gavan Duffy overturned the lower court fine, arguing that the 1937 Constitution established a new foundation for law making in Ireland. He went on to argue that:

> In a state where nine out of every ten citizens today are Catholics and on a matter closely touching the religious outlook of the people, it would be intolerable that the common law, as expounded after the reformation in a Protestant land, should be taken to bind a nation which persistently repudiated the Reformation as heresy.[18]

In the Tilson case,[19] Gavan Duffy upheld the pre-nuptial agreements between Catholics and non-Catholics in respect of educating the children of the union. Although the Supreme Court upheld his decision it did so in a narrower fashion than Gavan Duffy had maintained, but nevertheless placed what had been an informal arrangement on a legal footing that again privileged the Catholic majority in the state.[20]

The Tilson case demonstrates the shift in Irish life that resulted from Fianna Fáil's political dominance and the influence of the 1937 Constitution. Although the Supreme Court decision did not rest on the constitutional position of the Roman Catholic Church, nevertheless it did reinforce the Catholic nature of the society. It is telling that the only Supreme Court judge to question the ruling was himself a Protestant. What the decision did was provide a private body with legal authority to insist in perpetuity that the parties to an agreement be bound by that initial agreement. As only one side was insisting on compliance, the decision effectively bound members of minority religions to the wishes of the Catholic Church. The consequences of this were twofold. It increased the segregation of denominations within Ireland and made it a less pluralistic place, but also entailed that if a Protestant married a Catholic the

Protestant line would die out. The Hunt case in 1943 raised somewhat different issues for Church and state and indeed brought them into conflict. Hunt had married in a register office in London, the marriage broke down and he entered into a relationship with a Catholic woman, later himself becoming a Catholic. The Catholic Church did not recognise the first marriage and Hunt was urged by a Catholic priest to marry in a Catholic ceremony. As his original wife was still alive, this was bigamy under Irish law. While the government was not prepared to act in these circumstances, it could not prevent a private complaint from being made. This is what occurred in the Hunt case and he was found guilty of bigamy. On this occasion, the Catholic Church's position on marriage was not upheld by the state. The decision was condemned by William Conway in the *Irish Ecclesiastical Review*, who asserted that it was for the Church to 'determine the circumstances in which a marriage shall be valid and binding'. Catholic teaching accordingly rejected the right of the state to make this determination. The state itself was alert to this problem and embarrassed by the potential for conflict, but the Attorney General's office was not prepared to intervene to change the circumstances. While the Church complained about the differences between the state's position and its own view of marriage, this did not become a source of conflict. One of the reasons why it did not become a source of conflict was that the state was not prepared to prosecute the priest who advised Hunt to remarry and who carried out the ceremony knowing that he had been married previously. This was in line with the Attorney General's position on bigamy, as to take an active position would have exposed the government to clerical criticism.[21]

By the early 1950s the Catholic nature of Irish society had become more narrow and intolerant. Catholic sensibilities were easily roused as author Hubert Butler discovered when he challenged the official Catholic version of what had happened in Yugoslavia during and immediately after the war. Butler was effectively ostracised by his friends and neighbours in Kilkenny as a consequence of newspaper reports that he had 'insulted' the Papal Nuncio, when in fact the Nuncio had swept out of a public meeting because he did not like what Butler was saying. A further demonstration of this intolerance to minorities was shown in the West of Ireland when local Catholic farmers objected to the election of a remarried divorcee as joint master of the Galway Blazers hunt. That the woman was a Protestant was ignored; her divorced status caused local Catholic farmers to deny the hunt access to their land. The local bishops, who in a lengthy statement effectively challenged the right of Protestants to divorce and remarry, even if this were done outside the state, endorsed this popular prejudice. In effect, the bishops were saying that if an individual lived in Ireland then he or she would have to accept the moral position of the majority or suffer the consequences:

> A person who publicly acts counter to Catholic principles in this matter cannot expect to be received by a Catholic people with the same favour, and to be given the same honour and privileges as those who respect Catholic moral standards.[22]

The woman involved insisted that her actions were in conformity with her own church, but subsequently resigned as master. A sympathetic observer noted at the beginning of the 1950s that, even in urban Ireland, religious beliefs and behaviour remained conservative and traditional. Likewise, a little later in the decade the German author, Heinrich Böll described affectionately a society that was both conservative and theocratic in many respects.[23] The pervasive nature of Catholic power also had a political impact. In public it was rare for the government or opposition to challenge the Church or to question the type of behaviour meted out to Butler or to the Galway hunt. One of the leading Protestant politicians in Fianna Fáil, Erskine Childers, who was later to be President of Ireland, wrote to Seán MacEntee in 1945 complaining that his co-religionists were being discriminated against in public appointments. He also cited the Hunt case as an example of anti-Protestant bias. A little later, he again wrote to MacEntee suggesting that the climate of opinion was such that a Protestant could not become a cabinet minister in an Irish government. This may have been self-serving as Childers was at this stage parliamentary secretary to the Minister for Local Government and was perhaps concerned that his pro-motional prospects were limited by his religion. This concern was not realised, as Childers was later to play a prominent role in government, but that he expressed it does suggest nervousness on his part that was widespread among members of minority religions at the time.[24] Despite this, when Unionists criticised the position of Protestants in the south, Childers quickly defended his own party and his government. He rejected the charge that Protestants did not prosper or that they were not happy in an independent Ireland. Although he made this public statement at the same time that he was corresponding with MacEntee he retorted that such criticisms were, 'entirely baseless', continuing that:

> The Protestants of the 26 counties lived in an atmosphere of complete tolerance, their share in industrial and commercial activity far exceeding the proportion

of their numbers, and in connection with all government and local appointments where examinations were held, there was no religious test whatever.[25]

There is a clear contradiction between the public statement made by Childers with his private concerns that Protestants might be discriminated against. Whether this was due to fear on his part or for career purposes it is difficult to judge, but it was the public statement that was used subsequently to demonstrate that Protestants were not discriminated against.

The decade after 1945 was one when an intolerant strain of Catholicism dominated Irish life, as did a similarly intolerant and irredentist form of nationalism. The resultant Catholic nationalism reinforced the boundaries between North and South, but also deepened the divisions between Catholic and Protestant in the South. An informal religious apartheid became widespread with the denominations living very separate lives and inhabiting separate institutions. Archbishop McQuaid's campaign against Trinity College, Dublin was the most public expression of this, but the Tilson case and the decision to broadcast the Angelus on Radio Éireann in 1950 all reflect this denominational nature of Irish life after the end of the war. The political expression of this is more complex than the social consequence. The hierarchy's involvement in policy making and its influence was considerable. Many were shocked when Noël Browne published his correspondence with the hierarchy over the Mother and Child legislation, but what this showed was that the bishops were involved in the detail of legislation that concerned them. De Valera acknowledged this, when his government introduced legislation to deal with the issue after returning to office in 1951. The task of dealing with the hierarchy was given to Lemass, recognition that this was not simply another piece of legislation:

> I would suggest that each particular proposal of ours to which objection was made be taken up with the Archbishop, and that he be asked to make a draft with the qualifications which would satisfy him. This draft could then be examined from our point of view, and amended if necessary, until an agreed text was arrived at. That was more or less what happened in regard to the corresponding articles of the Constitution.[26]

Likewise, when Fianna Fáil decided to introduce legislation to regulate adoption in Ireland in 1952, McQuaid was intimately involved in framing the legislation. In 1944 the Department of Justice had dropped a proposal to introduce adoption when it was revealed that McQuaid was opposed. Even though circumstances had changed by the early 1950s, the government included a specific section in the Act after a recommendation from the hierarchy, while McQuaid was party to the drafting and redrafting of the legislation. Even more significant, there had been no adoption legislation in independent Ireland, largely because the Catholic Church vetoed any such proposal.

Events outside the control of the Church and the government changed this and made it more difficult not to legislate. As Mike Milotte has shown in his important research, Church and state had colluded after 1945 when American Catholics came to Ireland to adopt children born outside wedlock. It was only when this traffic was publicised in the United States that the Irish government was forced to act in order to regulate the circumstances under which such adoptions could take place. Furthermore, as Milotte persuasively argues, the Irish state effectively abdicated its responsibilities for the welfare of these children and ignored the rights of their mothers. The main concern of the legislation was to protect the spiritual welfare of the adopted children and to prevent any children being adopted by parents whose religion was not that of the mother. This reflected a deeper anxiety that 'many children are lost to the faith' if their mothers travelled to Britain to have their babies.[27] Two conclusions might be drawn from this. The first is that the Church was clearly not involved as an interest group in certain areas of legislation. Not only did it have a veto in some areas, but in others it actually established the policy environment and dictated in large part the detail of the legislation. This was explicitly recognised by the Attorney General in February 1951 when he stated publicly:

> This country is predominantly a Catholic country. This does not mean that Parliament should penalise any other creed, but it does mean this, that Parliament cannot surely be asked to introduce legislation contrary to the teaching of that great Church.[28]

It also questions Whyte's view that the hierarchy's position in the case of adoption was 'intelligible and not unreasonable'. Given the evidence now available this is a view that can only be sustained if the Church's view was the only one available, but other additional cases demonstrate that the role of the Church was one of close attention and intervention where necessary.[29]

In 1945 the government decided under pressure to amend the Censorship Act that controlled printed matter. There had been considerable criticism of the original act and some controversy in the Seanad when the banning of 'The Tailor and Ansty' was debated. However, the new legislation was based on a draft written for the Minister by William Magennis, the Chairman of the Censorship Board, confidant of McQuaid and like the Archbishop a member of the secretive Knights of Columbanus. The Minister welcomed the opportunity to depoliticise this area of controversy. In the past issues of censorship were discussed in the Dáil or Seanad and became public property. Magennis suggested that an appeal board be established which removed the issue from the government. All future questions of censorship would then to sent to the Appeal Board and reviewed there. The Censorship Board itself came to be dominated by the knights by the early 1950s. Moreover, the Minister for Justice who appointed these Knights to such a sensitive position was himself a knight, as were other ministers in both the Fianna Fáil and Inter-Party governments during this time. With the knights in control of censorship and concern being expressed by McQuaid and other bishops at the increase in objectionable literature the new censorship body accelerated its tasks. In 1954 over 1000 books were banned. Between 1950 and 1954 the Censorship Board banned twice as many books as were censored under the Board between 1930 and 1945.[30] The Knights were less successful when they gained control of the Meath Hospital in Dublin in 1949. The hospital was essentially non-denominational but the Knights organised a takeover intending to give it a Catholic character. The new dispensation now began to dismiss Protestant doctors from the hospital, but there was a swift reaction to this and legislation was enacted to secure the original control and independence of the hospital. It is likely that it was the publicity rather than the act itself that forced the political parties to respond, but it is significant that on this occasion Archbishop McQuaid, though himself a knight, opposed the action. This can be explained by the need to maintain a denominational structure in Ireland, though one that recognised non-Catholics (Protestants and Jews) within the Constitution, thus giving them a status that more extreme Catholics rejected.

What this also suggests is that there were limits to the influence that the Church could exercise, but also that the state had quite limited defences if the interests of the Church and that of the state did not coincide. On some issues the Church was concerned, but did not believe that matters of faith and morals were involved. On such occasions the hierarchy would make these concerns known, but it remained for the government to act. Emigration, for example, was seen as a great evil, but not one that the state could act decisively upon. Though some politicians and clerics called for a ban on emigration by young people, one priest writing in the influential *Irish Ecclesiastical Record* concluded that a ban would be 'morally inadmissible' as such an action would conflict with parental rights.[31] This is not to say that members of the hierarchy would have opposed vigorous action on the part of the government, but that they were not going to use their influence to achieve this end. Others issues were more complex. In 1959 the Bishops opposed Sunday opening of public houses in a fairly strong statement, but when the government decided to proceed with the legislation it largely ignored these objections. In this case the bishops had voiced clear opposition to the proposed legislation, but did not organise a campaign against the bill in private or in public. This is the difference between this case and others such as the Mother and Child Bill or the Adoption Bill. In these cases the hierarchy considered that its interests and those of faith and morals were directly involved, whereas in the cases of emigration or opening hours these considerations were less pertinent. Likewise when the Yugoslav soccer team arrived in Dublin to play Ireland in 1955, Archbishop McQuaid used his considerable influence on the Taoiseach in an attempt to undermine the match. The Government advised the President not to attend the match, though he had initially agreed to do so. A significant campaign was organised against the visit, though over 20,000 people including Fianna Fáil front bench member Oscar Traynor, who was a former soccer player himself, did attend. The issue here was persecution of the Catholic Church in Yugoslavia, though the outcome was mixed. McQuaid was able to intimidate the government, but a section of the population was not prepared to be as easily intimidated by him.

The key to understanding this relationship rests on an appreciation that the hierarchy believed that its areas of interest (especially those involving education and health/medicine) should be immune from secular interference. This was complicated further by an assertion that members of clergy should not be answerable to secular authority. The Church wished to protect its privileged position in all these respects. Thus when a group of Jehovah's Witnesses were attacked by a mob in the West of Ireland, the local parish priest was implicated in the assault. At a subsequent court case the charges against the assailants were dismissed, but the Jehovah's Witnesses were found guilty of blasphemy and bound to the peace. The local Bishop complained that the government had no right to bring a priest before the court 'for upholding and defending the fundamental truths of our treasured Catholic faith. . . . Are we to have legal protection in future against such vile and pernicious attacks on our faith . . . your Attorney General prosecutes one of my priests for doing what I and all good Catholics here, regard as his bounden duty and right.'[32] Nor was this an isolated case. In an earlier altercation the Bishop of Cork rejected the Department of Health and Local Government's right to remove a member of a religious order from her post as Matron of a maternity home and orphanage despite clear evidence of negligence on her part. James Deeny, the Chief Medical Officer, discovered during a personal visit to the home that large numbers of babies had died shortly after birth to unmarried mothers. The state had provided substantial funds for a new maternity unit, yet the mortality rate was so high that in one year alone over 100 newborn babes out of 180 died. Deeny closed down the unit on his own authority and dismissed the Matron and the Medical Officer in charge. At this point Bishop Cohalan took the view that Deeny had no authority in the matter, insisting that 'the removal or continuation of a religious superior in this office was not a matter for the civil authorities'. Deeny countered this on the grounds that the Department was concerned with the secular sphere and had no wish to interfere with the religious aspects of the convent. However, Cohalan retorted that no distinction could be made between the religious and secular positions held by the individual as to all intents and purposes, 'Reverend Mother Martina and Reverend Mother superior are the same thing'. For the bishop, canon law was the determining factor in this conflict and this did not justify any dismissal, whatever might be decided by the secular authorities. Although we do not have all the details of the outcome, the case was so serious and Deeny was so intent on proceeding with it that Cohalan eventually conceded 'that Sister Martin was gravely at fault and he had no difficulty in accepting the Government's view that she should be moved'.[33]

When the Report of the Commission on Vocational Organisation was published in 1944, the Chairman Bishop, Michael Browne, demanded that Lemass support its recommendations on the grounds that the principles embodied there 'have been taught to us by Pope Pius XI'. Despite this, Lemass and MacEntee, among other leading members of the government, rejected the report on the grounds that it was anti-democratic and would lead to the destruction of the parliamentary system. The dismissal of the report was both brutal and successful, though it did influence sections of the opposition for long after. The object of the commission had been to investigate the possibility of introducing a corporatist system in Ireland, though one that was compatible with Irish and Catholic conditions. The Portuguese corporatist state was frequently seen as a possible model, though Archbishop McQuaid told one visitor that he favoured the implementation of a system similar to that of Vichy France under Petain. The decision to continue the commission during wartime can be attributed to a fear that Germany would win the war and if so Ireland would have its own design for a corporate state in place to be implemented. German defeat undermined this rationale and made the report effectively redundant as the Fianna Fáil government was now anxious to demonstrate to the victorious allies its own liberal democratic credentials. While the prominent historian and political analyst James Hogan had supported vocationalism during the 1930s, by the end of the war he had come to recognise that implementing it would run counter to the parliamentary system. Despite this, there were many who wanted to see such a system implemented in post-war Ireland. The criticism of vocationalism by Lemass, MacEntee and the civil service was thus a defence of democratic politics and responsible government.

John Whyte in his authoritative study of Church and state misreads the conflict over vocationalism. In his view this was a conflict between the advocates of bureaucracy and those supporting the distribution of economic and social power among vocational groups in Ireland. Whyte suggests that while both sides of this argument had intellectual failings, those of the bureaucrats 'were, if anything, worse' than those of the vocationalists. What this misses is that the so-called bureaucrats were defending the existing representative system but doing so in the name of democracy. The charge made by critics of vocationalism is that it would lead to irresponsibility and that the role of the state would be seriously diminished. Lemass in particular defended the right of the state to play an active role in the development of the Irish economy and certain aspects of social policy, but he like others also concluded that the elected government had to exercise control over public expenditure and policy.[34] What Lemass was not prepared to do was to devolve power (and resources) to unelected organisations which were not publicly responsible for their actions. Despite the theoretical attractions of vocationalism as an alternative to the liberal democratic system, the reality was more threatening. When Bishop Cohalan rejected Deeny's right to dismiss the nun in charge of Bessboro convent in Cork, the logic of this position was that religious orders would operate hospitals, maternity units and orphanages without interference from the state. If this had been permitted in this case the negligence might not have been stopped by the Department of Health and Local Government. Similarly, if vocationalism had been introduced in the medical sector, it is questionable whether Fianna Fáil's or Noël Browne's campaign against tuberculosis would have been well organised. The Church and the Irish Medical Association wanted control of this sector for different reasons, but the outcome would have weakened any concerted campaign against this lethal disease. Furthermore, in the case of education, the effective control of secondary education by the Catholic Church prevented innovative policy departures, especially those associated with vocational education (as distinct from vocational organisation).

The Catholic hierarchy prevented the expansion of a crucial sector of skills-based education at a time when the country was in need of such expertise. Indeed, successive governments accepted the denominational nature of education, conceding a policy veto to the Catholic bishops in particular. De Valera was so concerned at Catholic criticism that at one stage he was prepared to hand over the entire vocational sector to a Catholic religious order, a decision that would probably have marked the end of this sector.[35]

There is no evidence for a conflict between Church and state in Ireland between 1922 and the 1970s at the earliest. What is evident is that Church and state were in dispute over where the interests of one institution extended and where the other ended, as in the case of education or health policy. But even in the case of the Mother and Child crisis, there was no conflict between Church and state as such. The state conceded to the Catholic Church on the issue and modified the legislation accordingly. The divisions over vocational organisation focused on the extent to which an authoritarian Catholic political system could be transplanted to Ireland, but it failed because there was not widespread support among the hierarchy for the changes and because political democracy was too deeply entrenched in Irish society. It could have provided the basis for a conflict between Church and state, but in the circumstances it did not. The current state of research suggests that while the Irish state had considerable power at its disposal, especially in respect of emergency legislation and its control over the economy, this did not extend to a number of policy areas, which in other states would have been controlled by the state. State control was thus circumscribed by the existence of a powerful counter-force in the Catholic Church. Here was an organisation with a strong sense of its importance and which demanded respect from the state. This respect was readily given during the period under review and was not to be challenged for the first time until the 1980s. The state was anxious not to come into conflict with the Church on any matter, but certainly not on those considered to be of primary importance to Catholic faith and morals. Thus, Lemass's claim in 1969 that there was little tension between Church and state has to be understood in this context. The extent to which the state remained cautious where the Church was concerned can be appreciated from the bizarre circumstances surrounding the decision to prosecute Alan Simpson, co-owner of the Pike Theatre, for producing Tennessee Williams's *The Rose Tattoo* in May 1957. Although there was no censorship of theatre in Ireland, the Department of Justice decided to prosecute on the grounds that it was an indecent play and pursued Simpson for over a year in what was a malicious and vindictive campaign to break the theatre owner. The evidence suggests that the decision to prosecute was taken at the highest level of government and that de Valera had agreed to the decision. The proximate reason for acting was the success of the play, as a result of which it was agreed to move the production to the Gate Theatre, a much larger venue, for a further run. In a memo produced for the Minister for Justice a case is made against the play and Simpson, but it also demonstrates the fear that possible Church criticism raised:

> In making this recommendation, [to prosecute] we have in mind the fact not only that the play as produced is, in our opinion, indecent but that if there is a delay in taking action you may be faced with a demand – possibly a demand made in public – from any one or more of several sources, including the Archbishop, for action and that you would then be put in the position of having either to take no action – though the play is believed to be indecent – or to give the impression to the public that you acted only at the dictation of the Archbishop or somebody else.[36]

Civil servants are normally cautious when offering advice to their Ministers, but this memorandum suggests deeper concerns on the part of the unnamed official [possibly the departmental secretary Thomas Coyne]. Gerard Whelan and Carolyn Swift (co-owner of the Pike Theatre and Simpson's wife) have provided the most satisfactory explanation for the government's decision and this makes uncomfortable reading. On this account, the state had hoped to intimidate Simpson to take the play off at the end of its Pike run and not transfer to the Gate. This would have resolved that issue, but Simpson was not prepared to agree to this. When he refused he was arrested, jailed overnight and then subjected to extensive intimidation by the police authorities. When that failed he was prosecuted with a degree of nastiness and vindictiveness that warrants further explanation, but the documentary evidence remains outside the public domain. While the state used all its resources to prosecute Simpson, it lost the case. However, this was a Pyrrhic victory for Simpson and his supporters, who were now in debt and the theatre fatally weakened. At one level, *The Rose Tattoo* was a victim of Catholic Ireland's self-righteousness in the face of a rapidly changing world. Ireland may not be changing during the 1950s, but Europe and the United States was, especially in the field of popular entertainment. New literary and dramatic trends were emerging, which challenged the moral sensibilities of Catholic Ireland, and by 1957 these were having an impact on Dublin if not Ireland generally. But there is a wider context that is established by Whelan and Swift in their persuasive research. The decision to prosecute Simpson should be linked to departmental concerns over the composition of the Censorship Board (which had been dominated by the Knights of Columbanus), the campaign against 'evil' literature initiated by the Archbishop and driven by the Knights and a little later the controversy over the Dublin Theatre Festival in 1958. This is not the place to rehearse in detail the argument developed by Whelan and Swift concerning the moves and counter moves in respect of censorship during the 1950s, but what the history of *The Rose Tattoo* demonstrates is an embattled state, fearful of Church intervention and ready to meet its concerns (even before these concerns were expressed).[37]

Little of this had changed when Lemass succeeded de Valera as Taoiseach in 1959. The moral community described above remained well entrenched, reinforcing the traditional pattern of Church–state relations. Lemass brought to government a different style, one that was more vigorous and active. He certainly believed that patriotism applied to the development of the society and not just in connection with Irish unity. He also prompted his ministers to consider where reform of institutions and practice was most appropriate. Lemass's brief period as Taoiseach is associated with change, and by the time he died in 1971 the first cracks in Ireland's homogeneous political culture had appeared. Despite this, the pace of change was slow when compared with Ireland's European neighbours. In a crucial sense Lemass's Ireland did not share in the permissive revolution that characterised most of the developed world at this time. De Valera's legacy loomed large, as did the constitutional, institutional and political constraints on change. However, change did occur as political elites in particular recognised the need to modernise the economy and some of the political institutions in the state. Yet, even when Ireland joined the Common Market in 1973, traditional attitudes remained dominant if no longer homogeneous. It is possible to obtain a sense of this change by comparing attitudes over time. While we do not have opinion poll data in any detail before the 1970s, there are some data that provide a basis for assessing continuity and change. The most important of these is the research carried out by Bruce Biever in 1961 when he studied the attitudes of Dublin Catholics to a range of religious and cultural issues. What he provides is a snapshot of the population that came of age during and immediately after the heroic period of Irish nationalism between 1900 and 1922 and which was socialised politically by Fianna Fáil. This is also a profile of a population before change takes place during the 1960s. Table 8.1 summarises the data collected by Biever in respect of Church and state, revealing a complex range of opinion on the part of these Dubliners.

Table 8.1 **Irish attitudes to Church and state questions**

Question	Agree %	Neutral %	Disagree %
Church cannot be compared to any other social institution	100	—	—
State to be preferred to Church on hypothesis of conflict	3.3	10	86.5
Rome control significant	3.0	5.0	92
Church too much involved in politics	7.5	10.5	82
Church usurping role of state	5.0	15	80
Irish Church a national church: nation and church inseparable	27	10	63
Church and state totally independent of each other	4.0	23	73
Church harms itself by political involvement.	28	13	59
Church should be more involved in state matters than it is.	28	13.4	57.6

Source: Adapted from Bruce F. Biever, *Religion, Culture and Values: A Cross-Cultural Analysis of Motivational Factors in Native Irish and American Irish Catholicism* (New York, 1976), p. 311, table 7.

Other data in the study demonstrates that Irish Catholic opinion was highly conformist when it came to Church teaching and often intolerant of other religions. In other ways this research confirmed the denominational apartheid that existed in Ireland at the time. While respondents agreed that members of other religions could be in theory better individuals than Catholics, over 70 per cent agreed that 'Catholics in fact have higher morality than non-Catholics'. Furthermore, 75 per cent of those questioned said that they would not marry a non-Catholic, while a massive 92 per cent rejected the view that one church was a good as another. Overall Dublin Catholics in 1961 were conservative and traditional when it came to religious attitudes and this affected how they perceived relations between Church and state. Most denied that a conflict between Church and state could occur, but if there were one then they would side overwhelmingly with the Church. The reason given for this was that the state was a secular and temporal institution whereas the Church was sacred and the Pope infallible. At the popular level there were strong theocratic influences at work, though one needs to assess carefully the ambiguous nature of some of the answers.[38]

Against this background, there was little pressure for change in the relationship between Church and state during the 1960s among the general population. Dissent did, however, appear on the major issues during this time. Liberals, socialists and feminists supported reform in many areas of concern to the

Church, including education, censorship, contraception and divorce. Precisely because these were considered areas of Church interest politicians were reluctant to take the initiative. Thus, what might appear a simple matter on the surface could embroil the government with the hierarchy or at least the powerful Archbishop of Dublin. On one occasion shortly after becoming Taoiseach, Lemass quickly deferred to McQuaid when he objected to a proposal to locate the National Library on a site owned by Trinity College, Dublin. McQuaid's hostility to TCD was well known but there were good reasons for adopting the policy. However, all plans were dropped once it was clear that the Archbishop would oppose the move. In similar fashion, when Lemass asked Brian Lenihan to explore the possibility of introducing divorce in a very limited way in 1965, no further action was taken once McQuaid indicated his opposition. When, in 1967, the Committee on the Constitution recommended that divorce should be introduced for Protestants, even this sectarian approach to policy making was quickly criticised by McQuaid and nothing more was heard of the suggestion.[39] This had its impact on opinion in the Dáil and especially in Fianna Fáil. Lemass's successor Jack Lynch was committed to liberalising aspect of Irish society, but he was taken aback by the opposition of his backbench deputies to any reform of the contraceptive ban in 1971. It is telling that the one change to the Constitution involving an issue with a religious aspect to it, the removal of article 44 that recognised the special position of the Catholic Church, went ahead when Cardinal Conway voiced support for its removal.[40]

Yet opinion was changing at different levels. The elite was dividing between liberal activists, moderate reformists and a more traditional group identifying with the older certainties. However, among the elite this latter group was increasingly on the defensive by the early 1970s. The Committee on the Constitution acknowledged in 1967 that the Supreme Court would no longer be bound by earlier decisions in respect of fundamental rights, suggesting that it might be creative in how these rights could be interpreted. Indeed, this view may well have originated with Lemass who told Brian Walsh when he was appointed to the Supreme Court in 1961 that he would like the court to operate in a similar fashion to that of the American Supreme Court. This view was vindicated in 1973 when the Supreme Court declared in the McGee case that the 1935 act prohibiting the importation of contraceptives was unconstitutional. This decision was to have significant consequences for Ireland and can be said to have initiated the cultural wars that divided the country for the next thirty years.[41] Opinion divided between liberal and conservative on this and many other issues and this divide became a major factor in political mobilisation and competition during the following decades. Mass opinion was also changing and challenging traditional aspects of the moral community. Opinion polls reported that while church going remained remarkably high into the 1970s, those who lived in urban areas, the better educated and those in non-agricultural occupations tended to be more liberal than the rest of the population on many issues. Ireland may not have been secularising in the 1970s but a significant section of the population (though not a majority by any means) were now more open to change and to a more tolerant attitude to moral issues.

Changes in attitudes were influenced by the belief that a more liberal Ireland would be more attractive to Unionists in Northern Ireland and also by the changes in the Catholic Church introduced by Pope John XXIII, but there was also a strong basis for this among the young urban population. Despite this there were very real divisions between liberals and conservatives on contraception, divorce and later on abortion, but also on Northern Ireland and other matters. The extent of these changes can be seen in the pioneering work carried out by MacGréil in Dublin in 1972. When compared to the survey carried out by Biever in 1961, this later study highlights the changes in attitudes over time. While the two cannot be directly compared, MacGreil's research demonstrated that it was possible to divide opinion along a liberal conservative spectrum. MacGréil's main concern was to identify the extent of tolerance and intolerance in Dublin, but in doing so he also highlighted the extent of change within the moral community. Some 46 per cent of respondents agreed that Catholic priests should be allowed to marry, with 44 per cent disagreeing; 45 per cent thought that homosexuality should not be a crime, though just under 40 per cent disagreed with this view. In the case of contraceptives 31 per cent considered that it was always wrong to use them, whereas 63 per cent disagreed with this. This latter finding was confirmed by a number of other surveys taken during the 1970s. There was divided opinion on whether something was right or wrong, while a clear majority (57 per cent) thought that premarital sex was always wrong. Taken as a whole, the MacGréil research disclosed that the moral community that had characterised Catholic nationalism since the nineteenth century was no longer homogeneous. Opinion was divided on most issues and in some cases views were evenly divided on matters of concern to the Catholic Church. What this also confirmed was that Ireland was displaying similar patterns of belief to other European states. The young tended to be more liberal, less intolerant and less conformist than older groups in the society. Women also tended to be less liberal and more religiously fundamentalist, as were those who lived in rural areas and with less education. The social divide was increasingly clear. Liberal views were closely associated with years of education, occupation, as well as age of respondent, while rural residents, those of lower socio-economic status, women and older age groups identified with conservative attitudes. One of the by-products of these changes was the emergence of a clear liberal–conservative political divide during the 1980s, though refigured by the divisions emerging here.[42]

These changes in attitudes did not lead directly to significant changes in the Constitution or in policy formation. These had to await further political developments during the 1980s and 1990s. What the changes draw attention to, however, is the divided nature of opinion and the demands that new and more liberal attitudes made on the political system. That system was very slow indeed to respond to these pressures. The influence of the Church remained strong among members of all political parties and, despite some liberal statements from individual Bishops or priests, the hierarchy generally took an increasingly conservative view on most issues. This became patently clear when legislation was introduced to address the contraception issue left open after the McGee case. Legislation to change the law was introduced by the Fine Gael–Labour Coalition government in 1974, but was defeated on a free vote. Most significantly, the Taoiseach himself voted against a piece of legislation introduced by his own government. When Fianna Fáil introduced legislation to address the issue in 1978, it followed closely the public position of the Catholic hierarchy in terms of the restrictions imposed. By this time a new Ireland was being shaped by the confrontation between liberal and conservative, but this confrontation was very much a result of the changes put in place by Lemass in the 1960s.

The relationship between economic change and political and social change is at best indirect. The causal connection is weak and the determinants often unclear. Notwithstanding this reservation, the policy changes introduced by Lemass from the late 1950s established the conditions for change in the social and political realm. This in turn both reinforced and was reinforced by trends in other areas. The growth of urban Ireland, changing demographics and a better-educated population provided a new constituency for more liberal politics. Lemass recognised earlier than most that constitutional change would be a key aspect of a changing Ireland and was instrumental in establishing the all-party Committee on the Constitution. While the report of the committee was cautious and tentative, it was the first time that de Valera's constitution became the focus for reasoned discussion. At the heart of this was the relationship between Church and state. It is perhaps no accident that some of fiercest political debates in Ireland since the 1960s have been concerned with this relationship. Though the issues have not been resolved, they remain central to the reformulation of the Irish moral community in the twenty-first century. This debate is concerned with whether this moral community will be conservative or liberal and how a new relationship between Church and state will be institutionalised. As yet, this outcome is not entirely clear. However, by cultivating change and promoting reform in various arenas Lemass, whether intentionally or not, laid the basis for the new social conflict that challenged the older moral community that had dominated Ireland for nearly a century.

CHAPTER NINE

The politics of educational expansion

JOHN WALSH

—

'Expansion would not have happened except for Lemass', commented Dr Patrick Hillery, who served as Minister for Education between 1959 and 1965, on Lemass's role in promoting educational expansion.[1] It is well known that Lemass appointed several younger, more dynamic ministers to the Department of Education, which had traditionally been dominated by conservative ministers and officials. Such appointments, however, formed only a single aspect of Lemass's pervasive influence on the politics of education during (and even after) his term as Taoiseach. It was Lemass's interaction with successive reforming ministers that provided much of the momentum for educational reform. Lemass played a central part in initiating and directing the radical reform and expansion of Irish education between 1959 and 1966.

The educational system between 1945 and 1959 was dominated by private interests, notably the Catholic and Protestant churches, while the state made little attempt to develop a new policy approach for education in the immediate post-war period. It was a period of very limited expansion in Irish education, due not only to financial constraints imposed on expenditure by the Department of Finance but also to the minimalist conception of the state's role in education held by ministers and officials.[2] Indeed, General Richard Mulcahy, who served as Minister for Education in the second inter-party government between 1954 and 1957, explicitly disclaimed responsibility for the formulation of educational policy and suggested that the minister should merely act to facilitate the work of the interests which controlled the educational system. He told the Dáil on 19 July 1956, 'You have your teachers, your managers and your churches and I regard the position as Minister in the Department of Education as that of a kind of dungaree man, the plumber who will make satisfactory communications and streamline the forces and potentialities of the educational workers and educational management in this country'.[3] Mulcahy's statement fully reflected the conservative approach of the Irish state in education, which was based upon the assumption that the policy initiative rested with private, mainly clerical, interests.[4] His restrictive definition of the role of the state was fully shared by the senior officials of the Department of Education.[5] James Dukes, who served as private secretary to Mulcahy, Jack Lynch and Dr Patrick Hillery, believed that the senior officials regarded Education as a junior department, under-staffed, under-resourced and unable to take on additional responsibilities: 'they were up to their ears with work and it was very tight where money was concerned'.[6] There was, however, some evidence of a new official attitude towards education in the late 1950s. *Economic Development*, composed by T. K. Whitaker and other officials of the Department of Finance, which was published in November 1958, drew attention to the potential contribution of vocational education to national development.[7] Jack Lynch, who served as Minister for Education in Eamon de Valera's final government, initiated reforms in primary education, notably the removal of the ban on married women teachers in July 1958.[8] But it was not until Lemass's election as Taoiseach that the government adopted a definite policy to promote educational expansion.

Lemass appointed Dr Patrick Hillery, who entered the government for the first time, as Minister for Education on 23 June 1959. The policy of the government towards education was clarified by Lemass and Hillery in a debate on a motion put forward by the two members of the left-wing National Progressive Democrat Party, Dr Noel Browne and Jack McQuillan, in October 1959, calling for the extension of the statutory school leaving age to at least 15 years. Hillery defended the educational system against criticisms by Browne, but the new minister also indicated that it was his 'earnest wish' to enable all children to continue in post-primary education at least up to the age of fifteen, arguing that the most effective way to achieve this objective was to accelerate the rate of increase of the necessary facilities for post-primary education.[9] The new policy was given the full support of the government through a statement made by the Taoiseach. Lemass intervened personally on 28 October 1959 in the debate on the Dáil motion.[10] He made a commitment that 'The aim of Government policy is to bring about a situation in which all childrenwill continue their schooling until they are at least fifteen years of age.'[11] Lemass pledged to achieve this objective as soon as possible, without extending compulsory attendance, on a statutory basis, up to 15 years of age. He summarised the government policy as a commitment to the gradual extension of both secondary and whole time technical educational facilities, combined with the expansion of scholarship schemes.[12] Lemass and Hillery outlined a policy based on a measured expansion of post-primary facilities and scholarships. It was not at all the radical approach sought by Browne, which involved the provision of free education by the state up to the age of 15; but Lemass's policy statement provided for the first time a definite gradualist approach by the state for the expansion of post-primary education.[13] Moreover Lemass's intervention in the debate, only four months after his election, underlined the priority which would be accorded to education by the new Taoiseach. His statement not only established a new policy commitment by the government to educational expansion, but also indicated that the new Taoiseach would not hesitate to intervene directly to clarify or promote a policy for which one of his younger ministers had responsibility. Lemass and Hillery established in October 1959 a cautious but definite policy approach by the state, which was designed to achieve a gradual expansion of the educational system, while avoiding any short-term commitment to the extension of the statutory school leaving age.

This gradualist approach to educational expansion soon provided for important practical improvements in the primary school system. Hillery introduced new state grants for national schools and acted to improve the pupil–teacher ratio.[14] The new Minister announced on 24 May 1961 a new scheme providing funding for the painting and decoration of national schools.[15] The scheme made state grants available from 1 April 1962 towards the cost of painting national schools externally every four years and for internal decoration every eight years.[16] While the maintenance of the schools remained a local responsibility, the department usually provided a grant of two thirds of the expenditure incurred on painting the building.[17] While the scheme was a relatively modest improvement, based partly on pragmatic official calculations designed to save money in the long term, it was the first state programme which directly funded the decoration and upkeep of national schools.

Hillery also acted to extend the post-primary and university scholarships scheme. The Local Authorities Scholarships (Amendment) Bill, which was introduced to the Dáil on 4 July 1961, was designed to establish a greatly expanded scholarship scheme.[18] The legislation provided for central state funding of approximately £300,000 for the local authority scholarships over a period of four years.[19] The Bill was also designed to encourage local councils to increase their contribution to the scholarship scheme by raising additional funding on the rates. The contribution from the Exchequer was intended to increase steadily in proportion to the funding raised by the local authority, to achieve a five to four ratio between state and local contributions after four years.[20] The most significant innovation of the Scholarships Act was the provision of direct payments by the national government towards the cost of local authority scholarships. While the department already provided limited scholarship programmes, mainly for the promotion of the Irish language, the legislation heralded a new approach by the state, which provided funding for a general scheme of scholarships for the first time.[21] The proposal, which was approved by the Dáil on 2 August 1961, transformed the financial provision for post-primary and university scholarships.[22] The new legislation also marked the first real attempt by the state to widen educational opportunity, especially with regard to post-primary education.

The Scholarships Act immediately contributed to a major increase in the number of scholarship candidates: 5,622 took the post-primary scholarship examinations in 1962, compared to only 3,122 in 1961. The Department of Education was providing £60,000 in a single year towards the cost of local authority scholarships by 1963–4.[23] The number of scholarships for post-primary schools more than doubled between 1961 and 1962, rising from 831 to 1927.[24] Similarly, the number of university scholarships showed a major increase from 155 in 1961 to 254 in 1962.[25] The revised legislation delivering direct state support for scholarships initiated a rapid and dramatic expansion in the scholarship scheme. The incremental reforming approach pursued by Hillery and Lemass delivered advances in post-primary education by dealing effectively with persistent educational problems which had been largely neglected by previous governments, such as the inadequate provision for the local authority scholarships. This incremental approach was firmly based on the government's gradualist policy, which gave priority to the expansion of educational facilities and scholarships in the first instance. This approach certainly had substantial limitations and was only beginning to have some impact with regard to post-primary education by 1962. But the government had initiated a viable policy for the expansion of post-primary education.

The government's policy towards higher education remained ill defined, however, for much of Lemass's term as Taoiseach. The government approved the establishment on 16 August 1960 of the Commission on Higher Education, which was requested to undertake a comprehensive review of higher education in the Republic.[26] Hillery appointed Cearbhall Ó Dálaigh, then a Justice of the Supreme Court, as chairman of the Commission: its membership included eminent academics, Catholic and Protestant clergy and representatives of business and the public service.[27] The Commission, which held its first meeting on 8 November 1960, was the first committee of inquiry appointed by an independent Irish government on higher education.[28] The Commission's deliberations proved lengthy and its report was not submitted until 1967, considerably later than Hillery had hoped and indeed after Lemass's retirement as Taoiseach. The lengthy deliberations of the Commission reduced its potential influence and delayed until the late 1960s the formulation of a definite state policy for the long-term development of third-level education. The decision to appoint the Commission, however, reflected the government's recognition that coherent educational planning was required for the future development of higher education.

Lemass and Hillery were increasingly influenced by policy ideas promoted by the Organisation for Economic Co-operation and Development, especially its advocacy of coherent planning of educational needs. The OECD held a policy conference in Washington on 'Economic growth and investment in education' between 16 and 20 October 1961, which was attended by two Irish representatives, Seán MacGearailt, assistant secretary of the Department of Education and John F. McInerney, deputy assistant secretary of the Department of Finance.[29] The Directorate of Scientific Affairs of the OECD proposed to the Conference the establishment of pilot studies on long-term educational needs in developed countries.[30] The OECD believed that investment in education was increasingly accepted as one of the main instruments in the creation of social and economic progress.[31] The Washington Conference agreed an international initiative, the Education Investment and Planning Programme (EIPP), which included the Directorate's proposal.[32] Although some of the national representatives at the conference were unenthusiastic about a study which would hold their educational provision up to international scrutiny, the Irish officials immediately agreed to recommend co-operation with the pilot study to the relevant ministers.[33] The delegations of Ireland and Austria were the initial volunteers for co-operation with the project, although the EIPP was subsequently joined by other European states.[34] The immediate offer of co-operation with the OECD by McInerney and MacGearailt proved an initiative with the most significant implications for Irish education.

Lemass and Hillery soon took up the OECD initiative with enthusiasm. The government, which was beginning the preparation of the Second Programme for Economic Expansion, regarded a survey of long-term educational needs as an appropriate element in a process of national economic planning.[35] Lemass informed Cearbhall Ó Dálaigh on 21 June 1962 that the government was undertaking the pilot study in part because the OECD approach heavily emphasised economic planning. Moreover the Taoiseach cited Ireland's application to join the EEC as another important element which influenced the government's support for the study. He considered that the government's acceptance of the OECD initiative 'could have a very important bearing on our future relations with the European Economic Community'.[36] Hillery announced the initiation of the pilot study of the state's long-term educational needs, which was to be implemented by a national survey team in conjunction with the OECD, on 22 June 1962 at a Labour/Management Conference on 'Employment in Productivity' in Shannon Airport.[37] The survey team, which was appointed by Hillery on 29 July 1962, was headed by Patrick Lynch, Professor of Economics at University College Dublin: the survey team also included W. J. Hyland of the United Nations Statistics Office, Padraig Ó'Nualláin, Inspector of Secondary Schools and Martin O'Donoghue, Lecturer in Economics at Trinity College, Dublin; Cathal Mac Gabhann of the Department of Education acted as secretary to the group. The survey team was asked to undertake a comprehensive survey of the state's long-term needs for educational resources.[38] Lemass drew attention to the new project on 8 July 1962 in a speech given to the Marist Brothers' centenary celebrations in Sligo.[39] Lemass declared that the new study was designed 'to frame a development programme and set the educational targets which must be realised if our facilities are to be kept in proper relation to our requirements as a progressive national community'.[40] The survey team would produce long-term objectives, which would facilitate a comprehensive programme of development. He emphasised the importance of education in supplying the country's growing need for qualified scientific and technical personnel, arguing that: 'It is in the growth and improvement of our education system that the foundations of our future prosperity must be firmly based.'[41] Lemass strongly asserted the government's commitment to the expansion of the educational system, not least because education would contribute to the economic development of the state. The Taoiseach's concern to relate the planning of educational developments to wider economic and social needs was evident.

Lemass also signalled that the government was considering a significant initiative for the expansion of post-primary education in an address to Muintir na Tíre in August 1962. Hillery made an initial proposal for a new type of post-primary school in a memorandum to the Department of the Taoiseach on 7 July 1962, following the report of the Inter-Departmental Committee on the Problems of Small Western Farms.[42] Hillery suggested the provision by the state of a number of new post-primary schools, offering a comprehensive course of three years for pupils aged 12 to 15.[43] Lemass included a short but positive reference to the department's proposal in his public statement on the report at Muintir na Tíre Rural Week, which was delivered on his behalf by Charles Haughey TD, Minister for Justice, on 14 August 1962.[44] The Taoiseach's statement acknowledged that special problems existed with regard to post-primary education in the western small farm areas and indicated that Hillery was preparing proposals to remedy these deficiencies.[45] Significantly Lemass's statement also announced that 'the Minister's ideas, which have not yet been fully developed, envisage a new type of post-primary school with a curriculum which, although broad-based, would also have a definite practical bias'.[46] The Taoiseach gave a firm indication that special measures were being considered by the government to overcome problems in the provision of post-primary education in specific areas. Lemass also publicly introduced the idea of a new type of post-primary school, provided by the state, as a solution to the under-development of post-primary education in thinly populated rural areas. The section of Lemass's statement on education attracted little public attention in August 1962.[47] Lemass had, however, signalled a new departure in educational policy, indicating that the government was considering an important initiative for the expansion of post-primary education.

A detailed proposal concerning the expansion of post-primary education was submitted by Hillery to the Department of the Taoiseach in January 1963. The Department of Education's proposal, entitled 'Proposal for comprehensive post-primary education: pilot scheme related to small farm areas', identified key problems in post-primary education. The basic structural defect of the system was summarised bluntly: 'under the present system of private enterprise', a large residue of pupils would never receive post-primary education.[48] Moreover the department's paper also identified further problems flowing from this 'fundamental structural defect' in the educational system.[49] Many rural secondary schools were too small, employing inadequate numbers of staff and therefore providing only a limited curriculum with little provision for continental languages or Science.[50] The department recommended the provision by the state of comprehensive post-primary schools, which were initially described as 'Junior Secondary Schools'.[51] The department's proposal made relatively rapid progress through the administrative and political obstacles which could have blocked its path, due to Hillery's effective advocacy and the support of the Taoiseach. The proposal was first submitted to the Department of Finance and was rejected.[52] Hillery then appealed directly to the Taoiseach, submitting a covering letter to Lemass on 9 January 1963, making the case for comprehensive schools, along with the draft proposal.[53] The Minister made a strong argument for a pilot scheme involving comprehensive schools in the western small farm areas. He hoped that the pilot scheme would provide a model of post-primary education, which could with time be extended to the whole country.[54] Hillery acknowledged both the considerable expense of the plan and the possible opposition of private interests, including the Catholic hierarchy, but urged Lemass that it was necessary and probably inevitable.[55] The Minister even argued that the comprehensive schools plan might well prove to be the only opportunity to introduce a 'really satisfactory system of post-primary education'.[56] Only four months elapsed before the Department of Education proposal became, in a modified form, the publicly acknowledged policy of the government.

Lemass played a crucial role in the rapid evolution of government policy on education. Hillery suggested that his department's proposal should be forwarded to the cabinet committee on small farms.[57] The Taoiseach fully supported Hillery's policy initiative but found a more effective means of progressing it. Lemass withheld the proposal from the cabinet committee, instead arranging a conference involving only Hillery, the Taoiseach himself and Dr James Ryan, the Minister for Finance.[58] Hillery then elaborated on his department's proposal in a further letter to Lemass on 12 January 1963, indicating that he hoped to achieve 'one system of post-primary education which would have a number of streams'.[59] This approach secured a rapid and positive response from Lemass. The Taoiseach explicitly stated his support for Hillery's policy initiative in his response on 14 January 1963, although he also noted his own lack of knowledge about the cost of the plan.[60] He warned the Minister that public confusion about the government's policy would persist until Hillery's plan was publicly announced.[61] Lemass gave Hillery clear directions on the procedure to be followed in the meeting with the Minister for Finance. The Taoiseach warned Hillery to 'come to this meeting with the nature of the decisions you desire very clear in your mind' and even sought in advance a draft of the decisions as Hillery wished to have them recorded.[62] Lemass indicated that Dr Ryan could not be expected to give full approval to the proposal at the first meeting.[63] But the Taoiseach's commitment to Hillery's proposal and his determination to fast track it through the normal procedures of the government were evident. The summary of the decisions requested by Lemass was drafted by Hillery's officials and contained three main elements. The summary envisaged a new system of post-primary education based on comprehensive courses and where necessary comprehensive schools; as a first step in this direction a pilot scheme would be introduced in more remote rural areas.[64] The Minister sought authorisation to consult with the Catholic bishop in each relevant area to give effect to the proposal, as it was envisaged that the pilot scheme would involve only Catholic schools.[65] Hillery secured agreement from the Minister for Finance to proceed with the proposal by following the procedure recommended by Lemass, despite some delay caused by the Department of Finance.[66] The Taoiseach then told Hillery to launch the scheme publicly without bringing it to the cabinet for formal approval, telling the minister bluntly: 'You'll never get it through the Government.'[67] The scheme for comprehensive schools was therefore launched by Hillery at a press conference on 20 May 1963.[68] Lemass not only played a crucial role in steering the proposal successfully past the procedural obstacles which might have frustrated it, but he also gave Hillery the authority to go ahead with the scheme without formal cabinet approval.

Hillery's policy announcement on 20 May 1963 identified major weaknesses in the existing post-primary system, including the failure of the system to provide post-primary education for a substantial segment of the population and the complete absence of co-ordination between secondary and vocational schools.[69] He announced that the state would take the initiative in resolving these problems by providing a number of new post-primary schools catering in the first instance for specific regions. Hillery proposed a comprehensive post-primary day school, providing a three-year course which would lead to the Intermediate Certificate Examination.[70] The Minister endorsed the concept of equality of opportunity as a guiding principle of state policy. He indicated that the school buildings would be financed largely by the state, while the running costs would be funded through annual grants from the department and the Vocational Education Committees (VEC). The salaries of the teachers would be paid as usual by the department.[71] Hillery's announcement marked a fundamental policy change from the practice of successive governments since the foundation of the Irish state. The direct intervention of the national government to establish a new form of post-primary school was unprecedented. The department made relatively slow progress in establishing comprehensive schools, due to the prolonged consultation required with the Catholic hierarchy.[72] The comprehensive schools proposal was initially implemented as a pilot project involving only three schools, in Cootehill, County Cavan, Shannon, County Clare, and Carraroe, County Galway, which opened in September 1966.[73] The policy announcement, however, marked the first major initiative by the Irish state to provide for post-primary education, outside the specific ambit of technical instruction.[74]

The initiative also involved a determined attempt by the government to raise the quality and status of technical education. Hillery initiated the revision of the Intermediate Certificate examination to provide a common system of assessment for all post-primary schools in the junior cycle.[75] The revised examination system marked the first real effort by the state to co-ordinate the activity of the vocational sector and the private secondary schools. The Minister also announced a radical new departure in technical education to accommodate pupils who did not intend to proceed with academic education after the age of 15. Hillery announced his intention to establish Regional Technical Colleges (RTCs) in conjunction with the VECs: the new regional colleges were effectively designed as a bridge to third-level education or skilled technical employment for students with technical aptitudes. The proposal marked the beginning of a dramatic development of higher education, which led to the foundation of the first RTCs as an element of the third-level sector in 1969.[76] Hillery's proposal was a serious attempt to widen educational opportunity for students with technical aptitudes and to enhance the status of the technical sector. The policy announcement was the first of the major reforms which transformed the Irish educational system in the era of expansion.

The emergence of educational expansion as a national priority under Lemass was underlined by the recommendations of the Second Programme for Economic Expansion. The Second Programme (Part I), which was published by the government in August 1963, indicated that 'special attention' would be given to education, training and other forms of human investment.[77] The *Second Programme* also identified educational expansion as a key national priority, asserting that better education and training would support and stimulate continued economic expansion. The government's programme for economic development confidently asserted that 'Even the economic returns from investment in education are likely to be as high in the long-run as those from investment in physical capital.'[78] Moreover the Second Programme, Part II, which was issued by the government in July 1964, indicated that the school leaving age would be raised to 15 years by 1970.[79] The government made a definite commitment to proceed with the extension of the school leaving age, although the time frame for the decision would depend on continuing prosperity.

The implications for educational policy of the Second Programme for Economic Expansion provided the major theme of an address given by Lemass on 13 February 1964, when he responded to a lecture given by Dr John Vaizey, lecturer in Economics at Oxford, on 'The economics of education', at St Patrick's Training College, Drumcondra.[80] Lemass's address fully reflected the approach to educational expansion outlined by the Second Programme, expressing with great clarity the government's rationale for investment in education. He commented that education was 'both a cause of economic growth and a product of such growth': education enhanced the general earning power of the nation, while increased production would provide the resources for educational advance.[81] Lemass indicated that economic planning made no sense unless it was accompanied with educational planning: the government had decided, in the Second Programme, that improvements in social services, including education, 'must go hand in hand with economic progress'.[82] Lemass's speech illustrated the extent to which economic progress and educational expansion had become inextricably linked in his approach to national development.

Lemass's address on this occasion drew public attention primarily to the announcement of a new scheme of building grants for secondary schools. Hillery recommended to the Taoiseach on 4 February 1964 that a scheme of building grants should be established to provide state assistance in financing the secondary school building programme.[83] The Minister summarised to Lemass the case for building grants made by a deputation representing the Catholic bishops on 5 December 1963, noting their view that they were 'at the end of their tether' in raising capital for the secondary school building programmes.[84] The proposed introduction of capital grants was designed to satisfy the Catholic hierarchy, whose co-operation was required by the Minister in establishing the comprehensive schools. The new measure was also desirable to discredit Fine Gael's criticism of the government's educational policy. Hillery warned the Taoiseach that the government would be damaged if the opposition appeared to take the initiative on educational matters, advising that it would be political folly to delay the introduction of building grants.[85] Lemass not only supported Hillery's initiative but also engineered the announcement of the new scheme with almost incredible speed. The Taoiseach indicated to James Ryan on 5 February 1964 that Hillery had outlined the necessity for a system of capital grants for the building of secondary schools.[86] Lemass then arranged a meeting on 10 February 1964 to discuss the issue, which was attended by Hillery, Ryan and the Taoiseach himself. The principle of the scheme was agreed by the Taoiseach and the two Ministers at this meeting.[87] Lemass was determined to arrange for the announcement of the new initiative as quickly as possible, although the details of the scheme had not yet been formulated. Lemass's urgency was explained largely by the imminence of two by-elections, to be held on 19 February, to Dáil seats in Kildare and Cork, which would determine the government's ability to retain power without calling a general election.[88] It was not surprising, therefore, that Lemass announced the new initiative in his address on 13 February 1964, only nine days after it had first been proposed by Hillery. The Taoiseach declared that the Government would initiate 'a new departure' for secondary education, indicating that Hillery would soon introduce a scheme of direct building grants to secondary schools.[89] The Taoiseach made only a brief statement concerning the new scheme: Lemass's announcement marked, however, a significant policy departure from the traditional approach followed by the Irish state, which had left capital provision for secondary education entirely to private interests. The *Irish Independent* on 14 February 1964 correctly commented upon 'a quite historic announcement' by the Taoiseach, which was also 'almost historic in its brevity'.[90] The scheme, which came into effect from May 1964, provided for grants to the secondary school authorities which would cover up to 60 per cent of the costs incurred in building or extending eligible secondary schools.[91] Despite strict conditions attached to the initiative by the Department of Education, the scheme of building grants introduced direct state aid in the provision of secondary schools for the first time. The rapid announcement and implementation of the scheme for building grants underlined Lemass's crucial role in guaranteeing effective intervention by the state to overcome long-standing educational problems.

The central importance attached by Lemass to educational expansion as a key element of national development was illustrated by his comments to the monthly periodical *Open* on 29 January 1965: 'The day of the unskilled worker, at any social level, is passing and with the development of modern science and technology, the future belongs to those who have trained themselves to meet its specific requirements in knowledge and skill.'[92] Lemass clearly reaffirmed his position that educational expansion was an indispensable element in the long-term economic development of the nation. Lemass's commitment to the expansion of the educational system provided a favourable political context for the radical reforms initiated by Hillery's successor, George Colley. Following his re-election as Taoiseach after the General Election in April 1965, Lemass appointed Colley as the new Minister for Education. Colley was a regular contributor to Dáil debates on education and was given his first cabinet portfolio as Minister for Education on 21 April 1965.

Lemass placed considerable public emphasis on the evaluation of the national economic requirements for skilled labour, which was undertaken by the OECD survey team between 1962 and 1965. He commented to *Open* that a key objective of future policy would be 'to relate the output of professional and technically trained personnel to estimated national requirements'.[93] He fully recognised the importance of the report *Investment in Education*, which was

submitted by the survey team to Colley in November 1965. The report identified severe deficiencies in the Irish educational system. *Investment in Education*
drew attention to 'significant disparities' in educational participation, which
involved considerable inequalities between different socio-economic categories
and regional groups.[94] The report also illustrated the prevalence of inefficient and
haphazard organisation of resources in primary and post-primary education,
due largely to the lack of co-ordination in the development of the Irish
educational system.[95] Moreover *Investment* identified a substantial shortfall in
the supply by the educational system of qualified manpower for the projected
requirements of the economy in the 1970s.[96] *Investment* was a seminal policy
analysis, which made a compelling case for educational reform to secure an
improved allocation of resources in the educational sector. Lemass strongly
encouraged Colley to publicise the report and act on its conclusions. The
Taoiseach wrote to Colley immediately after receiving the report on 27
November 1965, noting the Minister's view that *Investment* would be difficult
to summarise effectively.[97] Lemass told Colley that an official effort had to be
made to summarise the report and urged him to publish an official commentary
on *Investment*, to underline the key points of the report.[98] Colley immediately
assured the Taoiseach that he would arrange the publication of a commentary
summarising the conclusions of the report.[99] The report was published on 23
December 1965, along with a detailed press release drafted by the Department
of Education, which highlighted the report's conclusions concerning the
deficiencies of the educational system. Lemass clearly perceived the potential
for radical change in the critical evaluation of Irish education provided by the
survey team and was determined that the government would take up the issues
raised by the report in a proactive fashion.

The report's critical analysis of educational realities became an integral part
of government policy even before it was published. Colley announced a radical
new initiative in educational policy, which was largely inspired by *Investment
in Education*, in July 1965. The Minister was certainly aware at this stage of the
general conclusions of the report, as Seán MacGearailt, assistant secretary of
the department, chaired the steering committee which supervised the work of
the survey team. Colley informed the Dáil on 21 July 1965 that he intended,
where feasible, to replace small one-teacher and two-teacher national schools
with larger central schools, served by school transport schemes subsidised by
the state.[100] Colley argued, on the basis of the analysis made by *Investment in
Education*, that educational attainment on the part of pupils in smaller schools
was significantly inferior to the level reached by pupils in larger schools: school

facilities and teaching aids were also far inferior in small schools.[101] The new policy, which would involve the closure or amalgamation of small primary schools, also provided for proper planning of educational facilities.

Colley outlined the rationale for the new policy of amalgamation to Lemass on 24 September 1965.[102] The Minister told Lemass that there were about 730 one-teacher schools, frequently staffed by untrained teachers, who were obliged to cope with all classes in such schools.[103] He believed that a re-organisation of primary education was essential on educational and social grounds. Colley had privately discussed the initiative with Cardinal William Conway, Archbishop of Armagh, who 'agreed in principle with the policy' and suggested an area of his archdiocese where an amalgamation might be viable.[104] Lemass replied immediately to Colley's memorandum on 25 September 1965, fully supporting the case for the policy of amalgamation. He assured Colley that: 'I think the arguments in favour of your policy in this regard, as set out in the Memorandum, will be seen to be very convincing by all reasonable people'.[105] But Lemass also told the Minister that the case for larger central schools had not yet been 'sufficiently publicised', warning Colley to make a series of speeches in the near future to promote public understanding of the new policy.[106] Colley readily agreed that it was vital to publicise the case for amalgamation: he soon vigorously defended the new policy in a speech delivered at Ballinrobe, County Mayo, on 11 November 1965.[107] Lemass was concerned to promote public support for a radical educational reform, which soon proved highly controversial.

The initiative was opposed by local interests in many areas and by several members of the Catholic hierarchy, notably Dr Michael Browne, Bishop of Galway, who emerged as the principal spokesman of the opposition to the policy of amalgamation. The Catholic Bishops expressed 'their deep concern and anxiety' about the rapid introduction of the policy on 12 October 1965 and urged Colley to decide the case of each school on its merits.[108] Although the hierarchy did not oppose amalgamation in principle, Colley's policy change soon ignited a storm of controversy, which culminated in a public clash between the Minister and Dr Browne in February 1966. Following an address by Colley to the graduates of the National University of Ireland in Galway on 5 February 1966, Browne roundly denounced the new policy as 'a catastrophe – a major calamity for our Irish countryside' and claimed that the Minister's attempt to close small national schools was 'illegal and unconstitutional'.[109] Colley responded forcefully, immediately rebutting Browne's criticisms and strongly defending the right of the Minister for Education to initiate and manage policy reform.[110] Despite the severe criticisms levelled at Colley by

Browne and other opponents of the new policy, including Fine Gael TDs such as Oliver J. Flanagan, the government remained firmly committed to the reorganisation of primary education.[111] The controversial policy of amalgamation could not have been implemented without the full support of the Taoiseach for Colley's reforming approach. Lemass had fully endorsed the Minister's initiative and indeed correctly advised Colley to secure wider public support for the policy as a matter of urgency. The closure of small national schools proceeded rapidly, so that between 1966 and 1973 the number of one-teacher and two-teacher schools was reduced by about 1,100.[112] The policy of amalgamation represented a radical reorganisation of primary education, which would not have occurred without Lemass's unequivocal endorsement of the controversial initiative at an early stage.

The Taoiseach elaborated on the government's commitment to educational expansion, in the course of a general policy statement, which he delivered to the Dáil on 7 July 1966. Lemass argued that the state had to compensate for its limited resources by 'the fullest and most economical use of the resources which are available': this required the concentration of the available resources on the development of educational and technical training arrangements to utilise 'our main assets, the intelligence and adaptability of our people'.[113] He emphasised that the future economic development of the country would depend on enhancing the level of education and training secured by the Irish workforce. Lemass therefore pledged that the government would give educational development 'the priority it deserves' in the future allocation of public funds.[114] He commented that: 'To an ever-increasing degree the policy of the government will be directed to this end and we will have to endure the political criticisms which it may evoke from the unthinking as other desirable developments are necessarily slowed down to enable this essential educational programme to be fulfilled.'[115] Lemass's statement clearly established that the government would give precedence to education in the allocation of public expenditure. His commitment to give priority to education in the allocation of scarce national resources reflected the importance attached by the Irish state to educational expansion by 1966, which marked a fundamental change from the state's previous conservative policy approach. His approach provided the political context for the announcement by Colley's successor, Donogh O'Malley, of free post-primary education.

Lemass appointed O'Malley as Minister for Education on 13 July 1966. O'Malley, like his predecessor, soon proved to be a radical reforming minister. Lemass was, however, considerably less supportive of O'Malley's forceful efforts to promote rapid educational advances than he had been towards the more measured initiatives taken by the Minister's predecessors. O'Malley first proposed the introduction of some form of free post-primary education at a meeting with the Taoiseach on 7 September 1966.[116] The new Minister addressed a letter to Lemass, marked 'Personal – By Hand', immediately in advance of the meeting, enclosing a memorandum on free post-primary education.[117] The memorandum outlined two preliminary options, Scheme A and Scheme B, for the introduction of free post-primary education.[118] O'Malley told Lemass that he hoped, in a forthcoming speech, 'to make a general reference – without going into details – to some of the matters referred to in this Memorandum, should you so approve'.[119] The Minister warned Lemass that Fine Gael was about to launch its plan for education and emphasised the importance of pre-empting the largest opposition party with a policy announcement by the government.[120] Lemass's immediate response was not recorded in writing and O'Malley presented no definite scheme to the Taoiseach. The Minister's determination to pursue his initiative had the most profound repercussions for Irish education. On 10 September 1966 O'Malley announced at a weekend seminar of the National Union of Journalists in Dún Laoghaire that the state would introduce free post-primary education up to the end of the Intermediate Certificate course.[121] He emphasised that 17,000 primary school pupils, almost one third of the total age cohort, left school without receiving any post-primary education and were relegated to the category of unskilled labourers: 'This is a dark stain on the national conscience'.[122] O'Malley therefore announced that 'I am drawing up a scheme under which, in future, no boy or girl in this State will be deprived of full educational opportunity – from primary to university level – by reason of the fact that the parents cannot afford to pay for it.'[123] The Minister's announcement marked a dramatic new departure in the state's policy, which would have profound significance for the expansion of Irish education.

O'Malley evidently arranged the timing of his dramatic policy announcement to secure the maximum effect, not least in terms of favourable publicity by the media.[124] It is equally evident that the Minister acted to pre-empt critical consideration by the government of his far-reaching proposals. O'Malley's initiative was publicly announced without any consultation with the Department of Finance or the government as a whole. T. K. Whitaker reacted furiously to the announcement, complaining directly to Lemass on 12 September about O'Malley's disregard for official procedures: 'It is astonishing that a major change in educational policy should be announced by the Minister for Education at a weekend seminar of the National Union of Journalists.'[125] He asserted that such unauthorised announcements by Ministers would cause 'the negation of planning' and would make the development of national programmes 'increasingly futile'.[126] The Minister had also acted without the approval of the Taoiseach, although O'Malley subsequently claimed to have secured Lemass's support for his initiative at the meeting on 7 September.[127] This contention is clearly implausible. The Minister had presented only preliminary options, not a specific and definite proposal for approval, to the Taoiseach on 7 September. Moreover Lemass issued a definite rebuke to O'Malley on 12 September, bluntly warning the Minister that his announcement did not constitute a policy commitment by the government to any scheme advanced by O'Malley: the Minister's plans would be subjected to 'meticulous examination' by the Department of Finance and considered by the government in accordance with normal procedures.[128] Lemass pointedly observed that if other Ministers 'were to seek to commit the government, by making speeches about their intentions in advance of government approval of their plans, everything would become chaotic'.[129] The Taoiseach was sufficiently disturbed by O'Malley's unilateral initiative to issue a definite warning to the Minister, requiring closer adherence to government procedures in future.

Lemass's warning did not deter O'Malley, who replied on 14 September that it would have been 'disastrous' if Fine Gael was allowed to take the initiative on education: he also commented on the 'unprecedented' favourable response by the public to his initiative and hoped that Lemass would support him in getting his plans approved by the government.[130] The Taoiseach was, however, not only unhappy with O'Malley's attempt to circumvent normal government procedures but uneasy about the cost of the Minister's proposals. The Minister for Finance, Jack Lynch, raised O'Malley's announcement with Lemass on 21 September: the Taoiseach addressed another warning letter to O'Malley on the following day, conveying Lynch's 'grave concern' about the financial implications of the proposed scheme.[131] Lemass told O'Malley that 'any new proposals, even in the field of education, must be framed with strict regard to financial possibilities'.[132] He forcefully warned the Minister of the need to submit his proposals for consideration by the government, 'before any further public statement is made about them'.[133] Lemass did not oppose the proposals for free post-primary education in principle, but was concerned at the potential cost of the scheme and was clearly determined to ensure that O'Malley adhered to normal procedures in future.

Lemass intervened again in October to guarantee a measured consideration of O'Malley's plans by the government. The formidable Minister requested the government on 14 October 1966 to approve a memorandum concerning free post-primary education as a matter of urgency.[134] The memorandum proposed a wide-ranging scheme of free post-primary education, which involved various provisions to make free tuition available to all pupils in post-primary schools up to the end of the Leaving Certificate course: the proposal included a scheme of financial assistance to poor children for the purchase of school books. O'Malley also proposed the introduction of a scheme of state grants at university level for the first time.[135] He attached an urgency certificate to the memorandum which stipulated that 'the Minister requires decision before the television debate on Education' scheduled for 21 October.[136] Lemass acted rapidly to block this attempt to secure approval of a far-reaching and controversial reform, within a week of its submission to the government. He wrote to O'Malley on 17 October 1966, informing him that it would be 'unreasonable' to expect the government to consider his proposals without following the full cabinet procedure, including a detailed assessment of the scheme by the Department of Finance: it was also 'very improbable' that other Ministers would readily agree to the proposals, which involved additional expenditure of £3 million on education in 1968.[137] Lemass advised O'Malley that, 'You should therefore consider what it may be possible to achieve in the next few years in the post-primary education sphere at a lower cost.'[138] The Taoiseach was concerned about the scale and cost of O'Malley's plans, as well as the Minister's penchant for short-circuiting normal government procedures. As a result of Lemass's intervention, consideration of the Minister's memorandum was postponed until November. The Department of Education prepared a revised proposal, which was circulated to the government on 11 November 1966, the day after Lemass's retirement as Taoiseach.[139] Lemass's reservations about O'Malley's proposals did not indicate any retreat from the government's established policy of giving priority to education in the allocation of state expenditure. Lemass endorsed a request by O'Malley for a reassessment of the capital allocation for Education in 1967–8. O'Malley argued vehemently on 14 September that the allocation, which had been limited to £6 million by a cabinet committee, was entirely inadequate: he appealed to Lemass that it was 'unthinkable' to clamp down on national school building.[140] The Taoiseach agreed on 22 September to ensure that the capital provision for education would be reconsidered by the committee, with a view to increasing it.[141] Lemass remained committed to giving priority to educational expansion, especially with regard to capital investment, although he showed no inclination to give O'Malley unlimited scope to introduce free post-primary education.

Jack Lynch's first government, subject to several conditions sought largely by the Department of Finance, approved most of the revised proposals submitted by O'Malley. The cabinet approved the scheme for free post-primary education on 29 November 1966.[142] It appears, however, that Lynch's government shared Lemass's caution about the scheme. The conditions attached to the new scheme significantly modified the terms of O'Malley's original proposals. Certainly the government approved the scheme for free tuition in post-primary schools up to the Leaving Certificate, along with a new national scheme for free school transport to be provided by the state.[143] But the Minister's proposal for a scheme of higher education grants was not approved in November 1966 and the Cabinet did not agree a means-tested scheme until February 1968. Moreover a maintenance allowance proposed by O'Malley to subsidise 'very poor' pupils, which was designed to encourage the children of welfare recipients to remain in full-time education, was deferred by the cabinet for 'further consideration' and never implemented.[144] Despite its limitations, the scheme for free post-primary education was undeniably a landmark reform in Irish education, marking a decisive intervention by the state to transform educational participation at the post-primary level. Lemass, who sought to restrain O'Malley's individualistic approach to policy making, was cautious about the scope and content of the free education initiative. His caution was not surprising, as O'Malley had initiated a radical change in the government's educational policy, following only limited consultation, even with the Taoiseach. It was, however, Lemass more than any other political figure who created the conditions necessary for the achievement of free post-primary education. O'Malley's initiative made rapid progress at least in part because education had already been identified as the most urgent national priority in the allocation of scarce resources by Lemass himself. Moreover Lemass and Hillery established for the first time a coherent and definite role for the state in directing the expansion of the educational system, paving the way for more radical reforms. Even such a formidable political figure as O'Malley would have faced insurmountable obstacles if Lemass had not vigorously promoted educational reform and expansion throughout his term as Taoiseach.

The adoption by Lemass's government in 1959 of a definite policy for the gradual expansion of the educational system marked the first serious attempt by the Irish state to promote the expansion of post-primary education. Lemass not only provided essential support for initiatives proposed by the ministers or officials of the Department of Education, but often acted decisively to facilitate educational reforms. The Taoiseach approved the initiation of the Investment in Education study, which provided a road map for radical reform in Irish education. The launch of the comprehensive schools plan by Hillery in May 1963 owed much to Lemass's skilful promotion of the initiative within the government. Lemass both shared and helped to encourage the growing conviction, which took hold among Irish political elites in the early 1960s, that education made an invaluable contribution to economic development. This was a consensus fostered by Lemass at least from 1962 and it found clear expression in the Second Programme for Economic Expansion. The Taoiseach was concerned to build political support for controversial reforms, such as the amalgamation of small primary schools, which were designed to achieve a more systematic co-ordination of Irish education. Lemass's cautious approach to the provision of free post-primary education was underlined by his efforts to prevent O'Malley from circumventing government procedures; but the introduction of the scheme for free post-primary education was possible only because Lemass had made education a key national priority. Lemass's vigorous advocacy of long-term educational planning and his decision to give priority to education in the allocation of national resources shaped the political context for the reforms of the period.

CHAPTER TEN

A semi-state in all but name?
Seán Lemass's film policy

RODDY FLYNN

—

From 1937 until he succeeded Eamon de Valera as Taoiseach, Seán Lemass doggedly pursued, if not an Irish film industry, then at least a film industry in Ireland. Indeed there is some evidence that he continued to exercise a discreet but significant influence on film policy after 1959. This is not an aspect of Lemass's policy making which has received much attention. Film policy is not mentioned in the biographies by John Horgan, Michael O'Sullivan or Brian Farrell, nor does it merit a reference in Bew and Patterson's 1982 study. This is scarcely surprising: film is usually understood as coming under the rubric of 'cultural policy', not something commonly associated with Lemass, his involvement with the foundation of RTÉ notwithstanding. In any case, one might reasonably ask what point there is in studying a policy which, on the face of it, bore little fruit in the face of opposition from successive opposite numbers at the Department of Finance. Nonetheless the policy is worth considering because the nature of the film industry forced Lemass to consider an approach to film policy which presaged the turn to an open economy and foreign direct investment of the late 1950s. As this chapter will argue Lemass primarily understood cinema not as a cultural activity but as an industrial one.[1] Furthermore, this chapter also suggests that Lemass's labours to establish a film industry in Ireland may have been much more successful than was ever publicly acknowledged. Indeed it is arguable that a key element of the infrastructure underpinning the development of an Irish film industry in the 1990s would not exist but for Lemass's exertions forty years earlier.

As Minister for Industry and Commerce, Lemass was forced to grapple with film policy whether he liked it or not: the department was receiving proposals to establish a film studio at least as early as 1928.[2] However, the beginning of an explicit Lemass film policy dates from February 1937. In that month, de Valera received an unsolicited memo from one Eric Boden, a representative of the Hospitals Trust in the USA, outlining a detailed scheme for establishing an Irish film industry.[3] De Valera passed it to Lemass who sought the considered assessment of his own civil servants. The response was mixed. Some accepted the value of the proposal in the abstract:

> Nobody will dispute . . . the value of the Cinema as a form of entertainment or its potentialities as a medium for the promotion of education, the spread of culture and the dissemination of national ideals nor can there be any question that it is very desirable if economically possible to have an Irish film studio established.[4]

However, the financial prospects for an Irish film industry were considered very limited. The poor health of the contemporary British film industry (despite a domestic market much larger than Ireland's) was cited as proving that there was 'absolutely no hope of creating a large scale film industry in this country'[5] unless 'some large-scale American company' took an interest 'in the possibility of establishing a studio here'.[6] Failing that:

> One seems to be forced to the conclusion that if the industry is to be established here it can only be done with the assistance – and a very large measure of assistance – of the Government.[7]

Summarising his colleagues' thoughts on the matter, the ever-cautious secretary of the department, John Leydon, informed Lemass that, 'the prospect of establishing the industry on a healthy basis in this country is extremely remote. . . . I do not myself think that the stage has been reached when such a scheme should be seriously considered.'[8] Lemass, however, was more sanguine about the prospects for an industry and, in this respect, it is worth noting the passing reference above to American involvement. As would later emerge, for Lemass, the possibility of attracting foreign film capital to Ireland and state funding of the sector were not necessarily mutually exclusive options. Consequently Lemass dismissed Leydon's pessimism:

> The growing importance of this industry from many viewpoints is such that I think a detailed examination of the difficulties of its establishment should be undertaken before an adverse conclusion is reached. Please arrange for the setting up of a committee on the subject . . .'[9]

The reference to the importance of the film industry from 'many viewpoints' was somewhat vague – perhaps deliberately so. Over the course of the next two decades Lemass would cite national, cultural, social and economic concerns to justify the need for a film industry. Which of these concerns was stressed at any given moment in time varied according to his audience: the major challenge for the student of Lemass's film policy is to separate his real from his stated motivations.

Lemass's response to Leydon may well have been an example of this kind of dissimulation, since it appears his interest in film was piqued not by any manifest evidence of the industry's growing importance but by a fear that if Industry and Commerce was not driving film policy in Ireland then other agendas might. Specifically, in April 1937 – after the submission of the Boden proposal but before Leydon completed his assessment of it – the Jesuit priest Father Richard S. Devane began a campaign for the establishment of an official enquiry on the relation of film to the life of the nation. In a letter to the *Irish Press* on 8 April 1937 Devane argued that

> The sooner the enquiry is set up the sooner we shall advance towards the position of regarding the cinema, not as something suspect or as an enemy, but as a powerful instrument in the cultural development of our people.[10]

In an article written for the *Irish Press* four days later Devane tentatively suggested the following terms of reference:

> To enquire into the whole problem of the cinema in its various relations to national life, culture, education, agriculture, industry, film production and film distribution; furthermore, to examine into the best means of establishing central State control through a National Film Institute and to report accordingly.[11]

Finally, on 22 April, Devane, citing 'developing' public opinion, wrote to de Valera seeking a meeting with a view to pursuing the idea of an enquiry. Notwithstanding the progressive tone of Devane's proposal it is reasonable to conclude that Lemass viewed the priest's motives with some suspicion. Although the two never clashed directly, Lemass was not overly sympathetic with Devane's conservatism. Nearly a decade earlier, when 'the rhetoric and tactics' of Devanes's Irish Vigilance Association created the context for the 1929 Censorship of Publications Bill, Lemass had expressed 'measured reservations' about the bill, warning of the danger of going too far with censorship and arguing that 'public morality' was not a concept that should be treated of in the bill.[12]

Hence when in May 1937, as a precursor to meeting Devane, de Valera invited input from a range of departments on the cinema industry in the Saorstat, Industry and Commerce moved to stake a definitive claim on cinema as their 'territory'. The department's response stressed that it had been considering the establishment of a film-production unit 'for some time' and politely suggested that any response to Devane should wait until after a Lemass-appointed committee had reported. However, even if initially prompted by the need to head off Devane (and there is little in the available National Archive documents to support the assertion that Lemass or his officials had long been exercised by the question of a film industry), the considered nature of the Industry and Commerce response suggests that Lemass was now taking the industry seriously. Noting that although the £200,000 per annum taken at Irish cinemas meant the industry was quite small, the Industry and Commerce response to De Valera stated that

> it was hoped that this market might be sufficiently attractive to induce an experienced firm to submit proposals for the financing, erection, and equipment of a film studio in the ordinary way of private enterprise; the erection of a studio – at a possible cost of £150,000 to £180,000 – would be the first essential step towards the establishment of a motion-picture industry. It would, however, now appear that this expectation will not be fulfilled and that if the industry is to be launched and adapted to the national cultural and educational outlook of the country it can only be done as a State or semi-State undertaking.[13]

The Industry and Commerce memo stressed that economics entered very largely into the consideration and pointed out that the Irish market was a relatively small one, which could not possibly hope to support a native film industry without an export market. Furthermore it alluded to the fact that in Britain, where capital of about £50,000,000 was invested in cinema, the industry was in a very precarious condition, due to the limited size of the home market and to the failure of the English film industry to find a firm footing in the American market. The minute concluded that for Lemass, cinema was of growing importance and that a full examination should be made of all the difficulties standing in the way of a national film-production enterprise. This could best be investigated in the first instance by a small inter-departmental committee composed of representatives of Lemass's department, Finance,

Education and Justice. Their report should be awaited before any further examination of the question was undertaken.

The response is worth considering in the light of Lemass's overall industrial policy in the late 1930s. Firstly the 'experienced firm', which it was hoped would establish the studio, must, by definition, have referred to an overseas firm since there was no indigenous company even approaching that description. In this regard, John Horgan comments that Lemass's adherence to the economic doctrine of protectionism was conditioned by pragmatism – where an industry did not exist Lemass was not averse to actively courting foreign firms to establish in Ireland, even to the extent of promising exclusivity (i.e. a monopoly) within the Irish market.[14] Secondly, however, the reference to a putative semi-state undertaking suggests that for Lemass the film industry represented another case where a failure of nerve on the part of private capital necessitated that the state step in to remedy the situation.

The first steps to appoint the inter-departmental committee referred to in the minute had commenced a fortnight earlier when John Leydon wrote to the secretary of the Department of Finance, J. J. McElligott, proposing the establishment of a committee to assess the feasibility and approximate cost of establishing a film industry and the extent, 'if any, to which, and the conditions, if any, upon which, financial or other assistance should be afforded to such industry by the State'.[15]

The Department of Finance's response to this was spectacularly negative. For Finance the case against a film industry in Ireland was so obvious that merely to enquire into the question was a waste of human and fiscal resources. In a minute to Leydon, McElligott pointed out that even if an industry producing 50 films per annum were established in Ireland this would make only a minor dent in the country's cinematic balance of payments deficit given that approximately 1,000 films were imported every year. He also pointed to the severe losses experienced by the UK industry notwithstanding its much greater financial resources concluding that:

> In the light of these facts the Minister cannot see how a film industry could operate here without sustaining heavy losses, which would have to be borne by the Exchequer.[16]

McElligott firmly rejected the establishment of the committee. The dismissive tone of the response clearly irked Lemass:

The Department of Finance minute purports to be an answer to the question, or one of the questions, which the proposed committee was to examine. We are not trying to make a 'prima facie case' for the establishment of the film industry but to have examined whether it is practicable, and if so on what lines, and what are the advantages and disadvantages etc . . . There is no case which can be made against an enquiry directed to these aims. Please reply to Department Finance accordingly and say that I must insist on this committee being set up.[17]

Following Lemass's bidding, Leydon instigated a lengthy exchange of letters between the departments in which he and other Industry and Commerce officers repeatedly sought Finance's sanction of (and participation in) such a committee. The rationale for the committee underwent a subtle alteration in these letters, however, with Industry and Commerce stating:

It was, perhaps, not made sufficiently clear in our official minute that we were not as a Department desirous of making a case for the establishment of the industry but wished to have as much information as possible made available in the form of a considered report. Assuming even, that the report contained sufficient evidence that it was not possible, except at an unreasonable cost to State funds, to carry on film production in the Saorstat, it was felt that this would have the useful effect, at least, of enabling the Department to deal with the series of proposals which have been for several years past put to the Department from time to time.[18]

In effect this appeared to reverse Lemass's original rationale. Far from creating a potential basis from which to create a film industry, Industry and Commerce was now arguing that the committee was to gather information that would establish an authoritative basis on which the department could assess (and implicitly reject) the stream of film industry-related proposals it intermittently received. It is difficult to square this with the reference to the possible need for state intervention in the department's earlier minute to de Valera. After all, why mention such a possibility if such an active intervention was not even on the agenda? Given this, the portrayal of the committee as a disinterested information gathering exercise appears somewhat mendacious.

Nonetheless it worked; after a few more iterations Finance acceded to the committee's establishment and by January 1938 had agreed an outline terms of reference with Industry and Commerce. Still suspicious of Lemass's intentions, however, the agreement of the Minister of Finance, Seán MacEntee, was conditional on the understanding that the committee report would remain confidential and would be used purely for the information of ministers and for departmental guidance. The committee was formed by civil servants from Industry and Commerce (who provided both the chairman and secretary), Education and Finance. As such, it hardly constituted experts in the field of the cinema. In June 1939, Leydon wrote to McElligott seeking sanction for trips to observe the workings of British studios in London and to Killarney to examine the operation of the only extant (albeit small-scale) studio facility in Ireland.[19] Noting with regard to exhibition and distribution that the committee had already 'acquired a fairly intimate knowledge of these spheres of activity' Leydon admitted that the same could not be said of production:

> In this connection it may be stated that no member of the Committee has ever been inside a film studio, and, without a clear conception of what a film studio is like and some insight into the problem of production, any conclusion the Committee . . . will have on the feasibility of establishing a film industry in Ireland must necessarily be restricted.[20]

Hence the request (to which Finance largely acceded) to sanction the London trip.[21] The trip was scheduled to begin on 11 September, but the outbreak of war saw the visit indefinitely postponed. Although by October 1940 Industry and Commerce stated that 'on account of conditions arising out of the emergency', it had become necessary to 'suspend almost entirely'[22] the committee's activities, in practice it continued to work in fits and starts until March 1942 when it submitted a final draft report to Lemass. The report offered some interesting conclusions on exhibition, distribution and censorship of films in Ireland, but its comments on production are of greatest relevance to the current chapter. It commenced by burying the old canard that 'climatic conditions' would render impossible the establishment of an industry in Ireland, noting that technical advances had eliminated such problems 'if such difficulty ever existed'. Instead it pointed out that the main difficulty in establishing an Irish production sector was 'entirely an economic one'. It continued:

> The establishment of an organisation for the regular production of full-length films would involve an expenditure out of all proportion to the revenue which could be expected from our limited market. Apart from initial capital expenditure, the normal cost of producing a feature film of the less expensive kind is from £20,000 to £30,000. The maximum revenue that can be expected from

the distribution of a successful film in this country is from £3,000 to £4,000. From this it is clear that the Irish market alone would be unable to support a major film industry.[23]

This obviously led to considerations of the prospect of securing distribution for any potential Irish films overseas, especially in those countries such as the USA with a substantial Irish population. Yet here again the committee was pessimistic:

> In the United States competition is so keen and the market dominated to such an extent by the big Hollywood producer-renter-exhibitor trusts that the possibility of gaining a secure footing in that market is slight. In other countries, besides competition from Hollywood interests, opposition would be encountered from organisations endeavouring with Government support to develop a native film industry.

Nonetheless the committee suggested persuading US film distributors in Ireland to acquire one or two Irish features per annum 'in return for their Irish business', i.e. making a thinly veiled threat to introduce restrictions on US film imports if the distributors failed to play ball. (Although the committee also hinted darkly that given the small scale of the Irish market, US distributors might respond to such blackmail by simply withdrawing from the Irish market altogether.)

Moving on the committee pointed out that with the exception of the Killarney enterprise there was no studio in the country, nor any company regularly producing films on any scale. In this regard it noted that the situation was scarcely aided by the existing incentives to film in Ireland: these were limited to provisions in the 1932 Finance (Customs Duties) Act which allowed the duty free import of both films produced by Irish residents and featuring Irish-resident actors and of films produced mainly in Ireland and which employed a majority of Irish artistes. Since such concessions had proved inadequate to encourage the establishment of a film industry in Ireland, the committee concluded that more substantial state aid was required: the first step 'would be the setting up of a State film studio'. The scale of studio envisaged by the committee was – particularly in light of later moves by Lemass – modest. The committee opined that the building and equipping of a small but up-to-date studio would cost 'at least £25,000' plus a further £8,000 per annum in operating costs. Noting that it would be 'impracticable to charge the full costs of maintenance to the few producers who might be expected to make use of the studio in its early years', the committee conceded that government assistance would be necessary for 'an indefinite period'. They concluded, 'The erection of a studio, therefore, would be to a very large extent, speculative.'

Such was the small scale of any studio envisaged by the committee that their report gave serious consideration to the prospect of simply upgrading the existing Killarney facility which could be achieved for a more moderate sum than building a new studio. The committee argued that a single efficient studio could amply cope with any likely demand for such facilities 'for some considerable time' and thus recommended that 'in order to avoid uneconomic competition' it would be necessary to 'control the establishment of studios'. Finally the committee noted that whether the state supported the building of a studio or not, actual production of films by native enterprise would require financial stimulus from the state, specifically: 'grants representing a partial reimbursement of production costs'. They continued:

> Owing to the difficulty of securing adequate outside distribution, a native Irish film producing industry would be obliged, in the beginning at least, to depend solely on the home market. It might be possible for such an industry to produce an occasional full-length film of an inexpensive kind but the main scope of production would be confined to short films. A native film industry could never hope to replace to any large extent imported films by native films. Apart from an occasional full-length film its scope would be restricted to the production of short films and to films for education, industrial, agricultural tourist and general propaganda purposes. Its prospects of ever becoming self-supporting would depend on the extent to which a foreign market could be secured, and while this would depend to some degree on the quality, artistic merit and general appeal of the productions, *other obstacles in the way are so great that it would be wise in considering the question of the establishment of a small-scale film industry to proceed on the assumption that its products would seldom procure exhibition outside the country. The greater portion of the cost of films produced in this country would in these circumstances have to be met from public funds.*[24] (Italics added)

In sum, the committee concluded: first, that to be financially viable an Irish film industry would need to access export markets. Second, this would be virtually impossible given the oligopolistic nature of the US market and the protectionist nature of other national markets. Therefore any hypothetical

Irish production sector would necessarily be small-scale and probably state-subsidised.

On the face of it these were hardly encouraging conclusions for Lemass. In effect the report confirmed what Lemass's own civil servants and the Department of Finance had long asserted – that even with the protection of the Control of Manufactures Acts there was no prospect of establishing an economically viable Irish film industry since the domestic market could never be self-sustaining. In the event this conclusion did not deter Lemass but it prompted him to engage in some lateral thinking about the problem: namely, if an indigenous film industry was impossible, were there any alternative means by which film-making activity in Ireland might be encouraged? While he pondered this question, Lemass took a strategic decision to park the report lest its gloomy conclusions be seized upon by others (in particular Finance) as definitively closing the question. The report would remain largely mothballed until Lemass was 'in a position to put forward recommendations as to action on the lines of the report'.[25] This stasis continued through 1943 and 1944 despite several frustrated public and Dáil requests as to what action would follow the completion of the report. However, in the early months of 1945, a memo to Lemass from the acting secretary of the Department of Industry and Commerce, R. C. Ferguson and Lemass's response to that memo inaugurated a new approach to the film industry, which would ultimately lead to the drafting of a Film Production Facilities Bill in 1946.

Ferguson's memorandum was prompted by an application from a group styling itself National Film Studios Ltd, which proposed to produce newsreels for the Irish market. To facilitate this the company sought a guarantee of £5000 under the 1944 Trade Loans Act with a view to purchasing the Killarney studios. In assessing the application Ferguson surmised that the application was effectively a tacit request for an official state imprimatur for their activities:

> It is because of this element of securing official approval, amongst other reasons, that I think the whole question of policy in respect of the film industry ought to be considered now.[26]

Ferguson noted that the small scale of the National Film Studios Ltd proposal meant that it was unlikely to succeed in the absence of quota protection but argued that the institution of a quota 'when a small-scale affair like this is all we have to depend on' was 'hardly . . . attractive'. Instead he submitted that:

a better beginning for a national film policy would be made by the formation of a Government Company to build and run a modern, fairly large-scale, studio. If this step were taken such a Company would simply rent the studio on such terms as would service the capital involved. There should be little risk of losing money as the rental for the studio should be ample, without crippling those who might make use of it for the production of films. I think the establishment of a National Film Studio in this way, open to be rented by any firm desiring to produce a film, would be a solid and useful beginning for a national film industry.

Ferguson expressed the expectation that such a studio would be used for the production of newsreels and shorts but also:

> For the first years . . . it would be well to allow the studio to be rented, when it was free, by external companies, whether *American, British or other*, for the production of films . . . The example of *some competent external producing Company* using the studio for the production of a film here would, undoubtedly, lead to the creation of an interest in production amongst Irish Companies or groups.[27] (Italics added)

Ferguson's comments are significant because, hitherto, film policy had assumed as an objective the creation of a native film industry. In effect Ferguson's memo subordinated this to the main goal of simply encouraging film production in Ireland. Lemass's reply clearly signalled his approval of this direction. He agreed that if anything was to be done to facilitate the production of films in Ireland, it had to be done on the right lines and on an adequate scale, and that it would be bad policy to enter into any commitment at this stage to a private group proposing a small-scale project with second-hand plant:

> I think the idea of a national film studio deserves consideration in detail. There is, first, the question of direction. Can we secure competent persons to direct such an enterprise? Second, what field is open to it? *I have very little hope of ordinary entertainment films produced in this country by local enterprise finding an international market and doubt if such films could be a commercial proposition in any circumstances.* Conceivably, the Government might consider the matter of a subsidy for an attractive proposition, either one film or a series, but if so it would be a separate matter, and the proposed national film studio would need to have some prospect of regular business independently of any such special enterprise . . . What I wish to have examined is (1) the organisation required

(2) the probable cost of constructing and equipping such a studio and (3) some estimate of the business which may be available to it.[28] (Italics added)

In consequence, over the course of 1946 and 1947 Lemass's department prepared a series of memos to cabinet proposing the establishment of a National Film Studio. Indeed the department went to so far as attach a draft piece of legislation – the Films (Production Facilities) Bill, 1946 – to enact these proposals. Citing the 'national, cultural, social and economic significance of the cinema, the increasing public attention given to films and the various proposals which have been received in his Department on the subject' the first of these memos (dating from April 1946), argued that film production in Ireland would best be facilitated by providing studio and laboratory facilities. Thus Lemass proposed creating a statutory company to establish and run such facilities. He was at pains to stress that this company would not engage in actual film production:

> its main function would be to manage the National Film Studio facilities and to make them available on contract to approved concerns, domestic and foreign, desiring to produce films in this country.[29]

In effect the Irish state would not directly fund the making of films but – in a manner which anticipated the 1970s IDA policy of building advance factories – would create a facility to encourage private capital (film producers) to invest in film-making activity in Ireland. That these producers would come from outside Ireland was obvious as soon as Lemass outlined the scale of the proposed studios. Working on the basis that they were assessing the needs of a native industry, the report of the inter-departmental committee on the film industry had envisaged spending no more than £25,000 on a studio. The National Film Studios Ltd consortium planned on spending £50,000 on a one-stage studio and a laboratory 'for the production of Irish newsreels, documentaries and short pictures, with two or three longer pictures a year'.[30] A November 1946 memo on a National Film Studio, however, stated that, 'the Minister does not consider that assistance to small-scale enterprises of this kind would provide facilities adequate for the country's requirements'.[31]

Thus, Lemass sought 'upwards of £250,000' (a figure that he revised upwards to £500,000 from October 1946 on) to build two sound stages, an administrative building and a laboratory. (In addition he estimated that the annual administrative costs of the studio would be in the region of £70,000.)

Although such a studio would 'be available for productions by native concerns' (specifically educational/propaganda films for central and local government and semi-states such as Aer Lingus, CIE, the ESB, the Irish Tourist Board etc.), it was 'primarily intended for the production of long films.' Lemass then explicitly identified the likely clients for the studios:

> There are good prospects that *British and American* organisations would be prepared to avail of facilities for the production of feature films in this country for a considerable time to come.[32]

In effect from this point onwards Lemass's film policy would be based on the assumption that the only way to establish a film industry in Ireland was to work around the conclusions spelled out in the 1942 report. If, de facto, the English-language distribution market was dominated by US and UK companies, then the most pragmatic means of creating film-making activity in Ireland was to attract film production companies from those countries. Thus the requirements for the creation of a film industry in Ireland required the provision of a studio which, while suitable for the production of short films mainly by native enterprise, would also be capable of accommodating larger-scale productions, undertaken mainly by foreign enterprises in the initial stage and only later by domestic concerns.

Adverting to films shot in Ireland by 'outside organisations' in the preceding years (including most notably Laurence Olivier's 1945 production of *Henry V*), Lemass noted that the bulk of their activity had been 'confined to the filming of exterior scenes and special settings'. Given this it was 'reasonable to suppose that a good deal more work would be carried out in the country by outside organisations if adequate studio facilities were available here'. Indeed he explicitly cited commitments to this effect from 'persons prominent in the film industry in England' including J. Arthur Rank.[33]

The already globalised nature of the film industry in 1945 in effect suggested to Lemass a solution to the problem of a film industry that anticipated by more than a decade the 'solution' to the more general malaise affecting the economy in the 1950s: the opening of the economy to foreign capital with a view to developing an export-oriented industry. Lemass's response to the pessimistic conclusion arrived at by his 1942 committee was to change the question from considering how one might go about establishing a native film industry to how one might position Ireland as a base for international film-makers. Ironically the idea may in part have been suggested by a reference in the inter-departmental committee report to a proposal from a 'large American film producing company' (later identified as Columbia Pictures) to undertake production in Ireland 'in anticipation of production difficulties in Great Britain during the War'.[34] Such international prospects could not realistically be pursued whilst the war was still in progress – hence the temporary sidelining of the question after the publication of the committee report – but in the post-war era Lemass actively embraced a series of proposals from international filmmakers.

Typical of these was an approach made by producer Gabriel Pascal in August 1946. Hungarian born but UK-based, Pascal had a working relationship with George Bernard Shaw, films of whose plays he proposed as the basis for an 'Irish National Picture Industry'. Pascal sought to convince the Irish government to establish a studio in Ireland either as a state-owned company or as an Industrial Credit Corporation-funded private enterprise. With such a studio built, Gabriel Pascal Irish Picture Productions would:

> devote itself to the production of pictures by famous authors and produced and directed on an International scale so as to command a world market. In particular it would be devoted to the production of the works of Mr. George Bernard Shaw . . . *The general conception would be to produce pictures for the international market.*[35] (Italics added)

When, in October 1946, Pascal arrived in Ireland reporting that he had secured film-making equipment for a studio in Ireland, Lemass finally submitted to de Valera the (hitherto internal to Industry and Commerce) proposal for the establishment of a National Film Studio and a draft Film (Production Facilities) Bill. Although in the accompanying letter Lemass was at pains to stress that he had not overtly encouraged Pascal to seek such equipment he also noted that Pascal's association with the proposed National Film Studios raised the prospect of

> a long term arrangement for the renting of the facilities to be provided and the technical advice and assistance which he should be in a position to give in regard to the construction and equipment of such a studio.[36]

Lemass met Pascal in person on 17 October. At the meeting Pascal asked whether the government in fact intended to proceed with the establishment of a studio. Lemass stated that he was personally very interested in seeing a film producing company established in Ireland. He noted that many approaches had been made to him about the establishment of a film studio in Ireland by private interests, but that these had failed to materialise. Thus although he would prefer that such a studio be provided by private enterprise, it had been left to the state to take the initiative adding that 'it seemed likely that the Government would set up a statutory company to establish a studio'.[37] However, he also noted that the matter 'had not yet been finally determined by the Government and no substantial progress could be made until legislative authority to proceed had been obtained'.[38]

In fact the confidence that informed Lemass's talks with Pascal was not shared by the rest of the cabinet. Even his own department expressed doubts about the viability of the scheme.[39] But the most substantive critique of the proposals came from the Department of Finance headed by Frank Aiken. Pointing out that he was 'disposed in principle to the creation of a *native* film industry', Aiken was

> not convinced that a large scale studio would be continuously and economically employed during the next 5 to 10 years, and he considers that a smaller studio designed to deal with productions of the shorter types of films . . . would be more desirable.[40]

Accordingly he was more inclined to support a proposal along the lines of the 1942 report, with the caveat that 'an Irish film industry, of even the modest dimensions recommended by that Committee, would have little hope of financial success without a substantial foreign market; and the difficulties involved in the distribution of Irish film productions still have to be solved'. Just in case the point was not sufficiently explicit Aiken emphasised that:

> it would be most undesirable, nationally and culturally, that the shape and character of an Irish film industry should be determined on the basis of what might suit only the temporary requirements of wealthy foreign industrialists.[41]

Lemass's response to this was disarmingly honest: he conceded Aiken's point admitting that there was 'no definite assurance, nor even good grounds for expectation that the enterprise will be financially self-supporting'. However Lemass persisted that given 'the important nature of the project it is recommended as one for which the grant of financial aid from State funds is considered justified'.[42] There are two possible explanations for this response. On the one hand it is possible that Lemass considered the creation of a film industry so important from a cultural perspective that commercial considerations did not apply. Much more likely, however, given the rationale expressed else-where in the memos, is that Lemass assumed that possible losses on the studio investment would be more than offset by the net gain to the economy if overseas producers could be attracted to Ireland.

In any case faced with Aiken's refusal to sanction the half a million pound investment, Lemass was forced to formally submit his studio proposals to the Government in the hope that the cabinet as a whole would overrule Aiken. This was not to be. Apparently accepting Aiken's line, the cabinet quickly rejected the project at a meeting on 13 December 1946.[43] Never one to give up Lemass simply waited eight months and in August 1947 resubmitted the pro-posal to cabinet, albeit with one significant addition. Setting aside comments from Frank Aiken about the scarcity of money available to the state and the need to fund 'priority requirements of socially desirable projects such as those for houses, sanatoria and schools', Lemass actually sought more money:

> In order to encourage private enterprise it is proposed that the Minister for Industry and Commerce may . . . guarantee repayment of the principal of and payment of the interest on a loan proposed to be raised for the purpose of meeting a proportion of the cost of producing a film or films in the Studio.[44]

Lemass thus sought to allay concerns about the studio being under-utilised by offering to guarantee investments in film productions shot there. The cabinet duly considered the new submission on 16 September 1947. As far as Aiken was concerned nothing had changed. Predictably he noted 'the proposal for a system of guaranteed loans for the production of film in the studio renders the scheme even more objectionable from the financial point of view'.[45] The cabinet again decided not to proceed with plans for a National Film Studio although on this occasion a caveat was entered: 'Unless it becomes clear that there is no reason-able prospect of the establishment, through private enterprise, of a film studio, adequately financed and providing adequate facilities'.[46] With this second defeat of his proposals Lemass was forced to abandon active consideration of the film industry for a period, not least because of Fianna Fáil's defeat in the 1948 election. Nonetheless, the pro-FDI, export-oriented thrust of Lemass's 1946–7 proposals would remain the basis for his subsequent film policy.

While Lemass was in opposition, proposals relating to the establishment of film production or a related sector such as film processing continued to flood into Industry and Commerce. Most of these found their way to the Industrial Development Authority, which had been delegated 'all work in connection with the cinema industry'.[47] In May 1951, faced with a range of proposals to establish film laboratories, film equipment manufacturing, newsreel companies and indigenous production, the IDA initiated discussions with the film trade with a view to being able to make an informed assessment of these proposals.[48] These largely petered out after an inconclusive meeting with representatives of United States and United Kingdom distributors operating in Ireland. Nonetheless by the time Lemass regained the reins at Industry and Commerce a month later, there was a backlog of projects seeking state support for various aspects of film production. In consequence Lemass called a departmental conference on the subject in December 1951 and again in October 1953 to consider the proposals. The practical outcome of these conferences was negligible: for the most part they rehearsed the gloomy conclusion that feature production in Ireland was unlikely to be commercially viable. A civil service note prepared for the October 1953 conference noted with regard to the conclusions of the Inter-Departmental Committee in 1942 that:

> the remarks regarding the feasibility of full-length film production are fully vindicated by all the proposals which have come up in recent years . . . It is clear that production of full-length films cannot be undertaken economically here except in alliance with an external group who would ensure exhibition of Irish films abroad.[49]

By now, however, building such an alliance was the main focus of Lemass's film policy. Stating that 'on general principles' he favoured 'the setting up of a production unit to make short documentary films' he also stressed that he had not ruled out the possibility of having feature films made in Ireland. He specifically pointed to the tourist value of *The Quiet Man* which had been shot in Mayo three years earlier, adding that 'if other suitable films were made in Ireland, they would lead to an increase in the number of visitors'. Citing British state incentives for film-making he wondered 'whether some scheme could be devised under which foreign companies could be induced to make films in Ireland of Irish interest and background'. Describing himself as 'anxious that some scheme for promoting film production in Ireland' be devised he directed that 'consideration might proceed . . . on the lines indicated above'.[50] Indeed Lemass was willing to introduce such an incentive scheme even if it succeeded in attracting only a single major production company: in August 1951, representatives of Columbia Studios met with two departmental civil servants to outline a scheme whereby Columbia would make films in Ireland on condition that the state would meet 75 per cent of the production costs. In return, world-wide receipts from the films would be allocated 75 per cent to the state and 25 per cent to Columbia once costs of prints and distribution had been deducted.

Lemass had the proposal considered at a departmental conference. Although 'opposed to any scheme for the permanent financing of film production by the state',[51] the prospect of attracting a studio of Columbia's stature was sufficient for Lemass to declare himself prepared to recommend an initial government grant for the creation of a scheme on the lines of the Eady levy in the UK whereby 'a fund is maintained from exhibition rents for the financing of film production'.[52] Again, however, nothing came of the Columbia proposal. Apparently becoming frustrated with private capital Lemass had one further stab at encouraging the development of a film industry before the 1954 election. At a departmental conference on 12 April 1954, Lemass directed that a memo be drawn up outlining a proposal to establish a national film unit. With an eye to the earlier rejection of his studio proposals, the memo appeared to reverse Lemass's previous position stating that he now considered it, 'inadvisable to provide either a laboratory or a studio at present until production has reached a level to employ them economically'. Instead he now suggested (à la Frank Aiken) that:

> the most practical course in the setting up of a native film industry would be by means of a small beginning and to consider plans for future development in the light of experience. Accordingly . . . the Government should set up a national film company which would commence the production of documentaries and shorts on a limited scale.[53]

Lemass noted that initially at least (i.e. for the first five years of its existence) the company should not have any statutory standing, suggesting instead a limited liability company, financed directly by means of an annual grant-in-aid from the Department of Industry and Commerce's budget. Lemass identified as the immediate objects of the company the following: (a) to produce films, including films in Irish; (b) to encourage and co-ordinate film-making by other Irish producers; (c) to encourage the making of feature films in Ireland by outside organisations, and (d) to foster the general development of a film industry in Ireland.[54]

In addition he noted that:

> in discharge of its general obligation to develop the film industry, it would be the company's task to investigate and report to the Minister on the possibilities

of making, or inducing outside companies to make, feature films in Ireland, and on the possibilities of developing laboratory facilities, studios etc.[55]

In effect Lemass was suggesting a single institution that would undertake the not insubstantial functions of a production company, a national film board and a state screen commission. All of this would be funded by an initial capital outlay (on equipping a film unit with two production crews) of just £25,000 and annual outgoings of £35,000, which would largely be spent on the production of 12 films per annum. As such the proposal was, at best, disingenuous: while initially abandoning hopes of establishing a studio, it revived the prospect of just such an outcome in its latter stages.[56]

In the event Fianna Fáil's loss in the May 1954 election saw the proposal fall to the hands of Lemass's successor at Industry and Commerce, the Labour Party leader William Norton who deferred action on it. Norton could reasonably have done so on the grounds that the proposal was clearly impractical but officially it was sidelined in the light of the possibility that Four Provinces, a production company established by Lord Killanin with Tyrone Power and John Ford, might single-handedly form the basis for an Irish industry. Although the company did produce several features in Ireland after 1957, longer-term plans to establish a studio and laboratory were never realised. Despite this the Lemass proposal was effectively stalled at this point and Lemass himself would not directly revisit the idea on returning to Industry and Commerce in March 1957.[57] In any case, by the time Lemass returned to Kildare Street there was a much more attractive prospect in the air. On 6 January 1957 the *Sunday Independent* carried an interview with cinema owner and impresario Louis Elliman who was about to go into production on a 55 minute made-for-TV version of George Shiel's Abbey play *Professor Tim. Tim* was to be directed by Emmet Dalton, the former War of Independence hero, who had entered the film business in 1942 working with Paramount and the Samuel Goldwyn company before becoming an independent producer in 1955. *Tim* was to be produced under the auspices of Dublin Film and Television Productions Ltd of which Elliman and Dalton were directors. The two were joined on the board of a sister company – Dublin Film Productions Management Ltd – by Ernest Blythe, chairman of the Abbey.[58]

The relationship between these two companies (and Blythe's presence on the board of the latter) was explained by the fact that *Tim* was presented by Elliman as a 'pilot film to test the potentiality of the American market'. If *Tim* took off in the US, then the two companies would collaborate to produce film versions of a further 26 to 39 Abbey Plays. Dublin Film Productions Management Ltd would deal with the question of rights for the Abbey Plays and Dublin Films and TV Productions Ltd would actually shoot them. For the *Sunday Independent* it represented nothing less than the promise of 'the birth and growth of a new all-Irish film industry', provided the film was successful. However, Elliman also tantalisingly suggested that a successful foray into the US market would lead to a greater prize: the opening of a studio in Ireland to make TV films:

> This would be the first step towards the ultimate erection of a fully equipped film studio, with two stages, lighting, sound recording, etc. and its own technical crew. If such a studio were available as the basis of an Irish film industry, it is hoped that some of the major film companies would use it, and that the Government would use it for the making of propaganda films on health etc.[59]

By August 1957 Elliman and Dalton were apparently convinced that there was a US market for Irish-produced material. In that month they announced the acquisition of a site for a studio at Ardmore Place, Herbert Road in Bray, County Dublin. At a press launch, Elliman stated that their films would all have an Irish 'background', either in story content or 'in being the work of an Irish writer', suggesting that Ardmore would become 'a miniature Hollywood'.[60]

Industry and Commerce were well aware of these moves. At Norton's last departmental conference on the subject of film, it had been decided to defer any government action for six months pending developments in the intervening period. At Lemass's first departmental conference on the film industry in August 1957, these developments included the fact that Elliman and Dalton were now establishing a third company 'to be known as Ardmore Studios Ltd'. A memorandum on the development of the film industry in Ireland by the industries division of Industry and Commerce noted:

> The plans of the new studio company were discussed over the telephone with Mr Louis Elliman who said that it was intended that the studio would be available to all film producing companies in Ireland. Mr Elliman was very sanguine about the production of television films for the American and other markets.[61]

Specifically Elliman had made a deal with RKO Teleradio in New York to produce a series of Abbey plays as made-for-TV movies.[62] This apparent guarantee of regular work was the basis upon which Ardmore's construction was predicated, although an Industry and Commerce memo noted that the 'primary intention' in building the studios was to lease them 'to other film producers'.[63] Most intriguingly, however, the industries division memorandum continued:

> He [Elliman] said he had kept in close touch with the Minister in all that he was doing and that the Minister had been of great assistance to him. The Minister was already fully informed about his plans. He would be seeking further aid from the Minister.[64]

The impression gained here is that, unbeknownst to his own officials, Lemass had been communicating with Elliman. The nature of the assistance is unspecific here but was clearly significant. In any case the memo recommended that 'considerations for the setting up of a State-financed film organisation should be deferred pending development of the plans of the Elliman Group'.[65]

The studios were completed by March 1958 and the first film shot at Ardmore, an adaptation of Walter Macken's *Home is the Hero* began shooting there in April 1958. A month later Lemass officially presided over the opening of the studios. At the launch he described the enterprise as 'primarily aimed at the export market'. He continued that 'the aim of the company was to employ Irish staffs to the maximum extent and train them in the complex processes of the industry'. As a result, he added, when Elliman and Dalton had approached him, he had promised 'the greatest possible help the Department of Industry and Commerce could give them'. At the opening Elliman and Dalton were again at pains to describe the 'assistance' of the Department as 'absolutely invaluable' although they failed to specify the nature of that assistance.[66]

In retrospect it appears that the assistance was almost certainly financial. In an *Evening Press* article in June 1958, Kevin O'Kelly wrote:

> When he [Louis Elliman] and Emmet Dalton laid out a quarter of a million to build Ardmore, they may have wondered, as they signed the cheque, just how long it would take to get their money back.[67]

The irony is that – as would gradually emerge – for the most part it was not 'their' money at all. Ardmore's construction was initially budgeted at £161,000, but £45,000 of this was raised from an IDA grant.[68] Furthermore, it subsequently emerged that the Industrial Credit Corporation advanced a further £217,750 to Ardmore by way of debenture loan.[69] Some 'assistance' indeed: in effect, as a 1967 Industry and Commerce memo on Ardmore would ruefully admit, the state effectively bankrolled virtually the entire cost of building Ardmore. The absence of documentation about the funding decisions makes it hard to prove that Lemass had a hand in them but, given that both the ICC and IDA were very much creatures of Industry and Commerce, it would seem unlikely that Lemass was entirely out of the loop in allocating these funds.[70] The involvement of US studio, RKO, in the Abbey Plays would also have commended the project to the Minister. But the fact which most convincingly points to Lemass's involvement is the striking similarity of the Ardmore setup with that proposed by Lemass in his 1947 cabinet submission. This similarity lies not simply in the physical layout of the studio complex nor even the general business strategy of the studio – targeting overseas companies – but also in the fact that the establishment of the studios led indirectly to the practical realisation of Lemass's 1947 suggestion that the state should offers loans to encourage production companies to shoot at a National Film Studios.

This last similarity was not designed into the Ardmore scheme but came about as a result of changes in the operation of British Cinematograph Films Act of 1957. In promoting Ardmore, Elliman and Dalton assumed that Ardmore productions would avail themselves of UK Eady Levy Funding, a tax on all cinema seats in Great Britain, which was redistributed to the makers of registered British films. Prior to 1959 'a British registered film' included films made by Irish citizens or companies on the grounds that Ireland was legally considered a dominion within the Commonwealth. [71] Such generous (or imperialistic depending on your perspective) definitions had had no practical import before Ardmore's arrival, but on completion it immediately constituted competition for established British studios such as Pinewood and Elstree. Consequently in 1959 the British Board of Trade amended the operation of the levy limiting qualification to films made by UK residents or by companies registered, managed and controlled in the UK. The implications of this were identified in a letter from an official in Ireland's London embassy to C. A. Barry at Industry and Commerce:

> This would appear to mean that a film made in Ireland by a British citizen or a British company would, if shown afterwards in Great Britain, still qualify for a share of the Eady levy but a film made in Ireland by an Irish citizen or an Irish company would apparently not so qualify after the 1st January next.[72]

Within six weeks of the changes to the Eady Levy coming into effect, however, the Industrial Credit Company responded by establishing a subsidiary, the

Irish Film Finance Corporation Ltd. (IFFC) to 'consider applications from film producers in Ireland for financial assistance by way of loans'.[73]

As a later Department of Foreign Affairs minute would note, this was explicitly intended to shore up production at Ardmore:

> it became apparent that the absence in Ireland of an organisation to provide risk capital or 'end money' for producers wishing to make films at Ardmore Studios was proving a handicap to the full development and utilisation of the facilities at Ardmore.[74]

Thus, not only did the state build Ardmore but it also funded the films shot there; between 1960 and 1962, the IFFC would invest £385,000 of public funds into 15 films.[75] In effect, then, the combination of Ardmore and the operation of the IFFC saw Lemass's 1947 vision realised: and given the extent of state funding to Ardmore and the IFFC, both were, to all intents and purposes, semi-state bodies. Although Lemass would refer to the 'commendable initiative and enterprise' shown by 'the promoters of Ardmore Studios . . . in establishing this film-production unit' and though the studios were run by Louis Elliman they were de facto owned by the Industrial Credit Corporation.[76] When, in 1964, the studios ran into financial difficulties it was the ICC who appointed a receiver. Similarly when the studios were sold by the receiver to an Isle of Man registered company, the IFFC unproblematically noted that the studios were 'no longer a state liability'.[77]

Ultimately then, Lemass appears to have had his way. There was a post-script to his success, however. Although Lemass's 1947 proposal had assumed that the studios would mainly be used by foreign companies for feature film production, it also envisaged that, after a period of time, they would also be engaged by domestic companies for feature production. In this respect, Lemass's ambitions would not be fulfilled at Ardmore until the 1980s. Domestic concerns of a type likely to use Ardmore simply did not emerge until the support of the Irish Film Board became available in 1981. The establishment of the IFFC did little to address this lacuna: its policy of providing only 'end money' (or 'the remaining capital required by a producer to finance his film after he had been given credit by commercial institutions') meant that it was only of use to those producers with a track record impressive enough to convince banks or building societies to invest in their films. Since there was no history of consistent feature production in Ireland, there were no such producers based there. In consequence the bulk of the £385,000 advanced to production companies by the IFFC went to UK productions shot at Ardmore. Of the 15 films shot using this funding only two of them even dealt with Irish subjects let alone employed Irish crews. Unsurprisingly a 1967 civil service assessment of the IFFC concluded that it 'is serving no useful purpose as a credit institution for regular film production in Ireland'.[78]

Ardmore's failure to spontaneously spawn indigenous feature film production might have been more tolerable if the studios had at least achieved the aim Lemass had referred to at the studio's launch: the generation of Irish employment on the crews of the overseas productions shot at Ardmore. However, the stress laid on attracting overseas firms meant that, massive state cash injection notwithstanding, 'no provision was made for the training and staffing of Irish film technicians'[79] when Ardmore was set up. Lemass explicitly accepted that this should be the case. When, in 1958, some public concern was expressed about the fact that major roles in Ardmore films tended to go to foreign (mainly American) actors,[80] Lemass argued that the 'production of films here could not be economically based on the home market only and an undertaking such as this must aim at international distribution'. Given this he argued that

> while maximum employment of Irish personnel is desirable, those responsible for the conduct of the business must be granted reasonable facilities including the right to select such film stars, directors and technicians, as they may consider essential for its commercial success.[81]

In point of fact, the key determinant of crew nationality at Ardmore was often less the consideration of the box office and more a need to ensure that productions shot at the studios were able to continue accessing Eady Levy Funding after the 1959 changes. Although the IFFC may have been intended to replace Eady Levy funding, in practice producers using Ardmore continued accessing the fund by ensuring that their production companies were UK registered. A prescient March 1959 *Irish Times* article had pointed out that 'the exclusion of the Irish companies from the levy will make it difficult for a true Irish film industry to become established'.[82] Months later an article in the same paper by film correspondent (and later documentary-maker) Louis Marcus was more explicit:

> the much publicised 'Irish' films of Ardmore origins are, in fact, British Quota. Emmet Dalton, the producer of 'Sally's Irish Rogue' and 'This Other Eden' lives in London, employs British technicians on his films (one way of making

them qualify as quota) and must, in any case, have them processed in English laboratories (another quota regulation).[83]

As a result of the fact that 'the crewing of film technicians [i.e. the key creative positions] was arranged in London by whatever company had hired Ardmore for its film'[84] Irish employment at the studios was limited to some casual employment of Irish carpenters and plasterers, along with canteen and office workers whenever the studio was actually in production. One civil service minute could note of the 1964 filming of *The Spy Who Came in from the Cold* in Dublin, that

> under eleven different grades in camera, sound and production departments, 27 film technicians were given official credits of whom only two were Irish and these were employed as assistants to the Assistant Film Editor.[85]

Ironically then, if Ardmore represented a secret victory for Lemass it was also a pyrrhic one. It would be two decades after his death before indigenous production companies consistently used the studios and longer still before overseas productions shot in Ireland could be relied upon to source creative production roles from local crews. It is perhaps ironic that the industry which in the 1940s first drove Lemass to explore an open, export-oriented economy should have been such a poor exemplar of that policy in the 1960s when it had become commonplace.

CHAPTER ELEVEN

Introducing television in the age of Seán Lemass

ROBERT SAVAGE

—

By the time Seán Lemass made his most famous statement concerning Irish television being an 'instrument of public policy' the Taoiseach had been involved in shaping the form and structure of the medium in Ireland for close to a decade.[1] This chapter will consider the role that Lemass played in bringing television to Ireland in the last days of the de Valera government as Tanaiste (and Minister of Industry and Commerce) and while Taoiseach, when critical decisions were being made about establishing an Irish television service. It will also consider his vision of the role television should play in Irish society. Throughout the 1950s an often animated debate took place in Irish society and within both coalition and Fianna Fáil governments about television and how a native service should be structured and introduced to the nation. During the decade a consensus developed within these governments, which maintained that because of the costs involved, television simply was impossible for the state to encourage or support. The 1950s were, of course, a difficult period which witnessed seemingly relentless emigration, high levels of unemployment and stubborn economic stagnation. In this climate the notion of starting up a television service did not have much support in government circles.

In spite of this there was an understanding at many levels of society that television was inevitable and that basic questions had to be confronted. Much of the discussion in government circles and in the press during this time revolved around the question of who would control an Irish television service and the programmes it would transmit. Therefore the issue of what structure Irish television would take became critical. From the outset the state looked to Britain and saw two options to choose from. The first was to set up a state owned and financed 'public service' modelled on the British Broadcasting Corporation (BBC). This attractive, though costly, option was popular for many who advocated exploiting the medium to provide educational and cultural programmes. There was a belief that an Irish public service could produce high quality educational material that would explore the complexities of Irish history and literature; support the native language; and generally reinforce what many regarded was a frail national culture. The alternative was to follow the example of the Independent Television Authority in Britain and grant an exclusive broadcasting licence to a private firm. This option would not require government financing as television would be owned and operated by a corporation interested in making a profit by selling 'air time' to advertisers. As a market- driven enterprise it would seek the widest possible audience for its underwriters and therefore feature predominantly 'popular' American and British programmes. What clearly emerged during this period was a debate between those who favoured a service that would be set up as an independent, commercial, entity, versus those who endorsed a more 'Reithian'[2] concept of a government owned and operated 'public' service. Those that supported the latter option maintained that both radio and television should uplift and educate the nation and not simply provide popular entertainment for the masses. Advocates of each of these models or philosophies lobbied strenuously for proposals and schemes that conformed to their vision of television. Each model found support inside the government and the ensuing debate engaged politicians, civil servants, the press and a host of organisations anxious about how the new medium would affect cultural, economic and political issues.

Given the challenging economic climate of the period is not surprising that throughout most of the 1950s the Department of Finance was opposed to *any* form of television coming to Ireland. Finance was mortified by the notion of the state taking on television as a public service given the immense costs associated with building studios and transmitters, purchasing the required equipment and hiring a large staff to operate TV. The cost of 'home produced' programmes was also a matter of great concern for the Department. Finance was also convinced that the introduction of a privately owned commercial service which would not involve direct state expenditure would be problematic. It was worried about the prospect of consumers spending precious punts on what it defined as a 'luxury' and not putting their savings into Irish banks. Later, when it became clear that television was inevitable, Finance insisted that a television service should only be established with the clear understanding that no cost should fall on the exchequer. In these circumstances, the department preferred to see a commercial service established that would be modelled on the Independent

Television Authority in the United Kingdom or even the commercial networks in the United States.

The Department of Posts and Telegraphs, managed by the formidable secretary, Leon Ó Broin, was already heavily involved in telecommunications, as it was responsible for the state's national radio service, Radio Éireann. The radio service, which had gone 'on the air' in 1926 was operated by civil servants in Posts and Telegraphs and was much maligned for what many regarded as the poor quality of its programming. It had been granted a nominal degree of independence in the early 1950s when Maurice Gorham was hired as director and the Comhairle Radio Éireann was established to help supervise the service. In spite of this Radio Éireann remained underfunded and, in many respects, unpopular.[3]

As secretary of Posts and Telegraphs, Leon Ó Broin played an important role in developing the structure of the national television service that emerged at the end of the decade. Ó Broin was a highly cultured man, a linguist who wrote history in his spare time and translated books from English into Irish for An Gúm. Throughout the 1950s he relentlessly advocated the establishment of television as a 'public service' loosely based on the BBC. He maintained that it was imperative for cultural as well as political reasons that television be state owned and operated. The Department of Finance disagreed in the strongest of terms and these two departments engaged in frequent skirmishes in trying to influence governments throughout the decade. The structure of a future television service was the fundamental issue that had to be decided, as adoption of an independent commercial service or a government-owned public service, would determine the content of programmes, the paramount issue of the debate. Posts and Telegraphs argued that a public service following the model of the BBC could be an important asset to the nation as it would broadcast educational and cultural programmes that would uplift and enlighten the citizen. Finance and its supporters, focusing on economic development, believed that entrepreneurs should be encouraged to develop a service that would not impinge on scarce state resources. These two opposing concepts provided the terrain on which the television battle would be fought. This dialectical approach might seem somewhat superficial at first but the Irish television service that emerged in 1960 was a synthesis of these opposing ideas as it borrowed from both to produce what might be described as an Irish solution to an Irish problem.

Seán Lemass emerged as a key 'player' during this period both in his role as Minister for Industry and Commerce and Tanaiste and later as Taoiseach. Irish television is often regarded as a product of Lemass's Ireland, emerging in the

1960s as an agent that fostered cultural, social and political change. However the reality is that television emerged out of the 1950s, a period characterised by dire economic conditions. The decisions that were made about the structure of television in the state were informed by the crisis of the period. Joe Lee has pointed out that the 1956 census sent a shudder through Irish society and reverberated deep into the apparatus of the state. Simply put, the country was in deep trouble. Emigration was bleeding the country white as 500,000 people had emigrated between the conclusion of the Second World War and 1960. The 1956 census was a shock, 'that convinced some key figures, most notable in Finance of the necessity for a fundamental chance in direction. It was the closest Irish equivalent to the shame of surrender and occupation for continental countries in the Second World War.'[4]

In this climate, as debates about television developed, Lemass considered the commercial option as the best one for the government to adopt. He understood the arguments made by Ó Broin in favour of 'public service' television but did not see this as a practical or viable option. Lemass was also keenly aware of the proposals made by foreign corporations, interested in developing a television service in Ireland and intrigued by the notion of a commercial network operating a national service and freeing the state from the burdensome task of building and operating this costly new medium. It is important to remember that Lemass was focused on economic development and convinced that every effort had to be made to revive the national economy. He was therefore sympathetic with the arguments put forward by the Department of Finance and concerned that underwriting a mammoth project like television would retard efforts to realise economic development.

As the department responsible for broadcasting matters, Posts and Telegraphs attracted numerous proposals and queries concerning television throughout the 1950s. Ó Broin was, therefore, well placed to influence government policy and keenly interested in trying to shape the structure and form of Irish television. In 1950, acting on his own initiative, Ó Broin set up a television committee within his department to investigate the new medium and how a native service might be developed. During this decade, under both Fianna Fáil and coalition governments, his department conducted studies and produced a number of reports that explored the options that were open to the state. He consulted with the BBC on a regular basis and corresponded regularly with the Director-General, Sir Ian Jacob. He found an important ally in the BBC which supported his efforts to establish Irish television as a public service.[5] Ó Broin considered the BBC as the best model for the Irish television to emulate, regarding the programmes broadcast by commercial networks in Britain and America with deep suspicion. Much to the consternation of Lemass and Finance, he fully embraced the 'Rethian' philosophy of broadcasting.

While politicians, civil servants and interested citizens debated these issues, television was making its way into homes along the eastern coast and in border areas. These broadcasts made their way into Ireland initially from Britain and later from Northern Ireland. By 1953 the BBC had built a temporary transmitter on Divis Mountain in Belfast which enabled people on both sides of the border to witness the coronation of Queen Elizabeth II. Programmes routinely featured stories about the royal family and interviews with British and Unionist politicians. The Catholic Church complained about the 'immoral' element it detected in British programmes that were available as 'spillover' from Britain and Belfast. The inability of the state to offer an alternative created discomfort in Dublin and placed pressure on the state to come to a decision.

In 1957, while Neil Blaney was Minister for Posts and Telegraphs, Leon Ó Broin realised that the new Fianna Fáil government was seriously considering offering a licence to a private company to set up a commercial service. It is clear that one of the strongest voices behind this decision belonged to Lemass. An alarmed Ó Broin made a rushed and awkward effort to discredit the commercial option. His departmental television committee submitted a report to the cabinet, which challenged prevailing government policy and once again articulated the need for developing television as a 'public service'. The report argued that television was tremendously important but concluded that if the state could not afford to set up television as a public service it should simply not establish a native service. The report upset Lemass, because the committee refused to consider seriously that a private commercial service might be the best alternative. While in the past Ó Broin had tangled primarily with the Department of Finance, this report and Lemass's reaction to it ensured that the Tanaiste would stay involved in discussions centred on television policy. He was clearly disturbed with what he believed was as an ambiguous, incoherent document and expressed his concerns in a sharply worded letter to Neil Blaney. In this correspondence one can, for the first time, observe the future Taoiseach articulate his under-standing of how government policy should prepare for television.

The Tanaiste was quick to take Blaney to task for what he regarded as an inferior effort on the part of his department. He complained, 'the Memorandum is unsatisfactory from many viewpoints. It is just the type of Memo which, as a member of the Government, I hate to get because it does not convey a clear picture of the problem and appears to be, in some respects, self-contradictory.'[6]

He suggested a much more concise statement be made to the government, one that would not be the muddled, inconsistent submission that Posts and Telegraphs had produced. He told Blaney that the memo needed to be rewritten and that the issue should be put before the cabinet in a clear fashion. 'I suggest that you should put the T.V. issue to the Government in the following clear form:– (1) A state T.V. service is ruled out on grounds of cost. (2) A T.V. service must, therefore, be based on commercial advertising, and be provided by private enterprise.'[7]

As far as he was concerned the government had made a decision; there was no need for additional debate. Lemass suggested that Blaney and his department outline for the cabinet the requirements that any prospective applicant would have to conform to. 'My suggestion is that you should seek authority from the Government to make a public announcement that proposals for a commercial T.V. service be provided and operated by private enterprise will be considered subject to the following conditions: (1) No cost to the Government. (2) Suitable machinery for the supervision and control of programmes. (3) Free time for Public Services. (4) Nation wide coverage. (5) Encouragement of the Irish language.'[8]

Lemass wanted the government to have the luxury of a concise summary that would make a specific and coherent request. The 37 part, 17 page document that he had received from the Department of Posts and Telegraphs was simply too convoluted to enable the cabinet to take decisive action. The management strategy Lemass adopted in this instance would later be employed when he became Taoiseach. Rather than be burdened with a complex, contradictory submission that would confuse and frustrate members of the cabinet, Lemass wanted an explicit memorandum that would recommend a clear option. The government then could debate the submission and come to a decision.

In concluding his letter to Blaney, the Tanaiste suggested that, once adequate guidelines had been established, the department should quickly identify the one proposal that it thought was the most suitable. Blaney was told that he should then request the government's permission to make a commitment to the best applicant. Lemass wanted a decision made by the government, and a commitment given to a private commercial company that would allow a service to begin broadcasting. He certainly appreciated the argument that favoured a public service, but believed that the costs involved were beyond the state's resources. He saw no point in endless debate on the issue and was annoyed at the confusing memo produced by the Television Committee and Posts and Telegraphs. One can sense that Lemass had grown impatient and frustrated with both Blaney and Ó Broin. He believed commercial television provided a natural solution to the problem that confronted the government, a solution that fitted quite well with his philosophy of encouraging entrepreneurs and foreign investment.

However, he was unable to force the issue as amid these debates a cabinet committee was formed in October of 1957 to determine the most effective means of bringing television to Ireland. The establishment of the committee suggests Eamon de Valera's intervention, as the ageing Taoiseach always preferred the methodical approach to deciding difficult policy issues. The committee included Seán Lemass, the Minister for Posts and Telegraphs, Neil Blaney, the Minister for Finance, Dr James Ryan, and the Minister for External Affairs, Frank Aiken. This committee was established to examine television in light of the recent decisions that had been reached by the government. The new ministerial body was required to report to the government after exploring how an Irish television service could be introduced, 'as early as practicable, under public control . . . [and] . . . so far as possible, . . . without cost to the Exchequer'.[9] Lemass dominated this short-lived committee and was certainly not afraid to seize the initiative in this committee nor was he hesitant to make important unilateral policy decisions.

The relationship between Posts and Telegraphs and Lemass's cabinet committee proved difficult as Ó Broin and his associates were on the receiving end of policy decisions they considered unacceptable. In the not so recent past the department had been a proactive one able to influence policy and debate regarding television. With the creation of the cabinet committee, the staff at Posts and Telegraphs found itself reacting to the committee's proposals and declarations. This new relationship was difficult for Ó Broin to accept. He was uncomfortable with the commercial direction that he believed Lemass and the cabinet committee were moving towards, and frustrated by his inability to convince the ministers to change their approach to television. The first task of the cabinet committee was to draft a public announcement that would be made by Neil Blaney, the Minister for Posts and Telegraphs. The cabinet met in November of 1957 and decided that Blaney would issue a public statement inviting proposals from companies interested in television broadcasting in Ireland. This statement had been carefully drafted by Seán Lemass and approved by the cabinet committee. This was an important announcement as it provided an indication of the type of proposal Lemass and the government were looking for. It underscored the fact that a decision had been made to endorse the commercial option that would allow a private corporation to operate a television service.

Neil Blaney later addressed the Association of Advertisers in Ireland and revealed the government's new position on television. He announced that the government was:

> prepared to consider proposals from private interests for the provision of a transmission network, that will ensure satisfactory reception in all parts of the country, as well as necessary studios and complementary indoor and outdoor equipment. The entire capital and maintenance costs will be met by the promoting group . . . in consideration of a licence to operate commercial programmes for a term of years.[10]

Blaney revealed that his department had already received several very interesting proposals. Critically, he emphasised that it was anticipated that no cost would fall upon the Exchequer. He continued by outlining the structure of the Irish service and defining its relationship with the state. 'The television system will become state property and will be under the control of a Television Authority. . . . The authority . . . will . . . make special arrangements regarding such matters as the presentation of news and the position of the Irish language. It will be a condition that part of the time will be made available for programmes of a public service character.'[11] Blaney also addressed the issue of advertisements, indicating that the government had decided to discard the ban on foreign commercials, a policy that had been in force on Radio Éireann since 1934. This provision fits with the emerging reality in Lemass's Ireland where competition would be encouraged and special or preferential treatment of Irish firms would be phased out. He acknowledged that to succeed commercial television would be heavily dependent on advertisements and that limiting access of non-native companies would be a mistake. The minister expressed confidence that Irish companies would still make, 'the maximum use of the new medium for advertising Irish goods to Irish people.'[12]

The November 1957 address, initiated by Lemass, marked a turning point in the painfully slow development of Irish television. The government made it clear that television in Ireland would be a service 'largely commercial in character' with 'private interests' responsible for building and running the service. The fact that the announcement was made at a convention of advertisers underscored the extent of the commercial commitment that was being made. The speech clearly reflected the desire of Lemass to grant a licence to a private company, which would have an exclusive right to broadcast in Ireland.

If Ó Broin and the television committee were concerned with the decisions that the cabinet committee had made, a letter from the Department of Industry and Commerce in December 1957 caused genuine alarm. This concerned two proposals that had been submitted to and rejected by the government earlier in the year. One of the firms was the Texas based McLendon Corporation. The American proposal offered what amounted to a free television service for the country if the company was granted permission to set up a commercial radio service that could broadcast into Britain. A similar proposal was made by a Paris based company owned and operated by a Romanian exile, Charles Michelson. The price would be rather steep as these proposals would require the Irish government to withdraw from the Copenhagen Agreement, a treaty signed by the state, which governed the use of international wavelengths. In spite of this Lemass regarded each as attractive schemes, which deserved close consideration outside the cabinet committee. This signalled a new departure and an abrupt change because Lemass believed that the Michelson scheme could help promote the economic growth he was so desperate to cultivate. Michelson had spent considerable time in Ireland and tailored his proposal to the government's needs. The Romanian ex-patriot met with the heads of a number of semi-state boards and offered each free access to the commercial radio service that he wanted to build in Ireland. Lemass told Ó Broin that a decision had been made 'in favour of a combination of sound broadcasting and television on the basis which would meet the representations of Bord Fáilte Éireann, Aer Lingus, and Hospital Trust.'[13] A short time later Lemass informed the new Minister for Posts and Telegraphs, Seán Ormonde[14] that the cabinet committee had made a number of decisions about the direction television should take. He sent the cabinet committee's conclusions to Ormonde, and ordered Posts and Telegraphs to redraft the document into a formal memo that would be submitted to the government for a decision. Posts and Telegraphs was instructed to review all the proposals that had been submitted and to report back to the cabinet committee recommending the one company that best conformed to conditions that had been outlined by Lemass and his associates.[15]

Ormonde responded with a document that was highly critical of the decisions made by the cabinet committee. The response, written by Leon Ó Broin, but supported by Ormonde was clearly intended for Lemass, as it contained a robust critique of the cabinet committee's decision. It is clear that Ó Broin believed the cabinet committee's decision to reverse established government policy, concerning the Michelson and McLendon proposals, signalled a disastrous shift that would have terrible consequences for the country. Ó Broin expressed his disappointment with the cabinet committee complaining that he was 'profoundly unhappy' with the conclusion that it come to. He maintained that the decisions violated every feature of the policy that the television committee had developed since its inception in 1950. Ó Broin warned that if television was organised along the lines that the cabinet committee had suggested the government would experience 'constant trouble'.[16] Lemass responded to the Posts and Telegraphs memoranda quickly. He had hoped that the department would act on the cabinet committee's submission and prepare the memorandum he wanted to submit to the full cabinet. In his response one can sense a growing impatience with both Ó Broin and Ormonde. The Tanaiste tersely stated that the cabinet committee had envisioned a commercial monopoly in their report and dismissed Ó Broin's efforts to find an alternative.

> It has been accepted that a T.V. service must be provided on a commercial basis and while, like Mr Ó Broin, most of us would prefer a public service if this were possible, it is, as you know, out of the question for financial reasons. The Government have decided to proceed on the basis of a commercial service and this question must be regarded as settled.[17]

Lemass stated that he wanted Posts and Telegraphs to comply with the wishes of the cabinet committee and draft a submission to the government that would embrace the report his committee had issued. In responding to Ó Broin's polemic against McLendon and Michelson, the Tanaiste stated that the cabinet committee was aware of the complications that would be involved if one of these proposals were accepted. He maintained that although no decision had been reached the cabinet committee 'clearly understood' that accepting either of these proposals would require Ireland to withdraw from the Copenhagen Agreement.

Posts and Telegraphs complied with the wishes of Lemass and prepared a formal submission to the government, which endorsed the report of the cabinet committee. Seán Ormonde accepted Lemass's offer to submit the views of his department with the formal submission for the government. The formal document set out the procedure that would allow for a selection of what was described as a 'concessionaire'. Once the government had set the conditions of the contract that would be employed, Posts and Telegraphs would be responsible for nominating the candidate that best conformed to the conditions outlined by the cabinet committee. At this juncture it appeared that the wishes of Lemass and his cabinet committee would prevail and that momentum was building towards the establishment of a privately owned commercial service.

At the last minute, the efforts of Lemass were frustrated by a suggestion submitted by the Minister of Health. Seán MacEntee, Lemass's long time nemesis, suggested that the government should consider the procedure that was put in place in 1925 when an official government commission was established to consider how radio should be established in the state. His proposal to establish a television commission was quickly accepted by the government. Lemass had shown a desire to get a service 'on the air' quickly, and had illustrated a determination to take the difficult decisions to achieve this end. However once MacEntee's proposal had been circulated, it became difficult to justify opposition to the concept of an official commission that would review all proposals received by the state and provide a recommendation to the government. The decision to accept MacEntee's proposal suggests once again the influence of the Taoiseach, Eamon de Valera. It also highlights the limits of Lemass's influence in the last government of the elderly Taoiseach. De Valera's exhaustive, methodical style of management was in sharp contrast to the more determined Lemass who in a very short amount of time had immersed himself deeply in the government's evolving television policy. Although this may have been a tactical defeat for Lemass, he showed no interest in abandoning his opposition to 'public service' television and continued to be active in influencing the government's television policy.

The government announced in March 1958 that a television commission would be established by the Minister of Posts and Telegraphs to examine all aspects of television broadcasting and to make recommendations to the government. The fact that Posts and Telegraphs would oversee the work of the commission insured that Ó Broin would remain closely involved in the state's emerging television policy. Ó Broin and his staff worked closely with the television commission, and used every opportunity to try and influence the findings of this body. Posts and Telegraphs would also have to work with Lemass who limited the scope of the commission by personally writing its terms of reference. These terms had profound implications for the commission and certainly limited the scope and effectiveness of its work. Lemass drafted instructions, which were both concise and supported by Finance and the Taoiseach. Unlike the terms proposed by Ó Broin, the Tanaiste wanted the commission's work to be strictly defined when the question of financing television was concerned. He proposed that the Television Commission be created with instructions that would specify, 'that no charge should fall on the Exchequer, on capital or current account'.[18] This effectively eliminated the public service model from consideration.

This was the most critical qualification inserted into the commission's orders. This stipulation succeeded in limiting the ability of the television commission to conduct a thorough investigation and precluded it from submitting a truly comprehensive report to the government. It is clear that the Tanáiste was not interested in dredging up the subject of public service television, or the model advocated by the television committee. He clearly believed that such a proposal was out of the question given the financial difficulties that the state was experiencing. Lemass contended that the commission should investigate all the proposals that had been received by Posts and Telegraphs and make a recommendation as to which scheme should be accepted by the government. The terms of reference conformed to the proposal that had been made by Lemass and clearly supported the thinking of the Tanaiste and the Department of Finance.[19] The terms also proved that the government did not want to ignore any proposals that had been submitted to the government. It wanted the commission to evaluate closely all submissions received by the Post Office including those made by Michelson and McLendon.

The commission heard evidence from a wide range of groups, and sorted through proposals from domestic and foreign companies interested in gaining an exclusive licence to set up a television station in Ireland. Many of the proposals were from foreign companies, some with subsidiaries in Ireland, though Gael Linn submitted one of the more informed and comprehensive applications. The Gael Linn application made it clear that it viewed television as a tool to revive the Irish language. Gordon Mc McClendon, outfitted in cowboy boots and a ten-gallon hat, appeared before the commission to make the case that his company's proposal was an opportunity that was simply too good to be turned down. Charles Michelson spent weeks in Ireland meeting with politicians and businessmen trying to line up support for his scheme. The result was that his firm received support from a number of semi-state companies and intriguingly also from the Vatican. Lemass was intrigued by the Michelson proposal in spite of the difficulties inherent in the scheme. Michelson offered to provide a two-channel national service at no cost to the state. But there would of course be a price and this came in the form of a license to broadcast a commercial radio station from Irish territory into Britain. This would require the government to withdraw from the Copenhagen agreement to which Ireland was a signatory and which allocated wavelengths throughout Europe. The agreement restricted the use of wavelengths and made both the McLendon and Michelson proposals unfeasible.

Leon Ó Broin appeared before the commission to voice his opposition to the commercial option. Using the wealth of technical and financial information from the various proposals that had come into his department he offered an alternative. This proposed the state fund and operate a service that would generate revenue by selling 'air time' to advertisers. He also hoped to convince the BBC to offer programmes to the Irish service at greatly reduced rates. He was convinced this compromise could work and believed that popular commercial programmes could generate revenue while educational programmes could balance the commercial component. Importantly the state would maintain control of the medium and not turn it over to a private entrepreneur simply motivates by a desire to realise a profit.

The television commission submitted its report to the government in May of 1959. The document was a confusing, contradictory report that failed to reach any real consensus, or present a coherent recommendation to the government. Parts of the document were well researched and provided a great deal of information concerning how television might contribute to Irish society. In the final analysis the report was a disappointing effort. The failure of the commission can be traced directly to the terms of reference, which limited the scope, and depth of its investigation.

At this juncture and possibly seeing an opening Posts and Telegraphs submitted a revised proposal to the government that appeared much more attractive in light of the confused and contradictory report issued by the television commission. There can be little doubt that the three companies that the television commission had 'short listed' failed to impress Seán Lemass and other members of the cabinet including the Minister for Finance. Ó Broin and his associates were able to put together a more detailed proposal that requested financial support from the state, but also promised a return on the government's investment. The proposal indicated that by accepting the principle that no *ultimate* charge should fall on the Exchequer, a state-owned service could be up and running quickly. Post and Telegraphs argued that this state-run service would be able to make a profit and pay back the loan that would allow it to get 'on the air'. The Department of Finance reluctantly acknowledged that it would support a service along the lines that had been outlined by Posts and Telegraphs. Debates in the Dail illustrate that deputies realised that the television commission's report was not an enthusiastic endorsement of a private commercial service. At this juncture Ó Broin was perfectly positioned to try to persuade the government that a change in policy had to be made.

Lemass became Taoiseach in June of 1959 a short time later met with and Ó Broin, to discuss television. In this meeting the secretary for Posts and Telegraphs was able to put his case before the new Taoiseach. In his auto-biography, Ó Broin maintains that the change of policy endorsed by the government was due to Lemass:

> I can only surmise as to how the government's final decision was arrived at. Seán Lemass, who a couple of months before had taken over as Taoiseach from de Valera, had no doubt a lot to do with it. He asked me to go and see him. The interview was brief. I was concerned, I told him, about the quality of pro-grammes. We were fortunately placed in close proximity to what was probably the best service in the world, the BBC, an entirely public service organisation, and I suggested that we might explore the possibility of a special arrangement for an extension of their service as a back-up to such programmes of quality that as we could produce at home on a similar public service basis. He made no com-ment, but as I spoke of the BBC I felt that the chauvinists among us would not take too well to any arrangements with the *British* Broadcasting Corporation.[20]

Ó Broin, who had believed that the BBC could be a valuable part of an Irish public service, recognised at this juncture that this would be very difficult for political reasons. However, this did not preclude the government from consi-dering the Post Office plan *sans* BBC involvement. The government's ultimate decision surprised Ó Broin who described the announcement that was made in July 1959.

> An extraordinary *volte face* occurred. The government, again without consul-tation with us, but obviously returning to our television committee's reports, rejected the view of the commission and proceeded to set up a statutory authority to run both television and radio without any commercial promoters whatever.'[21]

John Horgan has indicated that other pressures were brought to bear on the Taoiseach, pointing to his 1969 interview with Michael Mills of the *Irish Press*.[22] In the interview Lemass explained that he was not in favour of setting up television as a semi-state body, 'I was in favour at that stage of giving it over to one of the private groups who were seeking the service. There was Gael Linn and another Irish group and a number of foreign groups were interested in the service. But the government decided it should be a State service.' This state-ment suggests that once again Lemass ran into trouble at the cabinet level on the question of the structure of television, but this time not as Tanáiste but as Taoiseach. In the end the Lemass government came to a final decision at a cabinet meeting on 31 July 1959.[23] A good deal of credit for keeping the medium out of the hands of private enterprise could be claimed by Ó Broin. He was successful in his persistent efforts to convince the government to accept the principle of a state-owned and operated public television service that would look to revenue from advertisers to sustain itself.

At the first meeting of the RTÉ Authority in June 1960, the new Minster for Posts and Telegraphs, Michael Hilliard delivered an address, which had been written, reviewed and edited by the Taoiseach, who remained engaged with television and concerned with its cost. Hilliard made it clear that there were important matters that he wanted to share privately with the new authority. It is revealing to note that the first issue on the Minister's agenda concerned the finances of the new service. This was unambiguously linked to the Authority's independence from the government. The Minister explained that the government believed that television should be 'self-supporting within a reasonable period'. He emphasised that this was 'a fundamental matter so far as the well-being of your organisation is concerned. Genuine independence may be a matter of outlook but it is, unfortunately, as often a matter of finances.'[24]

The new Authority had been put on notice that the financial stability of the new service was imperative and that any serious difficulty in this regard would place the independence of Irish television at risk. The Authority was promised that it was the government's intention to give the new organisation 'the greatest possible freedom from direct State control' but warned that as long as state funding was involved 'there will remain a temptation – and I will put it no stronger – for the state to interfere in matters which will be properly your concern'.[25] It is important to point out that the issue of financial stability was one that was critical to the Lemass government. The fear that had been expressed by the Department of Finance about television becoming a drain of the national exchequer remained a real concern for the state. The government's insistence that Telefís Éireann generate substantial income quickly influenced the character and ultimately the programmes transmitted by the fledgling service.

Although the new service was not scheduled to go 'on the air' until 1961, Lemass was concerned with the impact the new medium would have on Irish society. Like his predecessor, Eamon de Valera, the Taoiseach was uneasy with the advent of Irish television. Both men believed that the state should have a strong voice in determining what should and should not be broadcast on an Irish service. Lemass and de Valera argued that it was essential that the government protect the Irish people from what both considered the potentially insidious influence an unsupervised service might impart.[26] The concern of Lemass is evident in the strict instructions he wrote for the television authority that his government had recently appointed. The Taoiseach was clearly interested in trying to influence the authority, as can be seen by his decision to issue what he termed 'policy directives'. Lemass drafted these instructions a few months before the television authority was scheduled to convene for its inaugural session. In a detailed memorandum to the secretary of his department, Maurice Moynihan, Lemass stated that he felt it was imperative the authority understands that 'stage-Irishisms [and] playboyisms' should be avoided. Instead he argued that the station should produce an '"image" of a vigorous progressive nation, seeking efficiency'.[27] In regard to social and economic problems that challenged the country he emphasised that television should 'encourage objective presentation of facts and constructive comment. The "God-help-us" approach should be ruled out.'[28]

Although he believed television could be used in an intelligent manner, he cautioned:

> objectivity should not be allowed to excuse the undue representation of our faults. What you should aim to present is a picture of Ireland and the Irish as we would like to have it, although our hopes and aims may well be helped by the objective presentation of facts in association with constructive comment.[29]

He made it clear that Irish television needed to avoid coverage or comment about Northern Ireland that might upset the Stormont government and maintained that the issue of partition should be addressed only with the greatest of care. According to the Taoiseach, the new authority had to act with prudence when dealing with other sensitive topics such as sex, religion and education.

Lemass's memo met with resistance from the secretary of his department, who argued that the 'policy directives' were unnecessarily severe and would ultimately prove counterproductive. In a courageous memorandum, Maurice Moynihan tried to dissuade the Taoiseach from issuing orders he considered draconian. He argued that the recently passed broadcasting act made provision for the Taoiseach's concerns by establishing a strong, government appointed, public authority charged with overseeing Irish television. Moynihan argued that dictating terms to this new organisation would be seen, 'both at home and abroad, as an illiberal action, calculated to hamper unduly the freedom of the Broadcasting Authority'.[30] The secretary also pointed out that the proposed directives ran counter to the spirit of Article 40 of the Irish constitution that 'guarantees liberty of expression for organs of public opinion'.[31]

In spite of Moynihan's best efforts, Lemass insisted that the 'policy directives' be issued, as he believed they would provide important guidelines for the authority. To underscore this concern he ordered that the written directives be incorporated into a formal speech that would be delivered by the Minister of Posts and Telegraphs at the inaugural meeting of the board. He insisted that printed copies of the directives be distributed to each member of the authority in order to ensure that that all were aware of the government's position. Lemass rejected Moynihan's assertion that through the appointed authority the government would have the final word on television, declaring, 'On these matters it is not enough to have the last word, if we do not have the first.'[32] Lemass would one day claim that Irish television was 'an instrument of public policy'. One could make the case that this, perhaps his most famous statement about Irish television, had its roots in these policy directives.

One month after these directives were written, Isaac Kleinerman, the Executive Producer of the American television series, *The Twentieth Century*, visited Padraig O'Hanrahan, the Director of the Irish Information Bureau in Dublin. Kleinerman explained that he was interested in gaining government assistance for a programme his network was developing. CBS expressed interest in filming an information programme that would introduce contemporary Ireland to a large America audience. Kleinerman advised the director that the episode he envisioned would address social, political, economic and cultural developments in the country and provide an accurate portrayal of everyday life in Ireland. He explained that plans had been made to interview a number of 'principal people' in the country and that the network wanted to interview both the Taoiseach and the President.

The Twentieth Century was a commercial television series sponsored by the Prudential Life Insurance Company of America. Kleinerman explained to O'Hanrahan that the programme was a prestigious, critically acclaimed series that had developed a well-deserved reputation for excellence. He pointed out that the series had an audience of eleven and a half million informed and educated Americans. The programme's presenter was Walter Cronkite, a respected television personality whose name has become synonymous with professionalism in the field of television journalism. The series had begun broadcasting on Sunday evenings in 1957; by 1960 over one hundred programmes had been produced addressing issues that explored the turbulent history of the twentieth century.

   The request by the American network was greeted warmly by the director of the government's Information Bureau, who advised Kleinerman that the Irish government would be happy to cooperate if the programme would be 'serious and responsible'.[33] O'Hanrahan asked Kleinerman to forward an outline of the proposed programme detailing the topics the network intended to cover. CBS complied in a correspondence that caused a great deal of consternation in government circles. The response to the network's proposal and subsequent negotiations with CBS offer valuable insight into the image of Ireland that Seán Lemass sought to transmit to the United States. The negotiations also underscore the perceptions of the country from abroad at a critical juncture in the history of the state.

   On receipt of the network's 'shooting schedule', O'Hanrahan wrote to the Taoiseach and sent a copy of the proposal. He explained that the film 'could, if moulded on the right lines, be a very valuable opportunity of publicising Ireland abroad'.[34] However, he warned that the outline contained a number of 'wrong angles' that would have to be corrected if the programme was to provide a positive image of the country. When Lemass reviewed the 'shooting schedule' the fears he had articulated while drafting the 'policy directives' were, in his mind, confirmed. The outline validated his belief that without strict supervision, television could harmfully distort the image of the nation.

   At this juncture, the government was unaware that the Irish novelist Elizabeth Bowen, a writer with very distinct cultural and political prejudices, had been hired to write the script for the programme. The government never had the opportunity to read or review the actual script and only had access to the outline of the programme that had been provided by CBS. The involvement of Elizabeth Bowen and the considerable exposure given to Seán O'Faolain in the film underscore the influence that these two Irish writers brought to the project. Their hostility to de Valera's Ireland and to the government's Irish language policy is manifested quite clearly in the film. This is an important point: for what at first may seem like a rather awkward American effort to 'capture' the real Ireland, warts and all, was a more complex effort, strongly influenced by these two Irish intellectuals.

   Lemass and O'Hanrahan were upset with the outline the network produced. Both were convinced it was seriously flawed, pointing out that the network was starting off on the wrong foot by opening the programme in a Dublin public house. CBS explained that Walter Cronkite was scheduled to greet his American audience from Moody's Pub in Dublin to observe the Irish at 'two of their favourite occupations – talking and drinking'.[35] The programme created even more difficulties for the government as the 'shooting schedule' unfolded. CBS was interested in interviewing an IRA 'volunteer', a proposal Lemass found to be not only insensitive but also insulting. He believed any such interview would lend legitimacy to an illegal paramilitary organisation actively involved in unlawful acts and dedicated to the overthrow of the state. The network also wanted to explore the peculiar demographic situation it believed existed in rural Ireland by filming 'Square Dance scenes showing long stag line(s) because of the girl shortage.' In this segment of the programme, CBS also exhibited a desire to highlight 'the primitive' by filming, 'two farmer fathers arranging a marriage' and capturing what Kleinerman termed 'the dominant role of the mother' in Irish society.[36]

Another feature of the American's shooting schedule that caused government anxiety was the desire to film an intermission at the Abbey Theatre. Between acts a short Irish language play was often staged by Ireland's national theatre. CBS contended that by filming the audience rushing to and drinking at the bar, and therefore ignoring the Irish language performance, it could offer insight into the government's failed effort to restore the Irish language. CBS was thus interested in addressing issues that the Irish government found at best problematic and at worst offensive. The shooting schedule in many respects confirmed the government's fear that the network was ill informed about contemporary Irish society. Lemass believed that CBS intended to produce the type of story that would reinforce the very stereotypes he found so abhorrent.

Lemass and O'Hanrahan were keenly interested in trying to revise if not rewrite the outline that the network had submitted. With significant input from the Taoiseach, O'Hanrahan drafted a letter to CBS explaining that substantial changes would have to be made in the film if the network wanted to gain access to Lemass and de Valera. It is quite clear that Lemass and others in government felt that the film as outlined was seriously flawed and would portray Ireland as a nation that had not yet entered the twentieth century. Lemass believed the programme would portray Ireland as a backward peasant nation plagued by unemployment, political violence, relentless emigration, alcoholism, and an insincere effort to force an archaic language 'down the neck' of an uninterested populace.[37] This was hardly the image Seán Lemass wanted projected to the affluent, educated American audience that Kleinerman had described. It should be remembered that along with T. K. Whitaker, the secretary of the Department of Finance, the Taoiseach had put in place an innovative economic programme that among other things encouraged foreign investment. Lemass understood that a critical source of that investment would be American business and feared the proposed film might harm the vibrant, modern image of the nation that he wanted to project.

In writing to Kleinerman, O'Hanrahan outlined his governments concerns, explaining that Ireland had:

> unfortunately, only too often been represented as a country where the amenities of modern life are practically unknown, whose people live under conditions bordering on the primitive.[38]

The government took issue with the network's desire to open the programme in a public house and criticised the proposal to interview a member of the IRA. Other issues defined as unacceptable included the network's proposed treatment of rural Ireland, the state's language policy, and the desire to concentrate on emigration. Kleinerman was upset with the government's complaints and let it be known that he intended to film the programme with or without the co-operation of the state. While in Dublin, Kleinerman met informally with Frederick H. Boland, Ireland's Ambassador to the United Nations. Boland reported his conversation to the Taoiseach, indicating that the American producer was 'very upset by the comments on his proposed film'.[39] Boland argued that the government should do its best to work with CBS. He argued that without the involvement of the state the programme could be injurious to the image of Ireland in the United States. He advised the Taoiseach that *The Twentieth Century* was a reputable series, concluding, 'it would be a pity if we missed the opportunity of having Ireland presented in as good a light as we can'.[40]

Kleinerman soon demonstrated a new willingness to work with the government. Shortly after his meeting with Boland, he wrote to O'Hanrahan, maintaining that he intended to portray Ireland in a manner that was 'true and relevant. . . . We have no desire to alter, distort, or in any other way create a false or misleading impression.'[41] Kleinerman agreed to accept the government's recommendations and promised that he would make a number of substantial changes in the programme. He also promised that no attempt would be made to interview the IRA. However, he remained committed to opening the programme in a Dublin pub but 'with a view to dispelling the half-truths and myths which exist about Ireland today'.[42]

The government was convinced that CBS was making a number of important concessions as Kleinerman explained that other objectionable features in the outline would be eliminated. 'On the matter of the girl shortage and the segregation of the sexes . . . since these points do not exist they therefore cannot be included in this context. The same applies to the emigration story, arranged marriages, and the domineering role of mothers.' When addressing the Irish language, the government was assured that 'we are not looking for isolated incidents to disprove its worth. Rather we are looking for the true and factual record of its accomplishments.'[43] Kleinerman's letter convinced O'Hanrahan that CBS had made a commitment to correct the flaws contained in the original shooting schedule. He wrote to Lemass, explaining, 'I have come to the conclusion that his intentions are good and that by and large the finished project should not give rise to any really serious objections. The film may not be an ideal one from our point of view but on balance I feel the advantage will lie in our participation in it.'[44] Lemass reviewed Kleinerman's letter and accepted his advice. He agreed to be interviewed by the network, as did Eamon de Valera. The programme was broadcast on two consecutive Sunday evenings, 29 January and 5 February 1961.

The Irish Embassy in Washington and the Consulate in New York watched the programme with great interest. Both produced detailed reports for Dublin and both concluded that *Ireland, The Tear and The Smile*, was a poorly written programme that had denigrated Ireland. According to Irish officials in New York and Washington, the programme reinforced offensive stereotypes that ultimately damaged the image of Ireland. The Irish Ambassador, T. J. Kiernan, and members of his staff complained that the film projected a depressing image of as 'a poverty-stricken country riddled with backwardness, unemployment and emigration. [observing] There was a general air of fatalism and decay.'[45]

Embassy staff pointed out that the programme was a commercial one sponsored by a company hoping to sell life insurance to a rather affluent middle-class audience. The Ambassador referred to what he considered the offensive comparison made between Northern Ireland and the Republic, commenting:

Obviously the expert advertising agents decided that these Americans would be pleased with a striking contrast between North and 'South' Ireland, [including] a touch of superstition [emphasised by the cameras in the Knock scene], a heavy emphasis on the fecklessness and irresponsibility of the 'southern' Irish in contrast to the dignity, prosperity and stability of the descendants of Yorkshire and Scottish ancestors thriving in the north.[46]

Brian Faulkner, the Minister for Home Affairs for Northern Ireland, was interviewed by CBS while standing in front of the imposing edifice of Stormont. The Irish diplomats criticised the Minister for explaining to his American audience that Northern Ireland was a thriving democracy that had voted to remain part of the United Kingdom. His statements, and the decision of CBS not to challenge them, were attacked as containing 'outrageous inaccuracies'.[47]

The segment of the film that considered the issue of religion in Northern Ireland was seen as an example of the incompetent, even reckless journalism, practised by CBS. Irish officials in New York and Washington were incensed about a statement, which referred to 'persecutions of Protestants by the Catholics' in Northern Ireland.[48] The Consulate General's office in New York reported that when it had attended an advanced screening of the film it strongly protested this point to staff at CBS. The protests of the Consulate were ignored at the time, as they were informed:

> The Director said that they had relied upon Miss Bowen, who was Irish, for accuracy in her text and he regretted that it was not possible to effect any changes in the script at that late stage [three days before the public telecast].[49]

Irish diplomats in the United States complained that the individuals interviewed were cynical and at times incoherent. The students who appeared were described as smart alecks who had 'confused ideas'. The interview with Brendan Behan was dismissed as 'very meaningless but in view of Behan's notoriety in the US [it] had no doubt a good advertising purpose'.[50] The first half of the programme concluded on 29 January with what was described as 'a long drawn out tearful emigration scene which might have been taken from a scene of the refugees of the Hungarian Revolution or from a series of drawing of 1847. The background was a women singing "The Hills of Sweet Mayo".'[51]

One week later the second part of *Ireland, The Tear and the Smile* was broadcast and once again reviewed by Embassy and Consulate officials in Washington and New York. In reporting to Dublin it was agreed that the second programme was more hopeful than the first. However, the programme was criticised for a number of reasons. CBS was criticised for manipulating images and interviews to contradict Irish leaders and to suggest that the language was being forced upon an uninterested population. The network had addressed the role of women in Irish society but was taken to task for its decision to interview a decidedly unrepresentative woman, the editor of the woman's page of *The Irish Times*, which the network termed the 'leading Protestant paper in the country'. Irish officials viewing the programme described the woman's editor as 'very artificial and affected, [who] explained that Irish women envied American women in the comfort of their bathrooms and kitchens and said any well-to-do Irish woman who had a washing machine was lucky.'[52]

The Tear and the Smile disturbed Lemass. He clearly believed that his government had been misled by the American network, which he believed had given false assurances about the content of the programme simply to gain access to government leaders. He ordered Maurice Moynihan to conduct an investigation to determine if the network:

> could be held to constitute a breach of faith by CBS, in view of the under-standings reached in discussion and correspondence when the material for the programmes was being collected, and in particular before the president and himself gave their interviews.[53]

At an inter-departmental meeting convened to discuss the matter it was decided that even though the government believed that CBS had acted in bad faith a formal protest to the powerful American network would be counter-productive. Accusing CBS of a breach of faith was considered problematic as it 'might serve only to produce greater antagonism against us'.[54] Instead it was agreed that a strong letter of protest would be written to Isaac Kleinerman 'letting CBS know of our disappointment and surprise at the contents of the film'.[55] Lemass approved the letter of protest that was sent to Kleinerman in March of 1961. The letter expressed the Irish government's profound concern at the 'distorted image of Ireland which the film presents'.

The government condemned the manner in which the film was constructed, particularly the juxtaposition of interviews given by the Taoiseach and President in the film. It was believed that the two men had been 'set up' as their statements were sharply contradicted in the film by ensuing statements and images:

> I am bound, however, to express my horror at the treatment given to the interviews with the President and the Prime Minister, as regards to the selective technique applied to their presentation and the context in which they were incorporated in the film. My feelings are not in any way assuaged when I recall that in agreeing to give these interviews, the President and the Prime Minister were influenced to a large extent by your assurances, conveyed to them by me, as to the fairness and objectivity which were to characterise the film.[56]

Kleinerman was advised in the strongest of terms that the Irish government was deeply offended by the film.

The letter from the Irish government did not particularly impress Kleinerman. He responded that he was 'both surprised and shocked' by the government's complaints. 'On the basis of our research, our discussions with the people of Ireland, and our examination of all sources of material available to us, we feel that we covered the main points of the story of Ireland today.'[57] Kleinerman described O'Hanrahan's complaint of the de Valera and Lemass interviews as

> very unfair and unwarranted' and explained that it had not been the intention of CBS 'do another travelogue on Ireland', and lectured the director that he had made 'an effort to examine Ireland today as it is, not as it might be or as people imagine it to be'.[58]

Kleinerman continued by extolling the virtues of his network and his programme, arguing that honesty, fairness, and objectivity were critical components of the series. He continued in a rather dismissive tone:

> We cannot and do not take sides or plead special causes. . . . naturally we are not surprised when partisans are distressed at our non-partisanship in showing situations that they wish didn't exist. But for us to pretend that these situations did not exist would be journalistically dishonest as well as unconstructive.'[59]

In concluding his letter Kleinerman mentioned that his programme was an award-winning educational series that had received praise from all corners. The government was told that the network had received over one hundred letters, 61 per cent of which praised the show. A copy of letters from a chapter of the Ancient Order of the Hibernians and a chapter of the Knights of Columbanus were included to bolster the network's position. The Irish government decided not to answer the Kleinerman letter, believing that nothing further could be gained from writing to CBS.

Lemass believed that an arrogant American network that cared little for accuracy in producing its programmes had slandered government and country. The entire episode served as a warning to Lemass. Over the next six years the Taoiseach often clashed with the new authority over programmes and comments that were critical of government policy. However, the 1960 Broadcasting Act had given Irish television a remarkable degree of independence and the ability of the government to control or censor its programmes was limited. Television became an important part of the age of Lemass, and an agent in the transformation of Irish society that characterised his tenure as Taoiseach.

Notes

Chapter 1 Whose Ireland?

1   Frank Skinner, *Politicians by Accident* (Dublin, 1946), pp. 87–8.

2   Among the major contributions to the study of Lemass the following are of particular importance. J. J. Lee, *Ireland: 1912–85: Politics and Society* (Cambridge, 1989); John Horgan, *Sean Lemass: The Enigmatic Patriot* (Dublin, 1997); Paul Bew and Henry Patterson, *Sean Lemass and the Making of Modern Ireland* (Dublin, 1982); Richard Dunphy, *The Making of Fianna Fáil Power in Ireland* (Oxford, 1995); Brian Girvin, *Between Two Worlds: Politics and Economy in Independent Ireland* (Dublin, 1989); Brian Girvin, *From Union to Union: Nationalism, Religion and Democracy from the Act of Union to the European Union* (Dublin, 2002); Gary Murphy, *Economic Realignment and the Politics of EEC entry, Ireland, 1948–1973* (Bethesda, 2003).

3   UCDA MacEntee Papers, P67/299 Childers's report on 1948 general election.

4   Lars Mjøset, *The Irish Economy in Comparative Institutional Perspective* (Dublin, 1992).

5   As quoted in John F. McCarthy (ed.), *Planning Ireland's Future: The Legacy of T. K. Whitaker* (Dublin, 1990), p. 3.

6   Brian Girvin notes that people he has been interviewing for another study do not recall the 1950s as a period of crisis, but of fairly genteel living and a reasonable standard of living. As early as 1960 there were thousands of TV sets in Dublin at a time when the Irish TV service had yet to begin. Yet others who Gary Murphy has spoken to, mainly of college-going age and class in the late 1950s, maintain that they saw emigration as their main way of gaining satisfactory employment on graduation. It may be necessary to re-evaluate the meaning of crisis in terms of both class and status.

Chapter 2 Political and party competition in post-war Ireland

1   Only two European states, Ireland and Sweden held wartime elections. Cornelius O'Leary, *Irish Elections 1918–1977: Parties, Voters and Proportional Representation* (Dublin, 1979), p. 35.

2   Tom Garvin, *The Evolution of Irish Nationalist Politics* (Dublin, 1981), p. 166.

3 Donal Nevin, 'Industry and labour', in Kevin B. Nowlan and T. Desmond Williams (eds), *Ireland in the War Years and After, 1938–51* (Dublin, 1969), p. 102.

4 See Michael Gallagher, 'Party solidarity, exclusivity and inter-party relationships in Ireland, 1922–77: the evidence of transfers', *Economic and Social Review* 10:1 (1978), pp. 1–22; Brian Girvin, 'Politics in wartime: governing, neutrality and elections' in Brian Girvin and Geoffrey Roberts (eds), *Ireland and the Second World War: Politics, Society and Remembrance* (Dublin, 2000), p. 44.

5 See Tom Garvin, 'The destiny of soldiers: tradition and modernity in the politics of de Valera's Ireland', *Political Studies* 26:3 (1978) for an analysis of the election result.

6 Brian Farrell, *Seán Lemass* (Dublin, 1983), pp. 77–8

7 UCDA, MacEntee Papers, P67/299, Erskine Childers to Seán MacEntee, n.d. (after Feb. 1948).

8 See Niamh Puirséil, 'Labour and coalition: the impact of the first inter-party government, 1948–51', *Saothar* 27 (2002), pp. 55–6 for Labour's response.

9 See for instance the Fianna Fáil advertisement in the *Leader*, 31 Jan. 1948, which responded to complaints that the price of a bottle of stout had gone up by tuppence halfpenny by arguing that at least voters could 'eat and sleep in security for tomorrow – and the next day'.

10 See David McCullagh, *A Makeshift Majority: The First Inter-Party Government, 1948–51* (Dublin, 1998).

11 Kevin O'Doherty, 'Working for Seán Lemass, 1944–46: reflections of a private secretary'. Paper presented to the Research Seminar in Contemporary Irish History, TCD, 15 Oct. 2003.

12 Figures taken from Richard Sinnott, *Irish Voters Decide: Voting Behaviour in Elections and Referendums Since 1918* (Manchester, 1995), p. 299.

13 McCullagh, *Makeshift Majority*, p. 36.

14 See Fianna Fáil, *The Story of Fianna Fáil: First Phase* (Dublin, 1960), p. 101; UCDA, MacEntee Papers, Erskine Childers to Seán MacEntee, n.d. (after Feb. 1948), P67/299.

15 Childers to MacEntee.

16 Farrell, *Lemass*, p. 84; Horgan, *Enigmatic Patriot*, p. 144; Michael B. Yeats, *Cast a Cold Eye: Memories of a Poet's Son and Politician* (Dublin, 1998), p. 49.

17 Farrell, *Lemass*, p. 84.

18 Garvin, *Evolution*, p. 175. See also Tom Garvin, *Preventing the Future: Why Was Ireland So Poor for So Long?* (Dublin, 2004), p. 186.

19 Yeats, *Memories*, p. 49.

20 Quoted in Paul Bew and Henry Patterson, *Seán Lemass and the Making of Modern Ireland 1945–66* (Dublin, 1982), pp. 61–2.

21 *The Leader* quoted in Gary Murphy 'The politics of economic realignment' (PhD thesis, DCU, 1996), p. 57.

22 Lord Longford and T. P. O'Neill, *Eamon de Valera* (Dublin and London, 1970), p. 439.

23 See Farrell, *Lemass*, p. 53.

24 See Ronan Fanning, *The Irish Department of Finance* (Dublin, 1978), p. 470.

25 John Horgan, *Enigmatic Patriot*, p. 158.

26 UCDA, Fianna Fáil parliamentary party minutes, 3 Dec. 1952, P176/446.

27 UCDA, special meeting of the Fianna Fáil parliamentary party, 14 Jan. 1953 P176/446.

28 UCDA, Fianna Fáil parliamentary party minutes, 22 July 1953 P176/446.

29 Yeats, *Memories*, p. 55. There is a possibility that Yeats telescoped the events. The minutes show that the debate was resumed, not at the next meeting but the following January. It is likely that what Yeats refers to as a defeat on this occasion was in fact the shelving of the motion which as he saw it required immediate action.

30 *Irish Times*, 17 July 1953.

31 Brian Girvin, *Between Two Worlds: Politics and Economy in Independent Ireland* (Dublin, 1989), p. 186; Fanning, *Finance*, p. 496.

32 Fanning, *Finance*, p. 498; Girvin, *Between Two Worlds*, p. 187.

33 Fanning, *Finance*, p. 498.

34 *Irish Times*, 19 Nov. 1953.

35 *Irish Times*, 25–28 Dec. 1953.

36 *The Leader*, 5 June 1954, quoted in J. J. Lee *Ireland 1912–1985: Politics and Society* (Cambridge, 1989), p. 367

37 Horgan, *Enigmatic Patriot*, p. 160.

38 UCDA, Fianna Fáil Papers, *Gléas*, Nov. 1954, P176/985.

39 See C. S. Andrews *Man of No Property* (Dublin, 1982), p. 15; Farrell, *Lemass*, p. 13; Richard Dunphy, *The Making of Fianna Fáil Power in Ireland, 1923–1948* (Oxford, 1995), p. 84.

40 Report of the 25th Fianna Fáil Ard Fheis, 12–13 Oct. 1954, Fianna Fáil Papers, Centre for Contemporary Irish History (CCIH), TCD.

41 UCDA, Fianna Fáil Papers, Seán Lemass to Andreas O'Keeffe, 27 Sept. 1954, P176/283.

42 UCDA, *Gléas*, Feb. 1955, P176/985

43 *Irish Times*, 8–9 Apr. 1955.

44 Tuairim constitution, n.d.

45 Murphy, *Economic Realignment*, p. 80; Lee, *Ireland*, p. 341.

46 See for instance UCDA, MacEntee Papers, Memorandum on financial policy for party committee by Seán Lemass, 15 Apr. 1955, P67/468(3).

47 Horgan, *Enigmatic Patriot*, p. 165.

48 John F. McCarthy (ed.), *Planning Ireland's Future: The Legacy of T. K. Whitaker* (Dublin, 1990).

49 *Irish Times,* 15 Oct. 1955

50 Horgan, *Enigmatic Patriot,* pp. 166–7.

51 See John Horgan, *Irish Media: A Critical History Since 1922* (London, 2001), p. 68.

52 *Irish Times,* 18 Feb. 1956.

53 Report of the 26th Fianna Fáil Árd Fheis, 22–23 Nov. 1955, Fianna Fáil Papers, CCIH, TCD.

54 *Irish Times,* 12 May 1956.

55 *Irish Times,* 2 June 1956.

56 See McCarthy, *Planning,* pp. 28–9.

57 Ibid.; Fanning, *Finance,* p. 506.

58 *Irish Times,* 6 Oct. 1956.

59 Murphy, *Economic Realignment,* p. 93.

60 Report of the 27th Fianna Fáil Árd Fheis, 20–21 Nov. 1956, Fianna Fáil Papers, CCIH, TCD.

61 Murphy, *Economic Realignment,* p. 93.

62 McCarthy, *Planning,* pp. 68–9.

63 Coleman Tadhg O'Sullivan, 'The IRA takes constitutional action: a history of Clann na Poblachta' (MA thesis, UCD, 1995), p. 131

64 Basil Chubb, 'Ireland 1957', in D. E Butler (ed.), *Elections Abroad* (London, 1959), p. 198.

65 Chubb, *Ireland,* p. 198.

66 McCarthy, *Planning,* p. 35.

67 Although it had not won a plurality of seats in the new Dáil, it had a majority of sitting deputies as a result of the abstention of the four newly elected Sinn Féin deputies.

68 J. J. Lee, 'Seán Lemass' in J. J. Lee (ed.), *Ireland, 1945–70* (Dublin, 1979).

69 Farrell, *Lemass,* p. 95.

70 Horgan, *Enigmatic Patriot,* p. 175.

71 Tim Pat Coogan, *De Valera: Long Fellow, Long Shadow* (London, 1993), p. 91.

72 Horgan, *Enigmatic Patriot,* p. 180; Farrell, *Lemass,* p. 96.

73 Yeats, *Memories,* p. 71.

74 Lee, *Ireland,* p. 409.

75 Horgan, *Enigmatic Patriot,* p. 176.

76 Quoted in Ronan Fanning, 'The genesis of economic development' in McCarthy (ed.), *Planning,* p. 78.

77 Maurice Manning, *James Dillon: A Biography* (Dublin, 1999), p. 360.

78 Manning, *Dillon,* p. 333

79 Basil Chubb, *The Government and Politics of Ireland* (Oxford, 1971), p. 76

80 *Business and Finance,* 26 Mar. 1965

81 David Thornley, 'Irish politics and the left', *Hibernia,* June 1963.

82 Dunphy, *Fianna Fáil*, p. 25.

83 See Manning, *Dillon*, p. 311.

84 *Business and Finance*, 3 Mar. 1967.

Chapter 3 From economic nationalism to European Union

1   This figure is given in NAI DT S.16474A, Criticism of *Economic Development* by Departments of Health and Industry and Commerce with details of disparity between Ireland and Britain, 4 July 1958.

2   Jonathan Haughton, 'The historical background', in John W. O'Hagan, *The Economy of Ireland: Policy and Performance*, 6th edn (Dublin, 1991), p. 38.

3   See Alan Milward, *The Reconstruction of Western Europe: 1945–1951* (London, 1984); *Peter Katzenstein, Small States in World Markets* (Ithaca, NY: 1985).

4   T. K. Whitaker, *Economic Development* (Dublin, 1958), p. 218.

5   David O'Mahony, 'Economic expansion in Ireland', *Studies* 48:190 (1959), p. 134.

6   Tom Garvin, *Preventing the Future: Why Was Ireland So Poor For So Long* (Dublin, 2004), p. 118.

7   UCDA, Todd Andrews Papers, Notes for lecture in 1957 entitled 'Is emigration inevitable in Ireland?', P91/136(1), n.d.

8   Garret FitzGerald, 'Mr Whitaker and industry', *Studies* 48: 190 (1959), p. 149.

9   T. K. Whitaker, 'Financial turning points', *Interests* (Dublin, 1983), p. 91.

10   UCDA, Fianna Fáil Parliamentary Party Minutes, 11 Dec. 1958, P176/441/B.

11   UCDA, Fianna Fáil Parliamentary Party Minutes, 28 Jan. 1959, P176/441/B.

12   UCDA, Fianna Fáil Parliamentary Party Minutes, 4 Mar., 11 Mar., 29 Apr. 1959, P176/441/B.

13   NAI, DT S2850 F/64, Lemass to Margaret Greenan, 18 July 1959.

14   DF, F.121/15/59, Reasons for Reducing Protection, 14 Dec. 1959.

15   DF, F.121/15/59, MacCarthy to Whitaker, 24 Dec. 1959.

16   Andrews quotes Kavanagh's poem 'Memory of Brother Michael', 14 Oct. 1944, in 'Is emigration inevitable in Ireland?'

17   Bruce Arnold, *Jack Lynch: Hero in Crisis* (Dublin, 2001), p. 54.

18   Conversation with Dr Garret FitzGerald, 8 Dec. 2004 at an eyewitness seminar in Trinity College, Dublin on *Ireland in the 1950s* where I acted as the respondent to the eyewitness recollections of the eminent economist Professor Louden Ryan.

19   Brian Girvin, *From Union to Union: Nationalism, Democracy and Religion in Ireland – Act of Union to EU* (Dublin, 2002), p. 205.

20   DF, F.121/20/60, Note of Meeting of Secretaries held in Department of Finance, 6 Apr. 1961.

21   Author's interview with Tadhg O'Cearbhaill. Mr O'Cearbhaill served as private secretary to three Ministers for Industry and Commerce, Seán Lemass, Daniel Morrissey

and William Norton. He became assistant secretary at the Department of the Taoiseach in 1960 and was appointed the first secretary of the Department of Labour in 1967.

22 Comments of Professor Louden Ryan at eyewitness seminar, 8 Dec. 2004, and later conversation with the author.

23 Author's interview with the late Dr Aodogan O'Rahilly. Dr O'Rahilly was an industrialist during this period. He was chairman of Bord na Mona from 1959 to 1974. He was awarded an honorary doctorate by the NUI in 1974 for his contribution to the development of Bord na Mona.

24 Fitzpatrick is quoted in *Hibernia*, Mar. 1962.

25 *Industrial Review: The Journal of the Federation of Irish Industries* 18: 5 (Sept.–Oct. 1961).

26 Gary Murphy, 'Towards a corporate state? Seán Lemass and the realignment of interest groups in the policy process 1948–1964', *Administration* 47: 1 (Spring 1999), pp. 92–3.

27 National Archives and Records Administration, Washington, Record Group 59, Box 1652, 740/00(W)/5-2562, Dublin Embassy to State Department, 25 May 1962.

28 Author's interview with Colm Barnes. Mr Barnes was a major industrialist during this period with the textile company Glen Abbey; he became President of the FII in 1961 and represented that organisation on the Committee for Industrial Organisation in the early 1960s.

29 NAI, DT S.16877Y/62, Meeting between the Taoiseach, the Minister for Industry and Commerce and the Federation of Irish Industry, 8 Jan. 1962.

30 Confidential source who worked in the Department of Industry and Commerce, in conversation with the author.

31 Author's interview with Mr Joseph McCullough. Mr McCullough was an engineer and general manager of a number of manufacturing industries throughout this period.

32 Author's interview with Domhnall McCullough. Mr McCullough was a leading industrialist in the clothing trade during this period.

33 NAI, ICTU, Box 44 (Part 2) 4011, ICTU Economic Committee, Memorandum on the Application for entry to the EEC, July 1961.

34 NAI, DT S.17120A/62, Meeting between the Taoiseach, the Minister for Industry and Commerce and the Irish Congress of Trade Unions, 11 Jan. 1962.

35 NLI, ICTU Annual Conference, Cork, July 1961, p. 256. ICTU, Annual Conference, Galway, July 1962, p. 227

36 NLI, ICTU Annual Conference, Galway, July 1962, p. 227.

37 NAI, ICTU, Box 44 (Part 2) 4011, 'ICTU policy statement on entry to the EEC', July 1962.

38 NLI, ICTU Annual Conference, Galway, July 1962, p. 235.

39 NLI, ICTU Annual Conference, Cork, July 1961, p. 269.

40 NLI, ICTU Annual Conference, Killarney, 1963, p. 278.

41 NAI, ICTU, Box 43 (Part 2) Consultative Conference – Free Trade and Industrial Reorganisation, 4011/A, 22 Mar. 1963.

42 NLI, ICTU Annual Conference, Killarney, 1963, p. 278.

43 NAI, ICTU, Box 43 (Part 2) Consultative Conference. Lemass is quoted as speaking on 25 Feb. 1963. No place is given.

44 NAI, ICTU, Box 43 (Part 2), ICTU Consultative Conference, 22 Mar. 1963.

45 Committee on Industrial Organisation, *Final Report* (Dublin, 1965).

46 Conroy is quoted in the *Irish Press*, 10 July 1963.

47 Gary Murphy, '"Fostering a spurious progeny?": the trade union movement and Europe, 1957–1964', *Saothar* 21 (1996), p. 69.

48 DF, F.121/36/63, Whitaker to MacCarthy, 19 July 1962.

49 Ibid.

50 DF, F.121/36/63, MacCarthy to Nicholas O'Nuallain, 2 Aug. 1962.

51 DF, F.121/20/60, Note of Meeting of the Committee of Secretaries, 13 Nov. 1962.

52 NAI, DT S.16877Y/62, NFA statement on entry to the EEC, 20 July 1960.

53 Juan Greene, 'The next ten years in agriculture', quoted in DF D.306/10/61.

54 NAI, DT S.16877X/62, Whitaker to Minister for Finance, 5 Jan. 1962.

55 NAI, DT S.16877W, Memorandum for the Government: Application for membership of the European Community, 8 Jan. 1962.

56 *Dáil Deb*, vol. 185, cols 560–1, 1 Dec. 1960.

57 NAI, DT S.16877X/62, Lemass Statement to the Council of Ministers, 18 Jan. 1962.

58 *Dáil Deb*, vol. 199, col. 924, 5 Feb. 1963.

59 Maurice FitzGerald, 'Ireland's relations with the EEC: from the treaties of Rome to membership', *Journal of European Integration History* 7:1 (2001), p. 20.

60 Girvin, *From Union to Union*, p. 209.

Chapter 4 Emigration, political cultures and post-war Irish society

1   David Fitzpatrick, *Irish Emigration, 1801–1921* (Dublin, 1984), p. 1.

2   This is an estimate of net migration based on census data: gross migration flows would be considerably higher.

3   NLI, Frank Gallagher Papers, MS 18,339, p. 11. For the wider context, see John Horgan, *Seán Lemass: The Enigmatic Patriot* (Dublin, 1997), pp. 51–2.

4   Ruth Dudley Edwards, *Patrick Pearse: The Triumph of Failure* (Dublin, 1990), p. 183.

5   Enda Delaney, 'Placing postwar Irish migration to Britain in a comparative European perspective, 1945–1981', in Andy Bielenberg (ed.), *The Irish Diaspora* (London, 2000), pp. 341–4.

6   See, for more information, Tom Garvin, *Nationalist Revolutionaries in Ireland, 1858–1928* (Oxford, 1987).

7   Joseph Lee and Gearóid Ó Tuathaigh, *The Age of De Valera* (Dublin, 1982), p. 165; Richard Dunphy, *The Making of Fianna Fáil in Power in Ireland, 1923–1948* (Oxford,

1995), p. 236; Brian Girvin, *From Union to Union: Nationalism, Democracy and Religion in Ireland – Act of Union to EU* (Dublin, 2002), p. 172

8   J. J. Lee, 'Continuity and change in Ireland, 1945–70', in J. J. Lee (ed.), *Ireland, 1945–70* (Dublin, 1979), p. 169.

9   See Enda Delaney, *Demography, State and Society: Irish Migration to Britain, 1921–1971* (Montreal/Kingston and Liverpool, 2000), p. 296.

10 Kerby A. Miller, *Emigrants and Exiles: Ireland and the Irish Exodus to North America* (New York, 1985).

11 Ibid., p. 4.

12 Pauric Travers, '"The dream gone bust": Irish responses to emigration, 1922–60', in Oliver MacDonagh and W. F. Mandle (eds), *Irish Australian Studies* (Canberra, 1989), p. 326.

13 Delaney, *Demography, State and Society*, p. 296.

14 J. J. Lee, *Ireland, 1912–1985: Politics and Society* (Cambridge, 1989), p. 385.

15 Peter Pyne, 'The third Sinn Féin party: 1923–1926, part II', *Economic and Social Review* 1:2 (1969), p. 238.

16 Michael Gallagher, *Electoral Support for Irish Political Parties, 1927–1973* (London, 1976), p. 25, 54–8; Girvin, *From Union to Union*, pp. 138–9, 189–92.

17 For an assessment of the support base of Fianna Fáil and the relationship with its traditional ideology, see Tom Garvin, 'The destiny of the soldiers: tradition and modernity in the politics of De Valera's Ireland', *Political Studies* 26 (1978), pp. 345–7.

18 Delaney, *Demography, State and Society*, pp. 204–5.

19 Tracey Connolly, 'Irish workers in Britain during the Second World War', in Brian Girvin and Geoffrey Roberts (eds), *Ireland and the Second World War: Politics, Society and Remembrance* (Dublin, 2000), pp. 212–32; Delaney, *Demography, State and Society*, pp. 129–30.

20 Commission on Emigration and Other Population Problems, 1948–54, *Reports* ([Dublin], 1955), pp. 268–70.

21 Ibid., table 86, p. 115.

22 *Census of Population of Ireland, 1956: Vol. I* (Dublin, 1957), table x, p. xxi.

23 NAI, DT S 11582B, Department of External Affairs: memorandum for the government [on female emigration], 30 Aug. 1947, p. 8.

24 NAI, DFA 402/218/4, copy of letter from Sean MacBride to the Rev. T. J. Counihan, S.J., Feb. 1949 [exact date not on copy].

25 See Delaney, *Demography, State and Society*, pp. 186–92; Girvin, *From Union to Union*, pp. 149–50.

26 NAI, DT S 11582B, Department of External Affairs, memorandum on emigration, 30 Dec. 1947, p. 15.

27 Ibid., p. 21.

28 Quoted in Travers, '"The dream gone bust"', p. 328.

29 Commission on Emigration and Other Population Problems, 1948–1954, *Reports*, p. 1.

30 These surveys together with other materials relating to the Commission on Emigration and Other Population Problems are contained in the private papers of Arnold Marsh, a member of the Commission, held by TCD, MS 8297–8308.

31 Brian Girvin asserts that 'the delay was partly due to de Valera's reluctance to publish it while in office, given that the draft report had been available since the end of 1951 (Girvin, *From Union to Union*, p. 162).

32 *Dáil Deb*, vol. 159, col. 1708, 25 July 1956.

33 Commission on Emigration and Other Population Problems, 1948–1954, *Reports*, p. 134.

34 Ibid, pp. 135–6.

35 Ibid., p. 142.

36 NAI, DT S 14249 A/2, confidential note on the progress of the Commission on Population [*sic*] and other Population Problems, by W. A. Honohan, 28 Aug. 1951.

37 NAI, DT S 14249 A/2, extract from cabinet minutes, GC 7/16, 9 Aug. 1954.

38 Delaney, *Demography, State and Society*, p. 200.

39 *Irish Times*, 26 June 1956.

40 See Delaney, *Demography, State and Society*, pp. 200–1 for this line of argument.

41 Travers, '"The dream gone bust"', p. 326.

42 Delaney, *Demography, State and Society*, pp. 65–9, 134–5.

43 Ibid., pp. 65–9, 257–9.

44 NAI, DT 97/6/310, Welfare work amongst the Irish workers in Britain, summary prepared by the Department of External Affairs, 15 Dec. 1961, p. 1.

45 Ibid.

46 NAI, DFA 412/9, memorandum for the government: reports of the Commission on Emigration and other Population Problems, 22 July 1956, pp. 4–5.

47 *Irish Times*, 31 Aug. 1951. His comments were based on a report prepared by a full-time official of the Young Christian Workers' Association, Maurice Foley. For the context of de Valera's statement, see Delaney, *Demography, State and Society*, pp. 193–6.

48 This point was made in the contemporary newspaper coverage of the debate surrounding the speech (Delaney, *Demography, State and Society*, p. 195).

49 *Dáil Deb*, vol. 191, cols 671–2, 11 July 1961.

50 NAI, DT S 15398 B, James Fergus, Secretary of the Irish Catholic hierarchy, to Seán Lemass, 31 July 1965.

51 Ibid., Lemass to Fergus, 7 Sept. 1965.

52 Ibid.

53 For a brief overview, see Kieran O'Shea, *The Irish Emigrant Chaplaincy Scheme in Britain, 1957–82* (Naas, 1985).

54 NAI, DT S 99/1/287, Department of Labour: proposals in relation to official policy on emigration to Great Britain, 29 Nov. 1968, pp. 8–13.

55 Ibid., pp. 25–6

56 Ibid., p. 28.

57 Ibid., p. 29.

58 Ibid., p. 30.

59 NAI, DT S 2000/6/561, extract from Cabinet Minutes, G.C./12/171, 28 Mar. 1969.

60 Ibid.

61 Ibid., Secretary to the Government to Private Secretary, Minister of Labour, 2 Apr. 1969; *Irish Press*, 21 Apr. 1969.

62 *Irish Press*, 4 Oct. 1969.

63 NAI, DT 97/6/310, copy of statement by Seán Lemass on the proposed British legislation on immigration, 21 Nov. 1961, p. 1.

64 Enda Delaney, *Irish Emigration since 1921* (Dublin, 2002), p. 39, table 4.

65 Cormac Ó Gráda and Brendan M. Walsh, 'The economic effects of emigration: Ireland', in Beth J. Asch (ed.), *Emigration and its Effects on the Sending Country* (Santa Monica, CA, 1994), p. 100.

66 John A. O'Brien, 'The Irish enigma', in John A. O'Brien (ed.), *The Vanishing Irish: The Enigma of the Modern World* (New York, 1953), p. 3.

67 NAI, DT S 16066A, 'Has Ireland a future? Scheme of work' by T. K. Whitaker, 12 Dec. 1957, p. 1. For the general context of the preparation of this memorandum, see Horgan, *Enigmatic Patriot*, p. 176.

68 Whitaker, 'Has Ireland a future?'.

69 Delaney, *Demography, State and Society*, p. 161.

70 Ibid., pp. 205–6.

71 Ronan Fanning, 'The genesis of *Economic Development*', in John F. McCarthy, (ed.), *Planning Ireland's Future: The Legacy of T. K. Whitaker* (Dublin, 1990), p. 32; John F. McCarthy, *The Irish Department of Finance, 1922–58* (Dublin, 1978), pp. 515–16; B. M. Walsh, 'Economic growth and development', in J. J. Lee (ed.), *Ireland, 1945–70* (Dublin, 1979), pp. 28–9. The preliminary results of the 1956 census were published in June of the same year.

72 Department of Finance, *Economic Development*, p. 5.

73 Whitaker 'Has Ireland a future?', p. 2.

74 Ibid.

75 For example Paul Bew and Henry Patterson, *Seán Lemass and the Making of Modern Ireland, 1945–66* (Dublin, 1982), pp. 118–44; Lee, *Ireland, 1912–1985*, pp. 329–65; Girvin, *From Union to Union*, pp. 201–12.

76 Horgan, *Enigmatic Patriot*, p. 213.

77 J. J. Lee, 'Seán Lemass', in J. J. Lee (ed.), *Ireland, 1945–70* (Dublin, 1979), p. 23.

78 Líam Kennedy, *The Modern Industrialisation of Ireland, 1940–1988* (Dublin, 1989), p. 15.

79 Horgan, *Enigmatic Patriot*, p. 162.

80 NAI, DT S 16325 B, text of speech by Seán Lemass at the annual dinner of the Dublin Chamber of Commerce, 25 Oct. 1960, p. 1.

81 Ibid., p. 4.

82 *Dáil Deb*, vol. 184, col. 350, 2 Nov. 1960; for a similar statement of Irish government policy see NAI, DT S 16325 B, emigration to Britain: brief statement of the policy of the government of Ireland, 7 Oct. 1960.

83 NAI, DT S 97/6/310, text of speech by Seán Lemass at the annual dinner of Galway Chamber of Commerce, 19 Jan. 1961, p. 1.

84 Delaney, *Demography, State and Society*, pp. 253–4.

85 Ibid.

86 NAI, DT S 13101 F, memorandum from Seán Lemass to Secretary, 1 Apr. 1960.

87 This incident is documented in Horgan, *Enigmatic Patriot*, pp. 316–17.

88 NAI, DT 16325, copy of resolution adopted by the Corporation of Dublin in emigration, 9 Nov. 1960; copy of resolution adopted by Dublin City Council, 8 Dec. 1960.

89 NAI, DT S 16325 B, text of speech by Seán Lemass at the annual dinner of the Dublin Chamber of Commerce, 25 Oct. 1960, p. 3.

90 Quoted in Lee, *Ireland, 1912–1985*, p. 374.

91 This argument is based on Lee's thought-provoking analysis of post-war Irish emigration (Lee, *Ireland, 1912–1985*, pp. 373–86).

Chapter 5 Ireland and the productivity drive of post-war Europe

I am indebted to Brian Donnelly and to other members of the staff of the National Archives for their assistance.

1 NAI, DFA 305/57/226, Establishment of a Productivity Centre in Ireland: 'Memorandum for the government: establishment of an Industrial Productivity Centre: summary', 26 June 1950.

2 Bernadette Whelan, *Ireland and the Marshall Plan, 1947–57* (Dublin, 2000) p. 315.

3 NAI, DFA 305/57/226, Establishment of a Productivity Centre in Ireland. memorandum dated 22 June 1951: handwritten note conveying Minister's suggestion dated 3 July 1951.

4 Jacqueline McGlade 'Americanization: ideology or process? The case of the United States Technical Assistance and Productivity Programme', in Jonathan Zeitlin and Gary Herrigel (eds), *Americanization and its Limits: Reworking US Technology and Management in Post-War Europe and Japan* (Oxford, 2000), pp. 53–75.

5 Bent Boel, *The European Productivity Agency and Transatlantic Relations, 1953–1961* (Copenhagen, 2003), ch. 1.

6 Ibid., p. 136.

7 NAI, DETE R303/7/59, Establishment of National Productivity Centre in Ireland 'Extract from Report of Industry and Commerce Departmental Conference', 2 Mar. 1954.

8 NAI, DETE R303/7/59, Establishment of National Productivity Centre in Ireland: Industries Division 'A' 'European Productivity Agency' Eanair [January] 1958.

9 Ibid.

10 See NAI, DFA 99/3/70, OEEC Grant Counterpart Fund: Establishment of a Fund for defraying in whole or in part the cost of Technical Assistance Projects. NAI, DIC EPA/5/8, contains a letter of 23 Dec. 1958 from Industry and Commerce to Finance that lists the technical assistance grants made for participation in EPA activities using grant counterpart funding. For the negotiation of the Grant Counterpart fund agreement and sub-agreements see Whelan, *Ireland and the Marshall Plan*, ch. 7.

11 NAI, DETE R303/7/59, Establishment of National Productivity Centre in Ireland 'Extract from Report of Industry and Commerce Departmental Conference 12 October 1954': letter from Director IIRS to Secretary Industry and Commerce, 26 July 1955.

12 NAI, DETE R303/7/59, Establishment of National Productivity Centre in Ireland letter from Chairman IIRS and Director IIRS to Minister for Industry and Commerce, 30 Nov. 1956.

13 NAI, DETE/13/17, Minutes of Industry and Commerce Departmental Conference, 28 Jan. 1957; NAI, DETE R303/7/59, Establishment of National Productivity Centre in Ireland 'Diary of Events Leading to Formation of I.N.P.C.'

14 Tom Cox *The Making of Managers: A History of the Irish Management Institute 1952–2002* (Cork, 2002), p. 70.

15 NAI, DETE R303/7/59, Establishment of National Productivity Centre in Ireland 'Report of meeting: European Productivity Agency', 30 May 1958.

16 Ibid.

17 On the congress split see Charles McCarthy, *Trade Unions in Ireland 1894–1960* (Dublin, 1977), chs 6–11; for its effects on the IIRS-convened committee see NAI, DETE R303/7/67, Papers Regarding Productivity Committee and NAI, ICTU/2/378 (a) and (b), Economic Policy, Industrial Development, Industrial Productivity.

18 NAI, ICTU/2/378 (a) Economic Policy, Industrial Development, Industrial Productivity, letter from A. Vermuelen to Secretary ITUC 14 Nov. 1957; letter from V. Agostinone to R. Roberts, 13 Dec. 1957; NAI, DETE R303/7/59, Establishment of National Productivity Centre in Ireland Industries Division 'A' 'European Productivity Agency' Eanair [January] 1958.

19 NAI, DETE R303/8/25, Invitation by the Irish Trade Union Congress to the Deputy Director of EPA to address ITUC conference: NAI, DFA 57/168/412, Proposed Visit of Dr. King.

20 NAI, DIC TIW/1280/1, letter from Director of EPA to Head of Irish Delegation to OEEC, 3 May 1957.

21 NAI, DIC TIW/1280/1, contains the draft together with related notes and memoranda.

22 NAI, DETE/13/18, Minutes of Industry and Commerce Departmental Conference, 1 July 1957; for Denis Hegarty's career see Henry Boylan (ed.), *A Dictionary of Irish Biography*, 3rd edn (Dublin, 1998), p. 174.

23 NAI, DETE/13/18, Minutes of Industry and Commerce Departmental Conference, 15 July 1957.

24 Ibid.; for the correspondence between Lemass and Swift, who – while sympathetic – declined to act as a go-between and urged Lemass to approach the PUTUO leadership directly, see NAI, DIC TIW/1280/1. Swift's report on the EPA Collective Bargaining and Productivity seminar in Berlin is also to be found in this file.

25 See NAI, DIC TIW/1280/1, for correspondence and meetings relating to IMI's exploration.

26 See NAI, DETE R303/8/25, Invitation by the Irish Trade Union Congress to the Deputy Director of EPA to address ITUC conference; letter from Industry and Commerce to IMI 26 Nov. 1957.

27 NAI, ICTU 4/268/Box 30, Establishment of Human Sciences Committee and of Productivity Committee, Minutes of First Preliminary Meeting to Consider the Establishment of a Joint Committee to Implement EPA Project 405, 14 Mar. 1958.

28 Ibid. For the EPA Director's visit see Minutes of Second Preliminary Meeting to Consider the Establishment of a Joint Committee to Implement EPA Project 405, 6 June 1958; on the 'formation of a Body with wider functions' see Minutes of a Meeting held at 12 Leeson Park, 8 July 1958.

29 NAI, DETE R303/7/59, Establishment of National Productivity Centre in Ireland 'Report of meeting: proposed committee to deal with productivity matters', 11 July 1958.

30 On the HSC see Peter Murray, *The Transatlantic Politics of Productivity and the Origins of Public Funding Support for Social Science Research in Ireland, 1950–1979* NIRSA Working Paper No. 22, Apr. 2004 http://www.may.ie/nirsa/publications/WPS22.pdf.

31 NAI, DT S 15,453 G/62, letter from Chairman INPC to Secretary Industry and Commerce, 11 Apr. 1962.

32 NAI, DT S 15453 F/61, Memorandum 'Proposals for re-assessing the aims and functions of the Irish National Productivity Committee and for giving it a permanent organisation', Nov. 1961.

33 Copies of the final, agreed version of the Statement of Productivity Principles can be found in NAI, DT S 15453 E/61.

34 NAI, DT S 15453 D/1, letter from Lemass to President FUE, 29 Dec. 1960; NAI, DT S 15453 D/2/61, letter from Director General FUE to Lemass, 11 January 1961; FUE Memorandum on Draft Statement of Productivity Principles; undated Department of Taoiseach memorandum 'Observation on FUE Memorandum of January 1961 on draft statement of productivity principles dated 14th November 1960 and circulated by

the Irish National Productivity Committee'; undated memorandum from Chairman INPC commenting on FUE memorandum; notes by Taoiseach on meeting with FUE deputation 23 Jan. 1961.

35 NAI, DT S 15453 E/61, letter from Director General FUE to Chairman INPC, 26 Apr. 1961.

36 NAI, DT S 15453 E/61, letter from Chairman INPC to Lemass, 13 June 1961; letter from Director General FUE to Taoiseach's Private Secretary, 27 July 1961.

37 NAI, DETE/13/22, Minutes of Industry and Commerce Departmental Conference, 29 Nov. 1960; NAI, DETE/13/23 Minutes of Industry and Commerce Departmental Conference, 27 Mar. 1961; for a later, overt disagreement within the Committee on Industrial Organisation over redundant workers' rights see Garret FitzGerald, *Planning in Ireland: A P.E.P Study* (Dublin, 1968), pp. 63–4.

38 See Richard Griffiths (ed.), *Explorations in OEEC History* (Paris, 1997).

39 Boel, *The European Productivity Agency*, pp. 81–92.

40 NAI, DFA 305/57/15, VII B Minutes of Meeting of the Inter-Departmental European Recovery Programme Committee, 5 Oct. 1962: 'A discussion followed on the question of less-developed status . . . the representatives of the Department of External Affairs explained that they had been advised by the Department of Finance that it is essential for us to accept this status in such documentation (both UN and OECD) in order to safeguard our position on tax incentives for foreign companies investing in Ireland. On the other hand the Committee of Secretaries had recently decided that that it would not be advisable for us to participate in the OECD Technical Co-operation Programme for less-developed countries in view of our application for full membership of the EEC. Our position was therefore rather ambiguous but it did seem wiser not to highlight our industrially less-developed status in the OECD at the present juncture.'

41 NAI, DT S 15453 F/61, Memorandum 'Proposals for re-assessing the aims and functions of the Irish national productivity committee and for giving it a permanent organisation', Nov. 1961

42 NAI, DT S 15453 F/61, letter from Lemass to Minister for Industry and Commerce (Jack Lynch), 20 Nov. 1961; NAI, DT S 15453 G/62, letter from Lemass to Lynch, 26 Mar. 1962; letter from Lemass to Lynch, 2 Apr. 1962; Lemass to Minister for Finance (James Ryan), 2 May 1962; letter from INPC Chairman (Ruairi Roberts) to Lemass, 23 Nov. 1962; letter from Lemass to Lynch and Ryan 29 Dec. 1962.

43 The tone of these speeches sharpened noticeably as the economic situated deteriorated during 1962, producing a substantial visible trade deficit. NAI, DT S 15453 F/61 contains transcribed press reports of a speech by Lemass in Clonmel on 28 Sept. 1961. Here Lemass favourably contrasts wage rises accompanied by increased productivity with resort in Britain to a wages freeze and refers to the role of FUE and ICTU in framing the productivity principles. By contrast NAI, DT S 15453 G/62 contains a press clipping of a Lemass speech to an FUE dinner on 27 Feb. 1962 that again refers to the

productivity principles, accompanying it with a riposte to an *Irish Press* report of a union leader's claim that 'output rise can absorb wage round' which observed: 'but as faith without good works will not avail, so also must principles be backed up with action. We need the action – and we need it soon'. In another speech, to a Dublin Fianna Fáil Comhairle Ceanntair dinner, on 29 Dec. 1962 Lemass declared: 'there is a need in 1963 to "close the gap" between incomes and productivity . . . during 1963 "close the gap" must be our purpose and slogan'. A White Paper on Incomes and Output entitled *Closing the Gap* was published in February 1963. Accompanied by a pay standstill for all government departments and the state-sponsored bodies, this led to a hostile union response expressed through the withdrawal of representatives from a range of bodies that included the Committee on Industrial Organisation and the National Employer-Labour Conference. However, the launching of the National Industrial Economic Council marked a restoration of better government-union relations later in the year and the revamping of the INPC does not appear to have been jeopardised by the falling out occasioned by *Closing the Gap*. On relations between the Lemass government and the trade unions see Paul Bew and Henry Patterson, *Seán Lemass and the Making of Modern Ireland* (Dublin, 1982), chs 5 and 6 and Kieran Allen, *Fianna Fáil and Irish Labour: 1926 to the Present Day* (London, 1997), ch. 5.

44 See NAI, DT S 15453 F/61, for the speech delivered on 19 Sept. 1963.

45 Cox, *The Making of Managers*, chs 10 and 11.

46 NAI, DETE 2001/44/508, Correspondence and Discussions with the Irish National Productivity Committee, note dated 23 Sept. 1965.

47 NAI, DT 2000/6/349, Memorandum for the Government, 16 May 1969: in relation to advisory services the report of an OECD associated Research and Technology Survey Team, *Science and Irish Economic Development* (Dublin, 1966), had noted that 'the Irish Management Institute may also engage in advisory work, possibly instead of the Irish National Productivity Committee': the *Report* of the Public Services Organisation Review Group (Dublin: 1969), para. 30.4.1, p. 352, envisaged that 'the Industrial Development Authority will be the instrument through which industrial development policy will be co-ordinated . . . it should take over the functions of the Irish National Productivity Committee': on developments in the social research field see Murray, *The Transatlantic Politics of Productivity*, pp. 19–27.

48 *Irish Times*, 27 Oct. 1970.

49 NAI, DT 2003/16/341, Memorandum for the Government, 24 May 1972.

50 Irish Productivity Centre, *IPC – Who We Are*, http://www.ipc.ie/who_we_are.html

51 Tom Garvin, *Preventing the Future: Why was Ireland So Poor for So Long?* (Dublin, 2004), p. 164

52 Mary Daly, *The Spirit of Earnest Inquiry: The Statistical and Social Inquiry Society of Ireland 1847–1997* (Dublin 1997), pp. 169–70.

53 European Association of National Productivity Centres, *A Short History of the Association: Written on the 30th Anniversary of the Association, May 1996*, http://www.eanpc.org/eanpc/bg01.php.

54 Tony Hubert, *The Main Concepts of Productivity Centres in Europe and Overseas, and the Scope of their Activities.* http://www.eanpc.org/projects/downloads/s04_Tony_Hubert.pdf.

Chapter 6 The mainstreaming of Irish foreign policy

This chapter was completed with the considerable financial support of The Nuffield Foundation (Social Science Small Grants Scheme).

1 J. J. Lee, 'Sean Lemass', in J. J. Lee (ed.), *Ireland: 1945–70* (Dublin, 1979), p. 22.

2 Breandán Ó hEithir, *The Begrudger's Guide to Irish Politics* (Dublin, 1987), p. 138.

3 Patrick Keatinge, 'Ireland and the world, 1957-82', in Frank Litton (ed.), *Unequal Achievement: The Irish Experience, 1957–1982* (Dublin, 1982), p. 227.

4 The course of Anglo-Irish monetary relations is examined in more detail in Maurice FitzGerald, '"Ceart go leor": Ireland, the UK, EMU and the sterling area', in Francisco Torres et al. (eds), *Governing the EMU* (Florence: European University Institute, 2004), pp. 273–90.

5 Gary Murphy, '"A wider perspective": Ireland's view of western Europe in the 1950s', in Michael Kennedy and Joseph Morrison Skelly (eds), *Irish Foreign Policy, 1919–1966: From Independence to Internationalism* (Dublin, 2000), p. 251.

6 Democratic National Committee Papers (DNC), Harry S. Truman Presidential Library, Independence, Missouri (HST), Seán Lemass (Tánaiste and Irish industry and commerce minister) speech delivered to the National Press Club in Washington DC, 1 Oct. 1953, 'Foreign Affairs File', Box #151.

7 Robert Savage, *Seán Lemass* (Dundalk, 1999), p. 23.

8 Indeed, this is the central thesis put forward in Maurice FitzGerald, *Protectionism to Liberalisation: Ireland and the EEC, 1957 to 1966* (Aldershot, 2000).

9 Paul Bew and Henry Patterson, *Seán Lemass and the Making of Modern Ireland, 1945–66* (Dublin, 1982), p. 14.

10 DNC, HST Library, Lemass speech, 1 Oct. 1953.

11 John F. Kennedy Presidential Library, Boston, Massachusetts (JFK), Matthew McCloskey (US ambassador, Dublin) to John Kennedy (US president), undated (most probably January 1963), Box #119a, President's Office Files,

12 Kennedy speech delivered in Dáil Éireann on 28 June 1963, in *Public Papers of the Presidents of the United States: John F. Kennedy, 1963* (Washington, DC: 1964), pp. 534–9.

13 Lyndon Johnson Papers (LJP), Lyndon B. Johnson Presidential Library, Austin, Texas (LBJ), Central Intelligence Agency (CIA) report forming part of 'The President's European Trip', 'Vice-Presidential Security File', Box #3.

14 LJP, LBJ Library, 'President Kennedy's Travel: President's European Trip Briefing Book, June 1963 (I)', Vice-Presidential Security File, Box #3.

15 JFK Library, Sean F. Lemass oral history transcript, interview conducted by Joseph E. O'Connor, pp. 2–5.

16 Joseph Morrison Skelly, *Irish diplomacy at the United Nations, 1945–65: National Interests and the International Order* (Dublin, 1997).

17 JFK Library, Thomas J. Kiernan oral history transcript, interview conducted by Joseph E. O'Connor, pp. 11–15.

18 Peter Catterall, 'Senior editor's preface', in Kevin Theakston (ed.), *British Foreign Secretaries Since 1974* (London, 2004), p. viii.

19 Brian Farrell, *Seán Lemass* (Dublin, 1983), pp. 117–18.

20 Farrell, *Seán Lemass*, p. 118.

21 T. D. Williams, 'Irish foreign policy, 1949-69', in Lee (ed.), *Ireland*, pp. 138, 141.

22 John A. Murphy, *Ireland In The Twentieth Century* (Dublin, 1989), p. 148.

23 Murphy, *Ireland In The Twentieth Century*, pp. 148, 150.

24 LJP, LBJ Library, CIA report, 'The President's European trip', 'Vice-Presidential Security File', Box #3.

25 DNC, HST, Library, Lemass speech, 1 Oct. 1953.

26 Dwight D. Eisenhower Presidential Library, Abilene, Kansas, 'Frank Aiken (Irish External Affairs minister) to the Federation of American Societies for Irish Independence, *circa* mid-August 1958', cited in *Éire*, 18 Aug. 1958, 'General File 122', Box #816, Central Files.

27 The partition issue is examined within the context of Irish-American relations in Maurice FitzGerald, 'Ireland and the US in the post-war period', in Dermot Keogh *et al* (eds), *The Lost Decade: Ireland in the 1950s* (Cork, 2004).

28 John F. Kennedy Papers (KP), JFK Library, Benjamin H. Read (United States State Department official) to McGeorge Bundy (White House adviser), 30 Sept. 1963, 'CO 125 Ireland', Box #60.

29 Bew and Patterson, *Seán Lemass*, p.15.

30 Til Geiger, 'Ireland and the Committee for European Economic Cooperation', in Kennedy and Skelly (eds), *Irish Foreign Policy*, pp. 226–8.

31 Truman Papers, HST Library, CIA report entitled 'Ireland SR-48', 'Intelligence File', Box #261, President's Secretary's Files (italics in original).

32 DNC, HST Library, Lemass speech, 1 Oct. 1953.

33 Michael O'Sullivan, *Seán Lemass: A Biography* (Dublin, 1994), p. 172.

34 Dermot Keogh, 'Irish neutrality and the first application for EEC membership', in Kennedy and Skelly (eds), *Irish Foreign Policy*, p. 283.

35 LJP, LBJ Library, Lemass quoted in a report entitled 'Republic of Ireland', 'National Security File', Box #195.

36 KP, JFK Library, Report on the Lemass press conference of 5 Sept. 1962 in McCloskey to Kennedy, 14 Sept. 1962, National Security Files, Box #118.

37 Ronan Fanning, *Independent Ireland* (Dublin, 1983), pp. 148, 203.

38 KP, JFK Library, McCloskey to Dean Rusk (US Secretary of State), 27 Sept. 1963, 'National Security Files 2/63–9/63', Box #118.

39 Lemass speech delivered at a US State Department luncheon on 15 Oct. 1963, in *Public Papers of the Presidents of the United States*, p. 787.

40 Irish-American joint statement released on 17 Oct. 1963, in *Public papers of the Presidents of the United States*, p.788.

41 LJP, LBJ Library, Lyndon Johnson to Éamon de Valera, 29 May 1964, 'National Security File', Box #195.

42 LJP, LBJ Library, Report entitled 'Ireland', 'Vice-Presidential Security File', Box #3.

Chapter 7   Northern Ireland and cross-border co-operation

1   Paul Bew and Henry Patterson, *Seán Lemass and the Making of Modern Ireland* (Dublin, 1982), p. 11. A view echoed in Jonathan Bardon, *A History Of Ulster* (Belfast, 1992), p. 629.

2   Quoted in John Horgan, *Seán Lemass: The Enigmatic Patriot* (Dublin, 1997), p. 253.

3   See Michael Kennedy, *Division and Consensus: The Politics of Cross-Border Relations in Ireland 1925–1969* (Dublin, 2000), pp 43–91, for further details.

4   Author's interview with Dr T. K. Whitaker, Dublin, March 1997.

5   NAI, DT S16272.

6   See Kennedy, *Division and Consensus*; Horgan, *Enigmatic Patriot* and Brian Farrell, *Seán Lemass* (Dublin, 1983).

7   For example the thesis advocated in Bew and Patterson, *Making of Modern Ireland*, or Dermot Keogh, *Twentieth Century Ireland: Nation and State* (Dublin, 1994), p. 287.

8   See F. S. L. Lyons, *Ireland Since the Famine* (London, 1971), p. 587; a similar point is made, though less strongly, in Tim Pat Coogan, *Disillusioned Decades: Ireland 1966–87* (Dublin, 1987), p. 191.

9   O'Neill's failure to inform his Cabinet colleagues in advance of meeting Lemass, rather than his actual meeting with Lemass, caused concern in Unionist Party and Orange Order circles after the January 1965 meeting. See Marc Mulholland, *Northern Ireland at the Crossroads* (Hampshire, 2000), pp. 82–6.

10   Which is not to say, by extension, that Reynolds or Ahern were indifferent on partition.

11   'Gerry Boland's story', *Irish Times*, 19 Oct. 1968, quoted in J. J. Lee, *Ireland: 1912–1985* (Cambridge, 1989), p. 408.

12   An example being the reinterpretation of Lemass's religious beliefs to suggest that he was agnostic. See John Horgan, 'Lemass kept agnostic musings and religious faith

strictly private', where he weighs the evidence of whether Lemass was an agnostic or not, *Irish Times*, 27 Jan. 1998. For a deeper treatment of Lemass's religious beliefs see Horgan, *Enigmatic Patriot*, p. 325.

13 NAI, DT S9361G, 16 Apr. 1957.

14 Ibid.

15 Ibid., 23 Apr. 1957.

16 Ibid., 26 Apr. 1957.

17 *Irish Press*, 13 Dec. 1956.

18 *Seanad Deb*, vol. 47, col. 1309, 29 Jan. 1958.

19 PRONI, CAB 4/1085, Cabinet minutes, 19 Mar. 1959.

20 PRONI, CAB 4/1097, 9 July 1959.

21 *Dáil Deb*, vol. 176, col.157, 21 July 1959.

22 NAI, DT S16272A, 22 July 1959.

23 Ibid., 23 July 1959.

24 *Irish Press*, 13 Aug. 1959.

25 NAI, DT S16272.

26 NAI, DFA, 348/225 part one, 10 Oct. 1959.

27 NAI, DT S9361/94, 10 Nov. 1959.

28 NAI, DT S9361/94.

29 Ibid., McCann to Cremin, 11 Nov. 1959.

30 *Dáil Deb*, vol.181, col. 42, 26 Apr. 1960.

31 NAI, DFA 348/225 part one, 16 Mar. 1961, memo by Cahill.

32 NAI, DT S16272C61.

33 Ibid.

34 Ibid.

35 Ibid.

36 Fianna Fáil duly won the election, but was returned as a minority government.

37 NAI, DT S16272C/61, Lynch to Lemass, 13 Nov. 1961.

38 Farrell, *Lemass*, p. 104.

39 NAI, DT S16272C62, Murphy to McCarthy, 30 July 1962

40 Ibid., Memorandum, 7 Sept. 1962.

41 *Derry Journal*, 25 Sept. 1962.

42 PRONI, CAB4/1205, 17 Oct. 1962.

43 NAI, DT S16272E, 28 Sept. 1963.

44 NAI, DT S16272A62, 28 Nov. 1962.

45 *Irish Press*, 15 Dec. 1962.

46 For example the 'Mount Pottinger Speech' of 29 Nov. 1962 in which O'Neill called for a 'province of "do-ers"' and advocated industrial development, labour training and export-led growth to solve Ulster's problems rather than relying on the old heavy industries of the past. After becoming Prime Minister O'Neill told a meeting of the

Ulster Unionist Council that 'our task is literally to transform the face of Ulster [through] bold and imaginative measures'.

47 *Irish Times*, 16 Apr. 1963.

48 Lemass was not in attendance; his schedule that day would not permit him to meet the Northern visitors.

49 *Irish Times*, 17 Apr. 1963.

50 NAI, DT S16272D95.

51 *Irish Independent*, 30 July 1963.

52 NAI, DT S16272E63, Lemass to all ministers, 16 Sept. 1963.

53 NAI, DT S16272E63, 12 Sept. 1963.

54 *Irish Times*, 17 Sept. 1963.

55 NAI, DT S16272E, O Cearbhaill to Lemass, 30 Sept. 1963.

56 NAI, DT S16272E63, 16 Oct. 1963.

57 Ibid.

58 *Irish Times*, 18 Oct. 1963.

59 *Irish Press*, 8 Nov. 1963.

60 *Irish Times*, 14 Apr. 1964.

61 *Guardian*, 30 June 1964.

62 *Irish Times*, 29 Aug. 1964.

63 An Independent Television programme on discrimination in Northern Ireland had been aired in mid-December. With an estimated audience of ten to twelve million it showed a divided community controlled by the bayonets of the B-Specials and subsidised annually by Westminster to the tune of £90 m.

64 Author's interview with Dr T. K. Whitaker, Dublin, March 1997.

65 PRONI, CAB 9U/5/1, undated memorandum 'Meeting with Prime Minister of Irish Republic'.

66 NAI, DFA P363, memorandum by Whitaker entitled 'Taoiseach's visit to Belfast', 15 Jan. 1965.

67 *Irish News*, 16 Jan. 1965.

68 PRO, PREM 13/983, Wilson to O'Neill 15 Jan. 1965.

69 *Irish Independent*, 15 Jan. 1965.

70 NAI, DT S16272H, Communiqué issued after meeting.

71 NAI, DFA P363, McCann to Whitaker, 12 Feb. 1965.

72 *Irish Press*, 10 Feb. 1965.

73 A full analysis of these meetings and their results can be found in Kennedy, *Division and Consensus*, pp. 246–52.

74 *Dáil Deb*, 23 Nov. 1965, accessed on *Houses of the Oireachtas Parliamentary Debates 1919–2002* DVD (Dublin, 2002) at http://localhost:8780/D/0219/D.0219. 196511230002.html.

75 In June 1966 the Eccles Committee recommended that cross-border electricity interconnection was feasible and economically desirable and that a single 300-mega-watt interconnector be built between Maynooth in County Kildare and Tandragee in County Armagh.

76 A full analysis of co-operation during this period can be found in Kennedy, *Division and Consensus*, pp. 277–9.

77 NAI, DT 96/6/59, Lemass to Whitaker, 2 Nov. 1966.

78 *Belfast Telegraph*, 5 Oct. 1967.

Chapter 8 Church, state and the moral community

Brian Girvin would like to thank the British Academy for the award of a research grant (SG: 36711) which facilitated research for this chapter.

1   I have explored these claims in greater detail in *From Union to Union: Nationalism, Democracy and Religion in Ireland* (Dublin, 2002)

2   John Horgan, *Seán Lemass: The Enigmatic Patriot* (Dublin, 1997), pp. 20, 323–5.

3   Tim Pat Coogan, *De Valera: Long Fellow, Long Shadow* (London, 1993), pp. 489–90.

4   *Irish Press*, 27 Jan. 1969; cited in John Whyte, *Church and State in Modern Ireland* (2nd edn, Dublin, 1980), p. 353.

5   Ted Jelen and Clyde Wilcox (eds), *Religion and Politics in Comparative Perspective* (Cambridge, 2002).

6   Paul Blanshard, *The Irish and Catholic Power* (London, 1954), pp. 205–43 for the argument; John Cooney, *John Charles McQuaid* (Dublin, 1999); Dermot Keogh in *History Ireland* 8:3 (Autumn, 2000), pp. 53–5 in the course of a book review dismisses both Blanshard and Cooney without actually addressing the issues raised by these authors. Conor Cruise O'Brien, *States of Ireland* (London, 1972), p. 107.

7   The Minister for Health, Dr Noel Browne, attempted to introduce and Mother and Child health scheme in 1950 for maternity and child health with no means test or income limit. In essence this would have provided free health care for children up to the age of 16. The scheme was strongly opposed by the Catholic hierarchy on the principle that provision for the health of children was an essential part of the responsibilities of parents. Government support for Browne and the proposal faded away in the face of this determined opposition and he resigned in April 1951.

8   *Dáil Deb*, vol. 125, col. 784, 12 Apr. 1951; Brian Girvin, 'The state and vocational education 1922–1960' in John Logan (ed.), *Teachers' Union: The TUI and its Forerunners* (Dublin, 1999), pp. 62–92.

9   Éire is the term used for Ireland in the 1937 Constitution. When used in this chapter, Ireland refers to the territory that seceded from the United Kingdom in 1922.

10 I have examined the growing nature of this isolationism and insularity during the war in my book *The Emergency* (forthcoming, 2006).

11 Girvin, *From Union to Union*, pp. 80–105.

12 John M. Regan, *The Irish Counter-Revolution 1921–1936* (Dublin, 1999); Patrick Murray, *Oracles of God: The Roman Catholic Church and Irish Politics, 1922–1937* (Dublin, 2000).

13 Donal Barrington, *The Church, the State and the Constitution* (Dublin, 1959); Jeremiah Newman, *Studies in Political Morality* (Dublin and London, 1962).

14 James Deeny, *To Cure and to Care* (Dublin, 1989), p. 63.

15 Jean Blanchard, *The Church in Contemporary Ireland* (Dublin, 1963), pp. 68–9.

16 Cooney, *McQuaid*, p. 201; UCDA: Fianna Fáil/440, Parliamentary Party minutes, 11 June 1941; NAI, DT S. 1107A, Department of Justice, 'Admission of aliens', 24 Sept. 1945.

17 Girvin, *From Union to Union*, p. 111.

18 Cited in Blanchard, *Church in Contemporary Ireland*, p. 67.

19 On 5 August 1950, the Supreme Court, in delivering its judgement in the Tilson case, ruled that ante-nuptial promises about the religious upbringing of children were valid and that both parents – constitutionally – had equal rights in bringing up children. The Supreme Court accepted the principle that the paramount consideration was the welfare of the infants concerned. Previously Gavan Duffy in the High Court had ruled in favour of the wife who was the Catholic party. Her non-Catholic partner, Ernest Tilson, had originally promised to bring up any children as Catholic, but later placed three of four children born to the couple in a non-Catholic institution with the intention of rearing them in the Church of Ireland. Duffy rejected the English precedent which gave primacy to the father on the grounds that this deprived the wife of all rights in relation to the children's education. In effect Duffy overturned the legal precedent and concluded that husband and wife had equal rights in the matter, thus enforcing the pre-marriage agreement.

20 Girvin, *From Union to Union*, pp. 110–15.

21 NAI, DT S. 12952A, 'Marriage in Ireland, Constitutional and ecclesiastical position', which contains correspondence on various issues related to this; see note by M. Ó Muimhneachain, 22 Oct. 1940 on Taoiseach's intention to legislate; Note by O'Donoghue, Attorney General's Office, 17 Sept. 1942; *Irish Press*, 11 Dec. 1945; *The Standard*, 7 May 1937; W. Conway, 'Marriage in Ireland: Church and state' *Irish Ecclesiastical Review* 5th ser., 68 (1946), pp. 361–6; Whyte, *Church and State*, p. 55 identified only three cases of bigamy before the courts between 1937 and 1964.

22 Whyte, *Church and State*, pp. 171–2.

23 Alexander J. Humphreys, *New Dubliners: Urbanization and the Irish Family* (London, 1966), based on research carried out late 1949 early 1950; Heinrich Böll, *Irish Journal* (New York, 1967).

24 Private information.

25 UCDA, MacEntee Papers, P67/298 Childers to MacEntee (1945); P67/298, Childers to MacEntee 11 Dec. 1948; *Irish Times*, 16 Mar. 1946; Newman, *Studies in*

Political Morality, pp. 331–4, cites this speech as evidence that Protestants have full civil rights in the Irish Republic.

26 Horgan, *Enigmatic Patriot*, p. 151.

27 Cooney, *McQuaid*, p. 171; Mike Milotte, *Banished Babies* (Dublin, 1997), pp. 40–1; 60–5; 193; 275–7; NAI, DT S. 11582E, 'The problem of Irish girls immigrating to England', 25 Aug. 1953.

28 *Catholic Standard*, 16 Feb. 1951.

29 Whyte, *Church and State*, pp. 188–93.

30 Gerard Whelan with Carolyn Swift, *Spiked: Church-State Intrigue and the Rose Tattoo* (Dublin, 2002), pp. 198–208.

31 Rev. J. McCarthy, 'Morality of a state ban on the emigration of minors', *Irish Ecclesiastical Record* 5th ser., 71 (1949), pp. 269–72.

32 Cited in Whelan with Swift, *Spiked*, pp. 215–16.

33 NAI, DFA P. 99, Papal Nuncio to External Affairs 7 Apr. 1945 enclosing Bishop Cohalan's letter; Deeny to Walshe 29 May 1945; Walshe to Taoiseach 12 June 1945 reporting agreement with Nuncio.

34 Whyte, *Church and State*, pp. 116–19; Cooney, *McQuaid*, pp. 196–9; Don O'Leary, *Vocationalism and Social Catholicism in Twentieth Century Ireland* (Dublin, 1999) for a thorough review of these questions.

35 Girvin, *From Union to Union*, pp. 118–23; Girvin, 'The state and vocational education 1922–1960'.

36 Whelan with Swift, *Spiked*, p. 150.

37 Whelan with Swift, *Spiked*, provides the most comprehensive account of the period. I have drawn extensively on their research in this paragraph.

38 Bruce F. Biever, *Religion, Culture and Values: A Cross-Cultural Analysis of Motivational Factors in Native Irish and American Irish Catholicism* (New York, 1976) for the data. This is based on Biever's 1965 PhD thesis.

39 John Bowman, '"The wolf in sheep's clothing": Richard Hayes's proposal for a new National Library of Ireland, 1959–60', in Ronald J. Hill and Michael Marsh (eds), *Modern Irish Democracy* (Dublin, 1993), pp. 44–61; NAI, DT: 96/6/364, 'Marriage in Ireland' which contains the correspondence; Cooney, *McQuaid*, pp. 418–19.

40 *Irish Times*, 2 June 1971 cited in Whyte *Church and State*, p. 405; Dermot Keogh, *Twentieth-Century Ireland* (Dublin, 1994), pp. 265–6.

41 Horgan, *Enigmatic Patriot*, p. 202; *Report of the Committee on the Constitution* (Dublin, 1967), pp. 40–1; Whyte *Church and State*, pp. 408–9.

42 Mícheál MacGréil, *Prejudice and Tolerance in Ireland*, (Dublin, 1977), pp. 409–26.

Chapter 9 The politics of educational expansion

1 Interview with Dr. Patrick Hillery, 25 Feb. 2002.

2 Séamas Ó Buachalla, *Education Policy in Twentieth Century Ireland* (Dublin, 1988), p. 275.

3 *Dáil Deb*, vol. 159, col. 1494, 19 July 1956.

4 Sean O'Connor, *A Troubled Sky: Reflections on the Irish Educational Scene 1957–68* (Dublin, 1986), pp.11–12.

5 O'Connor, *A Troubled Sky*, p. 2.

6 Interview with Mr. James Dukes, 28 Apr. 2003.

7 T. K. Whitaker, *Economic Development* (Dublin, 1958), para. 9, ch. 11.

8 Department of Education, W26/30, M80/1, C.O. 704 (ii), *Progress Report for the Quarter Ended 30 June 1958*, July 1958, p. 1.

9 *Dáil Deb*, vol. 177, col. 202, 21 Oct. 1959.

10 *Dáil Deb*, vol. 177, col. 470, 28 Oct. 1959.

11 Ibid.

12 Ibid. col. 471.

13 Ó Buachalla, *Education Policy*, p. 307.

14 Department of Education, W26/30, M80/1, *Progress Report for the Quarter ended on 30 June 1961*, 21 July 1961

15 *Dáil Deb*, vol. 189, col. 842, 24 May 1961

16 Department of Education, Circular 22/61, Oct. 1961

17 Ibid.

18 *Dáil Deb*, vol. 191, col. 15, 4 July 1961; John Coolahan, *Irish Education: Its History and Structure* (Dublin, 1981), p. 139

19 *Dáil Deb*, vol. 191, col. 15, 4 July 1961

20 *Dáil Deb*, vol. 191, cols 1737–44, 25 July 1961

21 *Dáil Deb*, vol. 191, col. 1683, 25 July 1961

22 *Dáil Deb*, vol. 191, cols 2423–5, 2 Aug. 1961

23 *Dáil Deb*, vol. 206, col. 1083–6, 11 Dec. 1963

24 *Dáil Deb*, vol. 203, col. 384, 29 May 1963

25 Ibid.

26 NAI, DT CAB 2/20, G.C.9/90, 16 Aug. 1960

27 NAI, DT CAB 2/20, G.C.9/94, 13 Sept. 1960

28 *Dáil Deb*, vol. 210, col. 286, 27 May 1964; Department of Education 8223, *Commission on Higher Education, Minutes of Inaugural Meeting*, 8 Nov. 1960.

29 Séamas Ó Buachalla, 'Investment in education: context, content and impact', *Administration* 44:3 (Autumn 1996), pp. 10–20

30 NAI, DT S12891D/1/62, Pilot studies on long-term needs for educational resources in economically developed countries, OECD, 12 Oct. 1961, p. 1.

31 Ibid.

32 Ó Buachalla, 'Investment in education', pp. 10–20.

33 Ibid.; Eileen Randles, *Post-Primary Education in Ireland 1957–70* (Dublin, 1975), p. 78

34 Ó Buachalla, 'Investment in education'.

35 NAI, DT 97/6/437, S17913, N. S. Ó Nualláin to C. Ó Dálaigh, 21 June 1962

36 Ibid.

37 NAI, DT 97/6/437, S17913, Address by Dr P. J. Hillery TD, Minister for Education, on the occasion of his opening the Labour/Management Conference at Shannon Airport, 22 June 1962, pp. 1–6,

38 'Long-term educational needs will be investigated', *Irish Press*, 30 July 1962.

39 NAI, DT S12892D/1/62, Speech by Seán Lemass TD, An Taoiseach, at the Marist Brothers' Centenary celebrations, 8 July 1962, p. 1.

40 Ibid.

41 Ibid., p. 2.

42 NAI, DT S12891D/2/62, Memorandum from the Minister for Education concerning the Small Farms report, 'Post-primary education in the areas concerned', 7 July 1962, p. 1.

43 Ibid.

44 Ibid.; Randles, *Post-Primary Education in Ireland*, p.107.

45 NAI, DT S12891D/2/62, Outline of statement of government policy on suggestions in Report of the Inter-Departmental Committee on the Problems of Small Western Farms, 1 Aug. 1962, p. 8.

46 Ibid.

47 Randles, *Post-Primary Education in Ireland*, p. 107.

48 Ibid.

49 NAI, DT 17405 C/63, Pilot scheme related to small farm areas, Department of Education, proposal for comprehensive post-primary education, 9 Jan. 1963.

50 Ibid.

51 Ibid.

52 NAI, D/T S12891D/2/62, T. K. Whitaker to N. S. Ó Nualláin, 18 July 1962

53 NAI, D/T S17405 C/63, Hillery to Lemass, 9 Jan. 1963,

54 Ibid.

55 Ibid.

56 Ibid.

57 Ibid.

58 NAI, DT S 17405 C/63, Lemass to Hillery, 11 Jan. 1963

59 NAI, DT S 17405 C/63, Hillery to Lemass, 12 Jan. 1963

60 NAI, DT S 17405 C/63, Lemass to Hillery, 14 Jan. 1963

61 Ibid.

62 Ibid.

63 Ibid.

64 NAI, DT S 17405 C/63, Memorandum from the Department of Education, Proposals relating to comprehensive post-primary education.

65 Ibid.

66 Hillery interview.

67 Ibid.; John Horgan, *Seán Lemass: The Enigmatic Patriot* (Dublin, 1997), p. 295.

68 NAI, DT S 17405 C/63, Statement by Dr P. J. Hillery TD, Minister for Education, in relation to Post-Primary Education, 20 May 1963.

69 Ibid., p. 6.

70 Ibid., p. 8.

71 Ibid, pp. 9–10.

72 Department of Education, W26/30, M80/1, Secondary Education: Progress report for the Second Programme for Economic Expansion 1964, pp.1–2; Hillery interview.

73 Committee of Public Accounts, *Appropriation Accounts 1965–66* (Dublin, 1967), pp. 117–18

74 NAI, DT S17405 C/63, Statement by Dr P. J. Hillery TD, Minister for Education, in relation to Post-Primary Education, 20 May 1963, p. 7.

75 Ibid.

76 Committee of Public Accounts, *Appropriation Accounts 1967–68* (Dublin, 1969), p. 122.

77 *Second Programme for Economic Expansion, Part I, laid by the Government before each House of the Oireachtas, August 1963* (Dublin, 1963), p. 17.

78 *Second Programme, Part I*, p. 13.

79 *Second Programme for Economic Expansion, Part II, laid by the Government before each House of the Oireachtas, July 1964* (Dublin, 1964), p.193

80 NAI, DT S12891E/95, *Speech by Seán Lemass TD, Taoiseach, following address by John Vaizey on 'The Economics of Education', St Patrick's Training College, Drumcondra,* 13 Feb. 1964, p. 2.

81 Ibid.

82 *Second Programme part I*, p. 15.

83 NAI, DT S17592/95, Hillery to Lemass, 4 Feb. 1964.

84 Ibid. see also Archbishop John Charles McQuaid Papers, DDA, A AB8/B/XV/b/05, 'The Hillery scheme', 5 Dec. 1963.

85 Hillery to Lemass, 4 Feb. 1964.

86 NAI, DT S17592/95, Lemass to Dr James Ryan, 5 Feb. 1964.

87 Lemass to Ryan; NAI, DT S 17592/95, Internal memorandum, Department of the Taoiseach, 10 Feb. 1964.

88 Hillery to Lemass, 4 Feb. 1964; Randles, *Post-Primary Education in Ireland*, p. 145.

89 Speech by Seán Lemass TD, Taoiseach, following address by John Vaizey, 13 Feb. 1964.

90 'Grant for schools', *Irish Independent*, 14 Feb. 1964.

91 Ibid.; *Dáil Deb*, vol. 209, col. 1569, 14 May 1964.

92 NAI, DT 96/6/355, S 12891E, Interview by Seán Lemass with 'Open', 29 Jan. 1965.

93 Ibid.

94 *Investment in Education Part I, Report of the Survey Team appointed by the Minister for Education in October 1962* (Dublin, 1965) p. 391.

95 Ibid.

96 Ibid.

97 NAI, DT 97/6/437, S 17913, Lemass to George Colley, Minister for Education, 27 Nov. 1965.

98 Lemass to Colley.

99 NAI, DT 97/6/437, S 17913, Colley to Lemass, 30 Nov. 1965

100 *Dáil Deb*, vol. 217, col. 1968, 21 July 1965.

101 Ibid.

102 NAI, D/T 96/6/355, S.12891E, Colley to Lemass, 24 Sept. 1965.

103 Ibid. (*Investment* had identified 736 one-teacher schools).

104 Ibid.

105 NAI, DT 96/6/355, S 12891E, Lemass to Colley, 25 Sept. 1965.

106 Ibid.

107 NAI, DT 96/6/355, S 12891E, Colley to Lemass, 27 Sept. 1965; S 12891E, Speech by George Colley TD, Minister for Education, Rural Week, Ballinrobe, 11 Nov. 1965.

108 DDA, AB8/B/XV/b/05, McQuaid Papers, Minutes of the General Meeting of the Irish Hierarchy, 12 Oct. 1965.

109 'School closures unconstitutional, says Dr Browne', *Irish Press*, 7 Feb. 1966.

110 'Minister replies to Bishop's criticisms', *Irish Press*, 7 Feb. 1966.

111 *Dáil Deb*, vol. 220, col. 1712–59, 16 Feb. 1966.

112 John Coolahan, 'Educational policy for national schools 1960–85', in D.G. Mulcahy and Denis O'Sullivan (eds), *Irish Educational Policy* (Dublin, 1989), pp. 27–75, at p. 42.

113 *Dáil Deb*, vol. 223, col. 2194, 7 July 1966.

114 Ibid., col. 2195.

115 Ibid.

116 NAI, DT 96/6/356, S12891F, Donogh O'Malley, Minister for Education to Lemass, 7 Sept. 1966; Horgan, *Enigmatic Patriot*, p. 298.

117 O'Malley to Lemass, 7 Sept. 1966.

118 NAI, DT 96/6/356, S12891F, Memorandum to An Taoiseach on the necessity for improvement in full-time attendance at school at secondary level, Department of Education, 7 Sept. 1966

119 O'Malley to Lemass, 7 Sept. 1966.

120 Ibid.

121 'State plans free education for all children', *Irish Press*, 12 Sept. 1966

122 Ibid.

123 Ibid.

124 Horgan, *Enigmatic Patriot*, p. 298

125 NAI, DT 96/6/356, S 12891F, T. K. Whitaker to Lemass, 12 Sept. 1966

126 Whitaker to Lemass.

127 NAI, DT 96/6/356, S 12891F, O'Malley to Lemass, 14 Sept. 1966.

128 NAI, DT 96/6/356, S12891F, Lemass to O'Malley, 12 Sept. 1966.

129 Lemass to O'Malley.

130 O'Malley to Lemass, 14 Sept. 1966

131 NAI, DT 96/6/356, S 12891F, Lemass to O'Malley, 22 Sept. 1966

132 Lemass to O'Malley, 22 Sept. 1966.

133 Ibid.

134 NAI, DT 97/6/638, S 12891F, F 111668, Memorandum to the Government, Provision of Free Post-Primary Education, Office of the Minister for Education, 14 Oct. 1966

135 Ibid.

136 NAI, DT 97/6/638, S 12891F, Submission to the Government, Form A, Provision of Free Post-Primary Education, Office of the Minister for Education, 14 Oct. 1966.

137 NAI, DT 97/6/638, S 12891F, Lemass to O'Malley, 17 Oct. 1966

138 Ibid.

139 NAI, DT 97/6/638, S 12891F, F.111668, Memorandum to the Government, Provision of Free Post-Primary Education, Office of the Minister for Education, 11 Nov. 1966.

140 O'Malley to Lemass, 14 Sept. 1966

141 Lemass to O'Malley, 22 Sept. 1966

142 NAI, DT CAB 99/5/1, G.C. 12/2, 29 Nov. 1966.

143 Ibid.

144 Ibid.; Horgan, *Enigmatic Patriot*, p. 298.

Chapter 10 A semi-state in all but name

1 In this respect it is worth recalling that the first Irish ministry for Arts was only established in the 1990s. Hitherto film policy was mainly the responsibility of the Department of Industry and Commerce, although it was transferred to the Department of the Taoiseach under Charles Haughey's premiership in the 1980s.

2 NAI, DT S 13914A includes reference to a proposal from a John E. Harding and George Carney to establish a film producing company in Ireland and to a meeting between them and D. O'Hegarty who reported on it to Industry and Commerce Secretary Gordon Campbell. This meeting took place on 16 April 1928. This did not go ahead, perhaps because the government failed to accede to the terms proposed by the pair. What exactly these terms are, however, is not included in the archived material.

3 NAI, DIC R 303 3/5.

4 NAI, DIC R 303 3/5, Crotty to E. M. Forde, 22 Apr. 1937.

5 NAI, DIC R 303 3/5, R.C. Ferguson to John Leydon 21 May 1937.

6 Ibid.

7 NAI, DIC R 303 3/5, Forde to Assistant Secretary, Department of Industry and Commerce, 19 May 1937.

8 NAI, DIC R 303 3/5, Leydon to Lemass, 25 May 1937.

9 NAI, DIC R 303 3/5, Lemass to Leydon, 26 May 1937.

10 Richard S. Devane, Letter to the Editor, *Irish Press*, 8 Apr. 1937.

11 Richard S. Devane, 'The cinema and the nation', *Irish Press*, 12 Apr. 1937.

12 John Horgan, *Sean Lemass: The Enigmatic Patriot* (Dublin, 1997), pp. 53–4.

13 NAI, DT S 10136, Secretary Industry and Commerce to Private Secretary Department of the Taoiseach, 24 June 1937. In this regard it is worth mentioning the Industry and Commerce were probably familiar with a November 1936 report by a British Board of Trade Committee on the British Film Industry which offered a detailed explanation of the dominance of the UK market by US films and which stressed the importance for the US industry not only of its large domestic market but also of practices such as block and blind booking by renters (distributors) operating within the UK market. Note that the estimated cost of the studio appears to have been based on the Eric Boden memorandum discussed in NAI, DIC R 303 3/5.

14 See for example Horgan's discussion of Lemass and the Dunlop Tyre Factory, *Enigmatic Patriot*, pp. 76–7.

15 NAI, DIC R 303 3/5, R. C. Ferguson to the Secretary of the Department of Justice, 28 Jan. 1938.

16 NAI, DT S 10136, McElligott to Leydon, 14 July 1937.

17 NAI, DIC R 303 3/5, Lemass to R. C. Ferguson, 20 Aug. 1937.

18 NAI, DIC R 303 3/5, R.C. Ferguson to J. J. McElligott, 23 Aug. 1937.

19 The Killarney studio had been built by enterprising local garage owner Tom Cooper to facilitate the shooting of the only feature length indigenous film made in Ireland in the 1930s, *The Dawn*. See Kevin Rockett et al., *Cinema and Ireland* (Syracuse, 1987).

20 NAI, DIC R 303 3/5, Leydon to McElligott, June 1939.

21 The committee intended to visit Denham Studios in Buckinghamshire, Elstree, Pinewood, Pathe Studios in London and the lab of George Humphreys & Co. They also intended to visit the BBFC, the BFI and reps from the GPO Film Dept and the Cinematography Films Branch of the British Board of Trade. See NAI, DIC R 303 3/5, Ferguson to the Secretary of the Department of Foreign Affairs, 14 July 1939.

22 NAI, DIC R 303 3/5, Lorcan O'Brien to Assistant Secretary, Department of the Taoiseach, 18 Oct. 1940.

23 NAI, DIC R 303 3/5, Report of the Inter-Departmental Committee on the Film Industry, Mar. 1942.

24 Ibid. In passing, it is worth noting a proposal elsewhere in the report, which envisaged the creation of a National Film and Cinema Board. Amongst its duties it would 'in the case of schemes envisaging the grant of State assistance . . . consider whether and to what extent such assistance should be afforded'. In effect, then, the Committee envisaged an early version of the modern Irish Film Board.

25 NAI, DIC R 303 3/5, E. M. Forde to Secretary of the Department of the Taoiseach, 23 Aug. 1943.

26 NAI, DIC R 303 3/5, Ferguson to Lemass, 8 Mar. 1945.

27 Ibid.

28 NAI, DIC R 303 3/5, Lemass to Ferguson, 12 Mar. 1945.

29 NAI, DT S 13838, Department of Industry and Commerce, Memorandum for the Government: Proposals for the establishment of a National Film Studio, Apr. 1946.

30 NAI, DT S 13838, Department of Industry and Commerce, Memorandum for the Government: Proposals for the establishment of a National Film Studio, 30 Nov. 1946.

31 Ibid.

32 Ibid.

33 NAI, DT S 13838, Department of Industry and Commerce, Memorandum for the Government: Proposals for the establishment of a National Film Studio, version of 16 Aug. 1947.

34 Report of the Inter-Departmental Committee on the Film Industry, p. 19.

35 NAI, DT S 13914A, 'Preliminary heads by way of observations as to the proposed foundation of an Irish national picture industry', document attached to Gabriel Pascal letter to de Valera, 30 Aug. 1946.

36 NAI, DT S 13914A, John Leydon to Secretary, Department of the Taoiseach, 12 Oct. 1946.

37 NAI, DT S 13914A, Industry and Commerce Memorandum dated 18 Oct. 1946, sent to Secretary, Department of the Taoiseach, 29 Oct. 1946, outlining Pascal–Lemass discussions.

38 Ibid.

39 A comment pencilled in by an anonymous Industry and Commerce official queried the assumption that overseas producers would wish to avail themselves of Irish film processing facilities: 'would these foreign concerns not prefer to make use of their own processing arrangements?'

40 NAI, DT S 13838, Department of Industry and Commerce, Memorandum for the Government: Proposals for the establishment of a National Film Studio, Oct. 1946.

41 Ibid.

42 Ibid.

43 So quickly that the – rarely comprehensive – cabinet minutes for that date make no reference at all to Lemass's submission. It is only through references in Industry and

Commerce memoranda that one can divine that the cabinet took any such decision on the date in question.

44 NAI, DT S 13838, Department of Industry and Commerce, Memorandum for the Government: Proposals for the establishment of a National Film Studio, June 1947.

45 NAI, DT S 13838, Department of Industry and Commerce, Memorandum for the Government: Proposals for the establishment of a National Film Studio, 16 August 1947.

46 Ibid.

47 NAI, DIC, R 303 3/8, extract from Report of Departmental Conference no. 193, dated 2 Dec. 1950.

48 NAI, DIC R 303 3/8. For the full list see Industrial Development Authority Division C, Extract from Report of Minutes of Divisional Meeting no. 2, 9 May 1951.

49 NAI, DIC R 303 3/8, Film Production note for October 1953 Departmental Conference, 30 Sept. 1953.

50 All quotations from NAI, DIC R 303 3/18. Report of Departmental Conference no. 317 24 Oct. 1953.

51 Film Production note for October 1953 Departmental Conference.

52 NAI, DIC R 303 3/8, Film Proposals Memo prepared by D. Smyth, 8 Dec. 1952.

53 NAI, DIC R 303 3/14/2, 'Proposal to set up a National Film Unit', Memorandum for the government. Simply dated 1954 but must predate May 1954 election.

54 Ibid.

55 Ibid.

56 It is worth noting that at least some of the elements of this proposal appear to have been inspired by an unsolicited memo and subsequent letters to the department from one James McAnally, a photographer who had been attached to the Irish Tourist Board in New York between 1948 and 1950 (and who was the brother of then Abbey actor Ray McAnally). In September 1951, McAnally submitted a fourteen page memorandum recommending the establishment of a Government Film Board in Ireland. As a model he pointed to the Canadian Film Board as established by John Grierson in the 1930s: i.e. a body which would actually produce films rather than simply part-funding their production as the modern Irish Film Board does. He remained in contact with the department for the next three years. At a meeting in Industry and Commerce, McAnally outlined the specific structure of a potential documentary film unit. Interestingly he envisaged a two-crew unit producing up to 10–12 films per year, very much in line with Lemass's later proposal. See NAI, DIC R 303 3/18 on the establishment of a National Film Board.

57 NAI, DIC R 303 3/14/2, Memorandum on Film Industry for Departmental Conference, July 1955.

58 NAI, DIC R 303 3/1, Memorandum on Ardmore Studios, Bray, 22 Oct. 1958.

59 'Abbey cast on TV may be blazing a trail', *Sunday Independent*, 6 Jan. 1957.

60 Editorial 'An Irish film industry', *Evening Herald*, 8 Aug. 1957.

61 NAI, DIC R 303 3/14/1, Development of the film industry in Ireland, Memorandum prepared by Industries Division 'A', 4 Aug. 1957.

62 NAI, DIC R 303 3/1, Summary of proposals for providing film studios, not dated but by context late 1957–early 1958.

63 Ibid.

64 NAI, DIC R 303 3/14/1, Development of the film industry in Ireland, Memorandum prepared by Industries Division 'A', 4 Aug. 1957.

65 Ibid.

66 All quotations from 'Minister opens film studios', *Irish Independent*, 13 May 1958.

67 Kevin O'Kelly, 'Ardmore is a success', *Evening Press*, 16 June 1958.

68 NAI, DIC R 303 3/1, Summary of proposals for providing film studios, not dated but by context late 1957–early 1958.

69 NAI, DFA 323/272, 'Ardmore Studios', Department of Foreign Affairs minute, 1 February 1967.

70 Rockett, *Cinema and Ireland*, p. 99, asserts that Lemass arranged the funding but cites no evidence for this.

71 NAI, DIC R 303 3/14/1. J. P. Slevin, Irish Embassy, London, to C. A. Barry, Industry and Commerce, 16 Nov. 1959. It appears that this generous definition of Ireland's being part of the UK had been a factor in encouraging US production to take place in Ireland. In a note from the Consulate General of Ireland in New York to the Secretary of External Affairs in June 1946, reference was made to plans to shoot part of *The Wearing of the Green* in Ireland. The producer of the film had apparently told the Consulate that 'quite frankly they would not go to the trouble and expense of having the Irish scenes actually photographed in Ireland were it not for the fact that his company, like most other American film companies at present, had considerable funds block in England. The funds cannot owing to the British Exchange Control Regulations be exported to this country [the US]. Mr Binney's corporation has therefore decided to use portion of their blocked funds to defray the cost of their proposed operations in Ireland.' NAI, DFA 323/272, Sean Numan (CG of Ire) to Secretary of External Affairs, 27 June 1946. This might also account for Columbia's apparent interest from 1939 onwards.

72 Ibid.

73 'Loans to aid film-making in Ireland', *Irish Times*, 10 Feb. 1960.

74 NAI, DFA 323/272, Irish Film Finance Corporation minute, 1 Dec. 1967.

75 Ibid.

76 NAI, DIC R 303 3/1, Memorandum from Secretary Industry and Commerce to de Valera's private secretary, Oct. 1958.

77 NAI, DFA 323/272, Irish Film Finance Corporation minute, 1 Dec. 1967.

78 Ibid.

79 Ibid.

80 NAI, DIC R 303 3/1, *Sunday Press*, 8 June 1958, cited in Memorandum on Ardmore Studios, Bray, 22 Oct. 1958.

81 NAI, DIC R 303 3/1, Memorandum from Secretary Industry and Commerce to de Valera's private secretary, Oct. 1958.

82 'English ban hits Irish film-making', *Irish Times*, 28 Mar. 1959.

83 Louis Marcus 'Irish films and the British market: problems of distribution', *Irish Times*, 26 Nov. 1959.

84 NAI, DFA 323/272, Irish Film Finance Corporation minute, 1 Dec. 1967.

85 Ibid.

Chapter 11 Introducing television in the age of Lemass

1 See *Dáil Deb*, 12 Oct. 1966.

2 John Reith was the first Director General at the BBC. He advocated the use of radio for developing educational and cultural programmes and not simply as a source of entertainment.

3 See Robert J. Savage, *Irish Television: The Political and Social Origins* (Cork, 1996).

4 J. J. Lee, *Ireland 1912–1985: Politics and Society* (Cambridge, 1989), p 373.

5 Savage, *Irish Television*, pp. 117–28.

6 NAI, DC, TW 894, Letter from Lemass to Blaney, 25 July 1957.

7 Ibid.

8 Ibid.

9 NAI, DT S14996B, Cabinet notes, 25 Oct. 1957.

10 NAI, DC, TW894, speech drafted by Seán Lemass, approved by the Cabinet Committee and delivered by Neil Blaney, 11 Nov. 1957.

11 Ibid.

12 Ibid., p. 2.

13 NAI, DC,TW894, letter to Leon Ó Broin from the Department of Industry and Commerce, 12 Dec. 1957. The author of this correspondence was most likely Lemass, although the letter in this file is an unsigned copy.

14 In November 1957 Neil Blaney was replaced as Minister by Seán Ormonde.

15 NAI, DC TW 894, Memorandum from Seán Lemass to Seán Ormonde, Minister of Posts and Telegraphs, 17 Dec. 1957.

16 NAI, DC TW894, Memorandum from Ó Broin to Ormonde and Lemass.

17 NAI, DC TW894, Memorandum from Lemass to Ormonde, 6 Jan. 1958.

18 NAI, DT S14996B, Draft proposal by Seán Lemass, 28 Feb. 1958.

19 NAI, DF S104/1/50, Memorandum from Moynihan, Department of the Taoiseach to Ó Broin, 14 Mar. 1958.

20 Leon Ó Broin, *Just Like Yesterday* (Dublin, 1985), p. 210.

21 Ó Broin, *Yesterday*, pp. 209–10.

22 John Horgan, *Seán Lemass: The Enigmatic Patriot* (Dublin, 1997), p. 312.

23 NAI, DT S14996D.

24 RTÉ, Minutes of the Television Authority, 2 June1960.

25 Ibid.

26 See Savage, *Irish Television*, for discussion on de Valera's speech made at the opening of the television service on New Year's Eve 1961.

27 NAI, DT S14996D, Lemass to Moynihan, 30 Mar. 1960.

28 Ibid.

29 NAI, DT S14996D, Lemass to Moynihan, 30 Mar. 1960.

30 NAI, DT S14996D, Moynihan to Lemass, 4 Apr. 1960.

31 Ibid.

32 NAI, DT S14996D, Lemass to Moynihan, Apr. 1960.

33 NAI, DT S16882, O'Hanrahan to Moynihan, 5 July 1960.

34 Ibid.

35 NAI, DT S16882, O'Hanrahan to Kleinerman, 11 July 1960.

36 Ibid., p. 2.

37 NAI, DT S14996D.

38 NAI, DT S16882, O'Hanrahan to Kleinerman, 11 July 1960.

39 NAI DT S16882, Department of Taoiseach Memo, 10 Aug. 1960.

40 Ibid.

41 NAI, DT S16882, Kleinerman to O'Hanrahan, 12 Aug. 1960.

42 Ibid.

43 Ibid.

44 NAI, DT 16882, O'Hanrahan to Department of the Taoiseach, 12 Aug. 1960.

45 NAI, DT S16882 B/61, Report on 'Ireland the tear and the smile' written by Adrian Raferty and submitted by Dr T. J. Kiernan, Irish Ambassador to the US to the Department of External Affairs, 6 Feb. 1961, p. 5.

46 NAI, DT S16882 B/61, Covering memo, Kiernan to Department of Foreign Affairs, 6 Feb. 1961.

47 NAI, DT S16882 B/61, Report on 'Ireland the tear and the smile' written by B. Durnin and submitted by Dr T. J. Kiernan, Irish Ambassador to the US to the Department of External Affairs, 6 Feb. 1961.

48 NAI, DT S16882 B/61, Report from the Irish Consulate General of New York to the Department of External Affairs, 20 Feb. 1960, p. 3.

49 Ibid. It should be pointed out that an examination of the script reveals that this line was 'ad-libbed' by the presenter Walter Cronkite; it was not part of Bowen's written narrative. State Historical Society of Wisconsin, Archives Division, Kleinerman Papers.

50 NAI, DT S16882 B/61, Report on 'Ireland the tear and the smile', Part I, written by Dr T. J. Kiernan, Irish Ambassador to the US to the Department of External Affairs, 6 Feb. 1961, p. 1.

51 NAI, DT S16882 B/61, Report on 'Ireland the tear and the smile' written by Adrian Raferty and submitted by Dr. T.J. Kiernan, Irish Ambassador to the United States to the Department of External Affairs, 6 Feb. 1961, p.4.

52 NAI, DT S16882 B/61, Report on 'Ireland the tear and the smile' Part II written by D. T. J. Kiernan, Irish Ambassador to the US to the Department of External Affairs, 6 Feb. 1961, p. 2.

53 NAI, DT16882 B/61, Department of the Taoiseach memo, 16 Feb. 1961.

54 NAI, DT16882 B/61, Department of the Taoiseach memo, 22 Mar. 1961.

55 Ibid.

56 NAI DT16882 B/61, letter from O'Hanrahan to Kleinerman, 23 Mar. 1961.

57 NAI, DT16882 B/61, letter from Kleinerman to O'Hanrahan 6 Apr. 1961.

58 Ibid.

59 Ibid.

Select bibliography

Allen, Kieran, *Fianna Fáil and Irish Labour: 1926 to the Present Day* (London, 1997).

Andrews, C. S., *Man of No Property, An Autobiography*, vol. 2 (Dublin, 1982).

Arnold, Bruce, *Jack Lynch, Hero in Crisis* (Dublin, 2001).

Barrington, Donal, *The Church, the State and the Constitution* (Dublin, 1959).

Bardon, Jonathan, *A History of Ulster* (Belfast, 1992).

Bew, Paul and Henry Patterson, *Seán Lemass and the Making of Modern Ireland, 1945–66* (Dublin, 1982).

Biever, Bruce F., *Religion, Culture and Values: A Cross-Cultural Analysis of Motivational Factors in Native Irish and American Irish Catholicism* (New York, 1976).

Blanchard, Jean, *The Church in Contemporary Ireland* (Dublin, 1963).

Blanshard, Paul, *The Irish and Catholic Power* (London, 1954).

Boel, Bent, *The European Productivity Agency and Transatlantic Relations, 1953–1961* (Copenhagen, 2003).

Böll, Heinrich, *Irish Journal* (New York, 1967).

Bowman, John, '"The wolf in sheep's clothing": Richard Hayes's proposal for a new National Library of Ireland, 1959–60', in Ronald J. Hill and Michael Marsh (eds), *Modern Irish Democracy: Essays in Honour of Basil Chubb* (Dublin, 1993), pp. 44–61.

Boylan, Henry (ed.), *A Dictionary of Irish Biography* 3rd edn (Dublin, 1998).

Catterall, Peter, 'Senior editor's preface', in Kevin Theakston (ed.), *British Foreign Secretaries Since 1974* (London, 2004), pp. viii–x.

Chubb, Basil, 'Ireland 1957', in D. E. Butler (ed.), *Elections Abroad* (London, 1959), pp. 183–226.

Chubb, Basil, *The Government and Politics of Ireland* (Oxford, 1971).

Connolly, Tracey, 'Irish workers in Britain during the Second World War', in Brian Girvin and Geoffrey Roberts (eds), *Ireland and the Second World War: Politics, Society and Remembrance* (Dublin, 2000), pp. 212–32.

Conway, W., 'Marriage in Ireland: Church and state', *Irish Ecclesiastical Review* 5th ser., 68 (1946), pp. 361–6.

Coogan, Tim Pat, *Disillusioned Decades: Ireland 1966–87* (Dublin, 1987).

Coogan, Tim Pat, *De Valera. Long Fellow, Long Shadow* (London, 1993).

Coolahan, John *Irish Education: Its History and Structure* (Dublin, 1981).

Coolahan, John, 'Educational policy for national schools 1960–85', in D. G. Mulcahy and Denis O'Sullivan (eds), *Irish Educational Policy*, (Dublin, 1989), pp. 27–75.

Cooney John, *John Charles McQuaid: Ruler of Catholic Ireland* (Dublin, 1999).

Cox, Tom, *The Making of Managers: A History of the Irish Management Institute 1952–2002* (Cork, 2002).

Cruise O'Brien, Conor, *States of Ireland* (London, 1972).

Daly, Mary, *The Spirit of Earnest Inquiry: The Statistical and Social Inquiry Society of Ireland 1847–1997* (Dublin 1997).

Delaney, Enda, *Demography, State and Society: Irish Migration to Britain, 1921–1971* (Liverpool, 2000).

Delaney, Enda, 'Placing postwar Irish migration to Britain in a comparative European perspective, 1945–1981', in Andy Bielenberg (ed.), *The Irish Diaspora* (London, 2000), pp. 331–56.

Delaney, Enda, *Irish Emigration Since 1921* (Dublin, 2002).

Deeny, James, *To Cure and to Care* (Dublin, 1989).

Dudley Edwards, Ruth, *Patrick Pearse: The Triumph of Failure* (Dublin, 1990).

Dunphy, Richard, *The Making of Fianna Fáil Power in Ireland 1923–1948* (Oxford, 1995).

Fanning, Ronan, *The Irish Department of Finance 1922–58* (Dublin, 1978).

Fanning, Ronan, 'The genesis of economic development', in John F. McCarthy (ed.), *Planning Ireland's Future: The Legacy of T. K. Whitaker* (Dublin, 1990), pp. 74–111.

Fanning, Ronan, 'Raison d'état and the evolution of Irish foreign policy' in Michael Kennedy, and Joseph Skelly (eds), *From Independence to Internationalism: Irish Foreign Policy, 1916–1966* (Dublin, 2000), pp. 308–26.

Farrell, Brian, *Chairman or Chief? The Role of Taoiseach in Irish Government* (Dublin, 1971).

Farrell, Brian, *Seán Lemass* (Dublin, 1983).

Ferriter, Diarmaid, *The Transformation of Ireland, 1900–2000* (London: 2004).

FitzGerald, Garret, 'Mr Whitaker and industry', *Studies* 48, 190 (1959), pp. 138–50.

FitzGerald, Garret, *Planning in Ireland: A P.E.P Study* (Dublin, 1968).

FitzGerald, Garret, *All in a Life: An Autobiography* (Dublin, 1991).

FitzGerald, Maurice, *Protectionism to Liberalisation, Ireland and the EEC, 1957 to 1966* (Aldershot, 2000).

FitzGerald, Maurice, 'Ireland's relations with the EEC: from the Treaties of Rome to membership', *Journal of European Integration History* 7:1 (2001), pp. 11–24.

FitzGerald, Maurice, '"Ceart go leor": Ireland, the UK, EMU and the sterling area', in Francisco Torres et al. (eds), *Governing the EMU* (Florence, 2004), pp. 273–90.

FitzGerald, Maurice, 'Ireland and the US in the post-war period', in Dermot Keogh et al. (eds), *The Lost Decade: Ireland in the 1950s* (Cork, 2004). pp. 187–205.

Fitzpatrick, David, *Irish Emigration, 1801–1921* (Dublin, 1984).

Gallagher, Michael, *Electoral Support for Irish Political Parties, 1927–1973* (London, 1976).

Gallagher, Michael, 'Party solidarity, exclusivity and inter-party relationships in Ireland, 1922–77: the evidence of transfers', *Economic and Social Review* 10:1 (1978), pp. 1–22.

Gallagher, Michael, *The Irish Labour Party in Transition 1957–82* (Dublin, 1982).

Garvin, Tom, 'The destiny of soldiers: tradition and modernity in the politics of de Valera's Ireland', *Political Studies* 26:3 (1978), pp. 328–47.

Garvin, Tom, *The Evolution of Irish Nationalist Politics* (Dublin, 1981).

Garvin, Tom, *Nationalist Revolutionaries in Ireland, 1858–1928* (Oxford, 1997).

Garvin, Tom, *Preventing the Future: Why Was Ireland So Poor for So Long?* (Dublin, 2004).

Geiger, Till, 'The enthusiastic response of a reluctant supporter: Ireland and the Committee for European Economic Cooperation in the Summer of 1947', in Michael Kennedy and Joseph Morrison Skelly (eds), *Irish Foreign Policy 1919–1966: From Independence to Internationalism* (Dublin, 2000), pp. 222–46..

Girvin, Brian, *Between Two Worlds: Politics and Economy in Independent Ireland* (Dublin, 1989).

Girvin, Brian, 'Irish agricultural policy, economic nationalism and the possibility of market integration in Europe', in Brian Girvin and R. T. Griffiths (eds), *The Green Pool and the Origins of the Common Agricultural Policy* (London, 1995), pp. 238–59.

Girvin, Brian, 'Irish economic development and the politics of EEC entry', in R. T. Griffiths and S. Ward (eds), *Courting the Common Market: The First Attempt to Enlarge the European Community, 1961–63* (London, 1996), pp. 247–62.

Girvin, Brian, 'The state and vocational education 1922–1960' in John Logan (ed.), *Teachers' Union: The TUI and its Forerunners* (Dublin, 1999), pp. 62–92.

Girvin Brian, 'Politics in wartime: governing, neutrality and elections' in Brian Girvin and Geoffrey Roberts (eds), *Ireland and the Second World War: Politics, Society and Remembrance* (Dublin, 2000), pp. 24–46.

Girvin, Brian, *From Union to Union: Nationalism, Religion and Democracy from the Act of Union to the European Union* (Dublin, 2002).

Griffiths, Richard (ed.), *Explorations in OEEC History* (Paris 1997).

Hederman, Miriam, *The Road to Europe: Irish Attitudes 1948–1961* (Dublin, 1983).

Horgan, John, *Seán Lemass: The Enigmatic Patriot* (Dublin, 1997).

Horgan, John, *Noel Browne, Passionate Outsider* (Dublin, 2000).

Horgan, John, *Irish Media: A Critical History Since 1922* (London, 2001).

Humphreys, Alexander J., *New Dubliners: Urbanization and the Irish Family* (London, 1966).

Jelen, Ted and Clyde Wilcox (eds), *Religion and Politics in Comparative Perspective* (Cambridge, 2002).

Katzenstein, Peter, *Small States in World Markets* (Ithaca, 1985).

Keatinge, Patrick, 'Ireland and the world, 1957–82', in Frank Litton (ed.), *Unequal Achievement: The Irish Experience, 1957–1982* (Dublin, 1982), pp. 225–42.

Kennedy, Líam, *The Modern Industrialisation of Ireland, 1940–1988* (Dublin, 1989).

Kennedy, Kieran A. and Brendan R. Dowling, *Economic Growth in Ireland: The Experience Since 1947* (Dublin, 1975).

Kennedy, Michael, *Division and Consensus: The Politics of Cross-Border Relations in Ireland, 1925–1969* (Dublin, 2000).

Kennedy, Michael and Eunan O'Halpin, *Ireland and the Council of Europe: From Isolation Towards Integration* (Strasbourg, 2000).

Kennedy, Michael and Joseph Skelly (eds), *From Independence to Internationalism: Irish Foreign Policy, 1916–1966* (Dublin, 2000).

Keogh, Dermot, *Ireland and Europe 1919–1989: A Diplomatic and Political History* (Cork, 1990).

Keogh, Dermot, *Twentieth Century Ireland: Nation and State* (Dublin, 1994).

Keogh, Dermot, 'The diplomacy of "dignified calm": an analysis of Ireland's application for membership of the EEC, 1961–1963', *Journal of European Integration History* 3:1 (1995), pp. 81–101.

Keogh, Dermot, 'Irish neutrality and the first application for membership of the EEC', in Michael Kennedy and Joseph Skelly (eds), *From Independence to Internationalism: Irish Foreign Policy, 1916–1966*, pp. 265–85.

Lee J. J. (ed.), *Ireland 1945–1970* (Dublin, 1979).

Lee, J. J., 'Seán Lemass', in J. J. Lee (ed.), *Ireland 1945–1970* (Dublin, 1979), pp. 16–26.

Lee, Joseph and Gearoid O'Tuathaigh, *The Age of de Valera* (Dublin, 1982).

Lee, J. J., *Ireland 1912–1985: Politics and Society* (Cambridge, 1989).

Lee, J. J., 'Economic development in historical perspective', in John F. McCarthy (ed.), *Planning Ireland's Future: The Legacy of T. K. Whitaker* (Sandycove, 1990), pp. 112–27.

Longford, Lord and Thomas P. O'Neill, *Eamon de Valera* (London, 1970).

Lyons, F. S. L., *Ireland Since the Famine* (London, 1971).

McCarthy, Charles, *The Decade of Upheaval: Irish Trade Unions in the Nineteen Sixties* (Dublin, 1973).

McCarthy, Charles, *Trade Unions in Ireland* (Dublin, 1977).

McCarthy, John F., 'Ireland's turnaround: Whitaker and the 1958 plan for economic development' in John F. McCarthy (ed.), *Planning Ireland's Future: The Legacy of T. K. Whitaker* (Sandycove, 1990), pp. 11–73.

McCarthy, Rev. J., 'Morality of a state ban on the emigration of minors', *Irish Ecclesiastical Record* 5th ser., 71 (1949), pp. 269–72.

McCullagh, David, *A Makeshift Majority: The First Inter-Party Government, 1948–51* (Dublin, 1998).

McGlade Jacqueline, 'Americanization: ideology or process? The case of the United States Technical Assistance and Productivity Programme, in Jonathan Zeitlin and Gary Herrigel (eds), *Americanization and its Limits: Reworking US Technology and Management in Post-War Europe and Japan* (Oxford: 2000), pp. 53–75.

MacGréil, Mícheál, *Prejudice and Tolerance in Ireland* (Dublin, 1977).

Maher, D. J., *The Tortuous Path: The Course of Ireland's Entry into the EEC 1948–73* (Dublin, 1986).

Manning, Maurice, *James Dillon: A Biography* (Dublin, 1999).

Miller, Kerby A., *Emigrants and Exiles: Ireland and the Irish Exodus to North America* (New York, 1985).

Milotte, Mike, *Banished Babies: The Secret History of Ireland's Baby Export Business* (Dublin, 1997).

Milward, Alan, *The Reconstruction of Western Europe: 1945–1951* (London, 1984)

Mjoset, Lars, *The Irish Economy in a Comparative Institutional Perspective* (Dublin, 1992).

Moynihan, Maurice, *Currency and Central Banking in Ireland 1922–60* (Dublin, 1975).

Moynihan, Maurice (ed.), *Speeches and Statements by Eamon de Valera* (Dublin, 1980).

Mulholland, Marc, *Northern Ireland at the Crossroads* (Hampshire, 2000).

Murphy, Gary, 'Fostering a spurious progeny?: the trade union movement and Europe, 1957–1964', *Saothar* 21 (1996), pp. 61–70.

Murphy, Gary, 'Government, interest groups and the Irish move to Europe, 1957–1963', *Irish Studies in International Affairs* 8 (1997), pp. 57–68.

Murphy, Gary, 'Towards a corporate state? Seán Lemass and the realignment of interest groups in the policy process 1948–1964', *Administration* 47:1 (1999), pp. 86–102.

Murphy, Gary, 'A wider perspective: Ireland's view of Western Europe in the 1950s' in Michael Kennedy and Joseph Skelly (eds), *From Independence to Internationalism: Irish Foreign Policy, 1916–1966* (Dublin, 2000), pp. 247–64.

Murphy, Gary, *Economic Realignment and the Politics of EEC Entry: Ireland, 1948–1973* (Bethesda, 2003).

Murray, Patrick, *Oracles of God: The Roman Catholic Church and Irish Politics, 1922–1937* (Dublin, 2000).

Murray, Peter, *The Transatlantic Politics of Productivity and the Origins of Public Funding Support for Social Science Research in Ireland, 1950–1979*, NIRSA Working Paper no. 22, Apr. 2004.

Murphy, John A., *Ireland in the Twentieth Century*, 2nd edn (Dublin, 1989).

Nevin, Donal 'Industry and labour', in Kevin B. Nowlan and T. Desmond Williams (eds), *Ireland in The War Years and After, 1938–51* (Dublin, 1969), pp. 94–108.

Nevin, Donal, (ed.), *Trade Union Century* (Dublin, 1994).

Newman, Jeremiah, *Studies in Political Morality* (Dublin and London, 1962).

Nowlan, Kevin B. and T. Desmond Williams, *Ireland in the War Years and After, 1938–51* (Dublin, 1969).

O'Brien, John A., 'The Irish enigma', in John A. O'Brien (ed.), *The Vanishing Irish: The Enigma of the Modern World* (New York, 1953), pp. 3–10.

Ó'Broin Leon, *Just Like Yesterday: An Autobiography* (Dublin, 1985).

Ó'Buachalla, Séamas, *Education Policy in Twentieth Century Ireland* (Dublin, 1988).

Ó Buachalla, Séamas, 'Investment in education: context, content and impact', *Administration* 44: 3 (1996), pp. 10–20.

O'Connor, Seán, *A Troubled Sky: Reflections on the Irish Educational Scene 1957–68* (Dublin, 1986).

Ó Gráda, Cormac and Brendan M. Walsh, 'The economic effects of emigration: Ireland', in Beth J. Asch (ed.), *Emigration and its Effects on the Sending Country* (Santa Monica, CA, 1994), pp. 97–152.

O'Halpin, Eunan, *Defending Ireland: The Irish State and its Enemies since 1922* (Oxford, 1999).

Ó'hEithir, Breandán, *The Begrudger's Guide to Irish Politics* (Dublin, 1987).

O'Leary, Don, *Vocationalism and Social Catholicism in Twentieth Century Ireland* (Dublin, 1999).

O'Leary, Cornelius, *Irish Elections 1918–1977: Parties, Voters and Proportional Representation* (Dublin, 1979).

O'Mahony, David, 'Economic expansion in Ireland', *Studies* 48:190 (1959), pp. 129–37.

Ó'Muircheartaigh, F. (ed.), *Ireland in the Coming Times: Essays to Celebrate T. K. Whitaker's 80 years* (Dublin, 1998).

O'Shea, Kieran, *The Irish Emigrant Chaplaincy Scheme in Britain, 1957–82* (Naas, 1985).

O'Sullivan, Coleman Tadhg, 'The IRA takes constitutional action: a history of Clann na Poblachta', unpublished MA thesis, UCD, 1995.

O'Sullivan, Michael, *Seán Lemass: A Biography* (Dublin, 1994).

Puirséil, Niamh, 'Labour and coalition: the impact of the first inter-party government, 1948–51', *Saothar* 27 (2002), pp. 55–64.

Pyne Peter, 'The third Sinn Féin Party: 1923–1926, part II', *Economic and Social Review* 1:2 (1969), pp. 229–57.

Randles Eileen, *Post-Primary Education in Ireland 1957–70* (Dublin, 1975).

Regan, John M., *The Irish Counter-Revolution 1921–1936* (Dublin, 1999).

Rockett, Kevin et al., *Cinema and Ireland* (Syracuse, 1987).

Savage, Robert J., *Irish Television: The Political and Social Origins* (Cork, 1996).

Savage, Robert, *Seán Lemass* (Dundalk, 1999).

Sinnott, Richard, *Irish Voters Decide: Voting Behaviour in Elections and Referendums Since 1918* (Manchester, 1995).

Skelly, Joseph Morrison, *Irish Diplomacy at the United Nations, 1945–1965: National Interests and the International Order* (Dublin, 1997).

Skinner, Frank, *Politicians by Accident* (Dublin, 1946).

Travers, Pauric, '"The dream gone bust": Irish responses to emigration, 1922–60', in Oliver MacDonagh and W. F. Mandle (eds), *Irish Australian Studies* (Canberra, 1989), pp. 318–42.

Travers, Pauric, *Eamon de Valera* (Dublin, 1994).

Walsh, Brendan M., 'Economic growth and development, 1945–70', in J. J. Lee (ed.), *Ireland 1945–70* (Dublin, 1979), pp. 27–37.

Whelan, Bernadette, 'Integration or isolation? Ireland and the invitation to join the Marshall Plan' in Michael Kennedy and Joseph Skelly (eds), *From Independence to Internationalism: Irish Foreign Policy, 1916–1966* (Dublin, 2000), pp. 203–21.

Whelan, Bernadette, *Ireland and the Marshall Plan, 1947–57* (Dublin, 2000).

Whelan, Gerard with Carolyn Swift, *Spiked: Church-State Intrigue and the Rose Tattoo* (Dublin, 2002).

Whitaker, T. K., *Interests* (Dublin, 1983).

Whitaker, T. K., 'Economic development 1958–1985', in Kieran A. Kennedy (ed.), *Ireland in Transition: Economic and Social Change since 1960* (Dublin, 1986), pp. 10–18.

Whyte, J. H., *Church And State in Modern Ireland 1923-1979*, 2nd edn (Dublin, 1980).

Williams T. D., 'Irish foreign policy, 1949–69', in J. J. Lee (ed.), *Ireland 1945–1970* (Dublin, 1979), pp. 136–51.

Yeats, Michael B., *Cast A Cold Eye: Memories of a Poet's Son and Politician* (Dublin, 1998).

Index